Language Tree Jamaica

Second Edition

for the National Standards Curriculum

Student's Book 5

Writing and advisory team:
Leonie Bennett
Julia Sander
Ericka Forbes-Blair
Gillian Myers

macmillan
education

Macmillan Education
4 Crinan Street
London N1 9XW
A division of Springer Nature Limited

Companies and representatives throughout the world

ISBN 978-1-380-00985-2

First published 2015
This edition published 2018

Designed by Macmillan Education and Blue Dog Design Studio
Illustrated by Monica Auriemma c/o Sylvie Poggio; Blue Dog Design; Jim Eldridge; Pamela Goodchild c/o B.L. Kearley; Robin Lawrie c/o Beehive; Macmillan Education and TechType
Cover design by Antoine Cutayar and Macmillan Education
Cover illustration by Aleksandar Sotirovski c/o Beehive Illustration Ltd
Typeset by Blue Dog Design Studio
Picture research by Catherine Dunn

The author and publishers would like to thank Ericka Forbes-Blair and Gillian Myers for their help and advice throughout the development and writing of this series.

The authors and publishers would like to thank the following for permission to reproduce their photographs:
Alamy/John de la Bastide p9, Alamy/Darryl Brooks p11, Alamy/David Chapman p164(bl), Alamy/Kevin Elsby p164(tl), Alamy/FLPA p44, Alamy/fStop Images GmbH p55, Alamy/Dawna Moore p69(br), Alamy/National Geographic Creative p69(tr), Alamy/piluhin p61, Alamy/Friedrich Stark p137(tr), Alamy/Julian Worker p151; **Digital Vision** p8; **Getty Images** p56, Getty/Barcroft p45, Getty Images/Don Farrall p68, Getty/Franz-Marc Frei p42, Getty/Chris Jackson p137(br), Getty Images/koya79 p15(br), Getty/Ryan McVay p154, Getty Images/Oleksiy Mark p16(cr), Getty/ Robert S. Patton p43, Getty Images/Umberto Pantalone p16(tl), Getty/Photodisc p15(cl); **The Gleaner Company Ltd** p126; **Nature PL**/Roland Seitre p49.

The authors and publishers are grateful for permission to reprint the following copyright material:
P 22 'Lubricate the Joints' and ' Beneath my feet' from Centrally Heated Knickers by Michael Rosen reprinted by permission of Peters Fraser & Dunlop (www.petersfraserdunlop.com) on behalf of Michael Rosen; P 62 'Don' Ride No Coconut Bough Down Dere' by Valerie Bloom. Published in One River, Many Creeks by Macmillan Children's Books. © Valerie Bloom 2004. Reprinted with permission of Eddison Pearson Ltd on behalf of Valerie Bloom; P 64 'Scenery' by Joel McGowan, as printed in Journey at 9: Artistic Thoughts and Expressions. © Joel McGowan, 2011. Reprinted by permission of Sylinda Marks; P 64 'Habitats' by Joel McGowan, as printed in Journey at 9: Artistic Thoughts and Expressions. © Joel McGowan, 2011. Reprinted by permission of Sylinda Marks; P 165 'Dreamer' by Brian Moses. Published in Hippopotamus Dancing and Other Poems by Cambridge University Press, 1994. © Brian Moses 1994. Reprinted with permission of the author.

Printed and bound in Dubai

2022 2021 2020 2019 2018
10 9 8 7 6 5 4 3 2 1

Contents

			Page
How to Use this Book			4
Scope and Sequence			6

Term 1

Energy and Matter: Forces and Machines

Unit 1	Being an Airline Pilot	*dialogue*	8
Unit 2	Smart Science Facts	*webpage*	15
Unit 3	Lubricate the Joints, Beneath my Feet	*poems*	22
Unit 4	In Business	*realistic story*	29
Assessment 1	Traffic Survey	*various*	36

Diversity, Sustainability and Interdependence: Habitats

Unit 5	The Lower Morass, Cockpit County	*expository*	42
Unit 6	An Endangered Species	*realistic story*	49
Unit 7	Our Reef is a National Treasure	*poster, letters*	55
Unit 8	Don' Ride No Coconut Bough Down Dere	*poem*	62
Assessment 2	The Leatherback Sea Turtle	*expository*	69

Term 2

Health and Well-Being: Nutrition

Unit 9	A Healthy Diet	*labels and flyer*	75
Unit 10	The Party	*poem*	82
Unit 11	It Sounds Delicious	*realistic story*	89
Unit 12	The Food Fair	*formal letter*	96
Assessment 3	The Tree of Life	*traditional tale*	103

Institutions and Political Decisions: Parishes

Unit 13	An Important Visitor	*speech*	109
Unit 14	Visit to the Parish Library	*realistic story*	116
Unit 15	Stories from the Parishes	*legends*	123
Unit 16	The Debate	*persuasive speeches*	130
Assessment 4	Jamaica's Parishes	*various*	137

Term 3

Health and Well-Being: Air Pollution

Unit 17	Letter to the Traffic Division	*formal letter*	143
Unit 18	Caring for the Environment	*leaflet*	150
Unit 19	Out of Breath	*realistic story*	157
Unit 20	Poisoned Talk, Dreamer	*poems*	164
Assessment 5	Positive Results for NEPA Campaign	*newspaper article*	171

Practice Test			177
Strategies and Graphic Organisers			183
6 + 1 Traits of Writing			188
The Writing Process			189
Glossary of Grammar Terms			190
Skills Index			191

How to Use this Book

Modelled on the Jamaican National Standards Curriculum (NSC), *Language Tree Jamaica Second Edition* Level 5 follows an integrated, themed approach that ensures balanced and progressive teaching of all the language arts strands, in every unit. Key 21st century skills (critical thinking, creativity, communication and collaboration) are placed at the heart of the course, preparing students for real life as well as equipping them with tools that can be applied across the STEM subjects.

For the most comprehensive learning experience, this Student's Book can be used in conjunction with the grade 5 Workbook.

Teaching units

Student's Book 5 is divided into five themes across three terms, which correspond directly to the NSC units for grade 5. There are 20 teaching units, each comprising the following sections:

Get ready

Each unit opens with an opportunity to engage students: Lead a class discussion to introduce the reading passage and draw on the students' experience. Draw attention to the type of text (fiction, non-fiction, etc.) and text features (headings, diagrams, etc.). Introduce key vocabulary.

Reading

With a strong emphasis on literature throughout, reading passages cover a variety of text types. Students can read independently or take turns to read a section. Encourage students to work out the meaning of unfamiliar vocabulary from the context.

Comprehension exercises are modelled on Webb's Depth of Knowledge, with questions progressing from recalling simple detail ('right there') through application and analysis ('think and search'), to further extended thinking and research ('on your own').

Questions can be tackled orally or in writing, depending on the needs of students. It may be appropriate to talk through the questions before asking students to write answers to some of them.

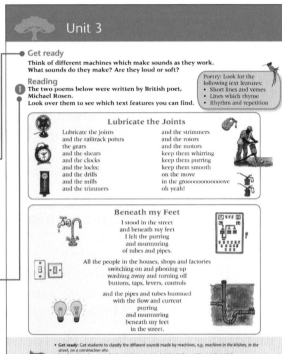

Speaking and listening

👥 This symbol indicates that students work with a partner or in a group, helping to improve **communication** and **collaboration** skills. Activities include discussion, planning and roleplay. Move around the class, checking on progress, or work alongside students who find oral work challenging.

This icon indicates a tip or suggestion for the student.

Language work

Teaching points allow students to explore new concepts and skills, which are then followed by a variety of practice exercises. Work through the examples together before asking students to work on an exercise. Some students can write their answers independently or in pairs. You may need to work orally with other students, writing the answers collaboratively.

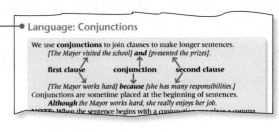

Language: Conjunctions

We use **conjunctions** to join clauses to make longer sentences.
[The Mayor visited the school] **and** [presented the prizes].

first clause   conjunction   second clause

[The Mayor works hard] **because** [she has many responsibilities.]
Conjunctions are sometime placed at the beginning of sentences.
Although the Mayor works hard, she really enjoys her job.
NOTE: When the sentence begins with a conjunction place a comma

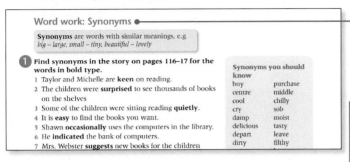

Word work: Synonyms

Synonyms are words with similar meanings, e.g. *big – large, small – tiny, beautiful – lovely*

1 **Find synonyms in the story on pages 116–17 for the words in bold type.**
1 Taylor and Michelle are **keen** on reading.
2 The children were **surprised** to see thousands of books on the shelves
3 Some of the children were sitting reading **quietly**.
4 It is **easy** to find the books you want.
5 Shawn **occasionally** uses the computers in the library.
6 He **indicated** the bank of computers.
7 Mrs. Webster **suggests** new books for the children

Synonyms you should know

buy	purchase
centre	middle
cool	chilly
cry	sob
damp	moist
delicious	tasty
depart	leave
dirty	filthy

Word work

Examples of word-level work, such as vocabulary, prefixes or homophones will be found in the reading passage.

Writing

See page 190 for an overview of the writing process that underpins all the writing activities in this Student's Book. The first stage – getting ideas – is very important. It provides the material for students to work with and sparks **creativity**. If students miss out this stage they are likely to say, "I don't know what to write." You may begin work as a class – brainstorming ideas and useful vocabulary on the board.Some students will be able to complete the writing task on their own or in mixed ability pairs. You may need to support other students by working alongside them, writing a group composition for which you act as a scribe.

Sometimes there are two writing activities at the end of a unit. Choose the one most suited to the needs of your class. One may be done as a collaborative writing task involving the whole class.

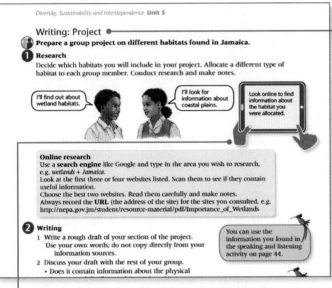

Diversity, Sustainability and Interdependence **Unit 5**

Writing: Project

Prepare a group project on different habitats found in Jamaica.

1 **Research**
Decide which habitats you will include in your project. Allocate a different type of habitat to each group member. Conduct research and make notes.

I'll find out about wetland habitats.

I'll look for information about coastal plains.

Look online to find information about the habitat you were allocated

Online research
Use a **search engine** like Google and type in the area you wish to research, e.g. *wetlands + Jamaica*.
Look at the first three or four websites listed. Scan them to see if they contain useful information.
Choose the best two websites. Read them carefully and make notes.
Always record the **URL** (the address of the site) for the sites you consulted, e.g. http://nepa.gov.jm/student/resource-material/pdf/Importance_of_Wetlands

2 **Writing**
1 Write a rough draft of your section of the project.
  Use your own words; do not copy directly from your information sources.
2 Discuss your draft with the rest of your group.
  • Does it contain information about the physical

You can use the information you found in the speaking and listening activity on page 44.

This feature supports the integration of technology into students' learning, ensuring ICT attainment targets are met.

On-the-page teacher's notes

There are suggestions for introducing and extending the activities at the bottom of each page.
DA This symbol precedes suggestions and instructions for differentiated instruction.
To help with planning, syllabus objectives are highlighted in bold type.

WB5 p127 This symbol indicates that a skill is practised further in the Workbook.

Assessments

Skills are revisited in five 'Assessment' units, which help students to evaluate their learning. Use the activities to assess in which areas students need further support.

Graphic organisers

Students are often referred to the appendix of graphic organisers (pages 183–188). These organisers offer vital support for planning and writing texts with differing structures plus flexible tools to support comprehension. Encourage students to regularly reflect on and apply **critical thinking** to their learning in their Learning Journals, using graphic organisers 1 and 2.

Scope and sequence chart and skills index

These sections will support your short- and long-term planning, enabling you to make sure that you are covering the syllabus.

Scope and Sequence

Unit	Speaking and listening	Reading and comprehension	Language	Word work	Study skills/IT	Writing
Energy and Matter: Forces and Machines						
1 page 8	Discuss machines	Audience and purpose Environmental print	Nouns: types, singular and plural	Compound words	IT: research jobs	Design poster to inform. Write about a job.
2 page 15	Identify machines and describe function.	Scanning, text features, signal words Paragraphs	Sentences: types and punctuation Subject and predicate	Syllables	IT: collaborative research	Report about machine
3 page 22	Discuss comic strips.	Elements of poetry: rhyme, rhythm, lines and verses	Verbs: subject–verb agreement with simple present tense	Onomatopoeia Interjections Exclamation marks		Compose acrostic poem
4 page 29	Use diagrams to describe process	Predicting Identify question types Story elements: problem / solution	Personal pronouns	Root words, prefixes	Use a dictionary IT: create word bank	Plan and write story using writing process
Assessment 1 page 36	Literal and inferential comprehension		Nouns, simple present tense, pronouns, sentences, compound nouns, prefixes and root words, onomatopoeia			Paragraphs
Diversity, Sustainability and Interdependence: Habitats						
5 page 42	Find information, make notes Present report	Cause and effect Deduction	Adjectives, adjectival phrases Comparative and superlative	Parts of book	IT: collaborative research	Collaborative project about habitats
6 page 49	Retell a story, roleplay	Skimming Inferring	Simple past tense	Suffixes	IT: research online and create fact sheet	Write story Apply writing process
7 page 55	Discussion: pros and cons of tourism Make notes	Author's purpose Text organisation and structure, illustrations	Quotation marks Simple and compound sentences		Interpret graphs and tables	Email to editor stating opinion
8 page 62	Sensory description of a place	Language awareness, JC and SJE ICT: prepare poster	Adverbs: time, manner, place	Similes, metaphors	Use a thesaurus	Descriptive poem and description of a place
Assessment 2 page 69	Text features Fact sheet		Adjectives, adverbs, simple past tense, compound sentences, quotation marks, suffixes			Report on animal and its habitat Narrative
Health and Well-Being: Nutrition						
9 page 75	Discuss diet, conduct survey	Fact and opinion	Colons in lists Abbreviations	Classify foods	IT: create word bank	Design advertisement Notice about healthy foods
10 page 82	Group recitation	Elements of poetry Alliteration	Present and past continuous tenses Comparative adverbs	Homographs	IT: find poems online	Description of fruit Poem about a fruit or vegetable
11 page 89	Perform skits in JC and SJE	Convert comic strip to narrative	Future tense	Compound words	Interpret diagrams	Informal letter to pen pal about Jamaican food
12 page 96	Presentation, record, play back	Text features: formal letter, poster	Direct and reported speech	Word building: prefix–root–suffix	IT: create an invitation	Write a grace Formal letter of thanks Plan using RAFTs
Assessment 3 page 103	Predicting Cause and effect		Identify tenses, continuous present and past, reported speech, colons and commas, homographs, word building Abbreviations			Informal letter of apology Report about celebration

Unit	Speaking and listening	Reading and comprehension	Language	Word work	Study skills/IT	Writing
Institutions and Political Decisions: Parishes						
13 page 109	Introduce speaker, vote of thanks	KWL chart Formulate questions Summarise talk	Complex sentences Subordinating conjunctions	Spelling *ie*/*ei* It's or its Silent letters: k,g,w	IT: research municipal corporations	Letter of thanks to mayor Report on work of emergency worker
14 page 116	Find information in a library	Skimming Classifying books	Possessive adjectives and pronouns Possessive nouns	Synonyms	Complete a library application form	Book report
15 page 123	Discuss story, present to group	Compare and contrast Context clues	Relative clauses Relative pronouns: who, which, where, whose	Consonant blends, morpheme triangles	IT: research Jamaican legends	First person narrative Proofreading
16 page 130	Arguments for and against Express own views.	For and against	Conditional sentences Semi-colons Signal words	Silent letters: b,l,n,t	Fill out a form for an activity programme	Persuasive composition
Assessment 4 page 137	Compare and contrast Arguments for and against		Possessive nouns, relative pronouns, conjunctions, punctuation, spelling			Informal letter If I were Mayor… (persuasive writing)
Health and Well-Being: Air Pollution						
17 page 143	Debate on banning cars	Cause and effect, signal words Summarise	Present perfect tense Past participles	Synonyms Antonyms	Interpret graphs	Persuasive letter Six traits of writing
18 page 150	Panel discussion Formulate questions	Problem/ solution	Passive voice Fused sentences, comma splice	Homophones False homonyms	IT: research agencies, e.g. NEPA	Collaborative research project
19 page 157	Retell a story	DRTA Phrased cued text	Contractions Prepositions of place	Easily confused words Reader response journal		Journal entries
20 page 164	Create adverts/ jingles with message	Compare poems on same theme	Helping verbs Subject–verb agreement review	Signal words		Poster Haiku
Assessment 5 page 171	Signal words Context		Present perfect tense, antonyms, passive voice, homophones, prepositions, synonyms			Journal entry Persuasive letter

Get ready

An airline pilot flies a plane. What else do you think a pilot does? What questions would you like to ask an airline pilot?

Reading

Captain Gordon is a pilot for Island Airways. She has come to talk to the Grade 5 class at Shannon's school about her work.

Remember : When we speak or write, our audience is the person or people with whom we wish to communicate. Our purpose is our reason for communicating. Who is the *audience* and what is the *purpose* of the dialogue below?

Being an Airline Pilot

Airliners have a **cruising speed** of between 800–900 km/h. and they fly at an **altitude** of 30,000 to 40,000 feet

A car would have to drive non-stop for over a month to use as much **fuel** as an airliner uses in one hour.

Captain Gordon: Good morning students. Thank you for inviting me to talk to you about the work of an airline pilot. It's a responsible job which takes years of training. Pilots have to know about communication and navigation. In addition to flying the plane, they must also learn how to deal with emergencies. Now, who has the first question?

Shannon: Please can you tell us how you trained to become a pilot?

Captain Gordon: I went to pilot school where my initial training took 18 months. After that I worked for five years as a co-pilot, assisting a fully trained pilot.

Dwayne: What does the pilot do before a flight?

Captain Gordon: We study the route we will take and the weather forecast. With the help of the on-board computer, we calculate how much fuel will be needed for the flight. Once the pre-flight checks are completed and all the passengers are on-board, the plane is ready to take off.

Chantelle: Do you ever fly the plane alone?

Captain Gordon: No, there are always two pilots in the cockpit, the captain and the co-pilot. Both have controls, but only one actually flies the plane. On a long flight, the co-pilot may have control of the plane for some time under the supervision of the pilot.

- **Get ready:** Use this section to help students to engage with the topic. Encourage *text-to-self* connections by asking students to draw on their prior knowledge of flying.
- **Reading:** Ask students to predict content from the picture. Ask about the text type, e.g. *What type of text is it? How do you know that?* Encourage students to use reader response journals (see page 183) to record their reactions to texts.

Shannon: How do you manage not to lose your way in the air?

Captain Gordon: When we fly from one airport to another, we follow 'air corridors' which are like imaginary roads in the sky. If there is bad weather, we may need to alter our route. Throughout the flight, we remain in touch with air traffic control, which informs us about weather conditions. It also ensures that we keep a safe distance away from other aircraft.

Shawn: Is it difficult to land the plane?

Captain Gordon: We have to get permission from the control tower at the airport before we touch down as there may be other planes on the runway. This is important as the plane may still be travelling at more than 240 kilometres per hour when it lands.

Dwayne: Is your work over after you've landed the plane?

Captain Gordon: Oh no! Before going off duty, we have to make a post-flight report recording in detail what happened on the flight.

Chantelle: Do you like being a pilot?

Captain Gordon: Good question! I work very hard and spend a long time away from my family, but I can't imagine ever wanting to do anything else.

1 What must pilots learn when they are training?

2 How long did it take for Captain Gordon to become a fully trained pilot?

3 Why do you think that both pilots in the cockpit have controls?

4 What is the job of air traffic control?

5 Why does the pilot stay in touch with air traffic control throughout the flight?

6 Why might a pilot decide to change course during a flight?

7 Explain in your own words the meaning of the words *pre-flight* and *post-flight*.

8 Suggest three things a pilot might write in his post-flight report.

9 Why do you think Captain Gordon says that being a pilot is 'a responsible job'?

10 Do you think she enjoys her work? Why/Why not?

Use your Learning Journal to reflect on your progress. Complete a 'Reading response' chart (page 183) about this text.

- Discuss with students where they can find the answers to the comprehension questions.
- **Question 1:** The answer is right there in the text. Question 2: Students have to combine separate pieces of information. Question 10: The answer is not in the text. Students must use inference to work it out.
- Encourage students to regularly reflect on their learning in their Learning Journals. They can use the graphic organisers on page 183 to help them.

9

Context means the words and phrases surrounding a particular word that can help you understand what it means. Reading unfamiliar words in their context will help you to work out what they mean.

1. communication	a. an unexpected situation involving danger
2. navigation	b. height above sea level
3. emergency	c. checking that someone is working correctly
4. cockpit	d. sending and receiving information
5. supervision	e. travelling at a steady speed
6. runway	f. following a planned route using instruments
7. cruising	g. strip used by planes to take off and land
8. altitude	h. part of plane where pilot sits

Flight	Airline	Country	Arrival	Status
1675	Jet Blue	JFK - New York	8.27	Landed – on time
458	Caribbean Airlines	ANU - Antigua	9.45	En route – delayed
1589	American Airlines	MIA - Miami	10.10	Landed – on time
6718	Avianca	PTY – Panama City	11.35	Cancelled
821	Amerijet International	BG – Bridgetown	12.10	En route – on time
339	Delta Airways	ATL - Atlanta	13.15	En route – delayed
526	Caribbean Airlines	MIA - Miami	13.45	Scheduled
2235	Virgin Atlantic	LGW – London	14.40	En route – on time
1802	Air Canada	YYZ Toronto	15.45	Scheduled

1 Where would you expect to see this information?

2 Who would find the information useful?

3 How many flights are scheduled to arrive in the morning?

4 What sort of information is given under the heading 'Status'?

5 A flight that is 'en route' is:
   a) a flight that has been delayed.
   b) a flight that has been cancelled.
   c) a flight that has arrived.
   d) a flight that is in the air.

6 Two of the flights are 'scheduled'. What do you think this means?

Look online to see which flights are scheduled to arrive at Montego Bay airport today.

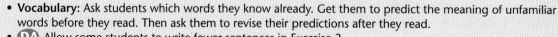

- **Vocabulary:** Ask students which words they know already. Get them to predict the meaning of unfamiliar words before they read. Then ask them to revise their predictions after they read.
- **DA** Allow some students to write fewer sentences in Exercise 2.
- Note: The symbol **DA** is always followed by a suggestion for working with students of different abilities.

Speaking and listening: Discussion

1 An aircraft is a big machine used to transport people and goods. Which other machines are used for transport?

2 What machine can you see in the photograph? What kind of work is done by this machine?

3 a) What kind of machine might be used by these people?

> carpenter   cook   doctor   fire officer   farmer   mechanic

b) For what purpose do they use machines?

> Example: A carpenter uses a drill to bore holes in wood.

c) Name three other groups of people who operate machines. Which machines do they use?

Language: Noun types

> **Nouns** are **naming words**.
> They name people, animals, places, things and events.
> **Common nouns** are **general** names: *pilot, airport, runway, passenger*
> **Proper nouns** name **specific** people, things, places, times and events.
> They always begin with a capital letter: *Captain Gordon, Caribbean Airlines, Saturday, Ocho Rios Jazz Festival*

WB5 p5

1 Find eight common nouns and five proper nouns in this paragraph.

> Last August Mrs. Campbell travelled by plane to visit her sister in Toronto. At the airport, she checked in her luggage at the Air Canada desk. She had to wait two hours for her flight to leave, so she called her friend Verna.

2 Rewrite these sentences. Use capital letters where they are needed.

> Example: the plane will arrive at montego bay today.
> *The plane will arrive at Montego Bay today.*

1 my aunt travelled to miami last week.
2 my brother dean works in new york.
3 many tourists visit dunn's river falls.
4 my grandmother went to london in march.
5 jordan often sees her cousin tiffany on weekends.
6 the airport in kingston is named after norman manley.

> We add 's' to most nouns to make them **plural**, e.g. *pilot – pilots*.
> For nouns ending in **-s**, **-sh**, **-tch** or **-x** we add **es**: *box – boxes*
> Nouns ending in **-y** change **y** to **i** and add **es**: *country – countries*
> Nouns ending in -ay, -ey, -oy just add **s**: *key – keys*
> Most nouns ending in **f** change **f** to **v** and add **es**: *loaf – loaves*
> Most nouns ending in **o** add **s** or **es**: *mango – mangoes*

- **Speaking and listening:** Discuss communication protocol with students, e.g. *listening respectfully, not interrupting*. Draw up a code of practice and display it in your classroom.
- Students can record machines in action on an electronic device and describe what they see.

3 **Write the plural forms of these nouns.**

1 passenger *passengers*
2 bus
3 city
4 airport

5 runway
6 half
7 mango
8 watch

9 thief
10 brush
11 journey
12 body

4 **Research irregular plurals and create a list.**

Search online to find information about irregular plurals. Type a list and save it in a special file.

Remember: Some nouns have irregular plurals, e.g. child – *children*, goose – *geese*

Collective nouns name groups of people, animals and things.

There is a **bank** of computers in the control tower of the airport.

It is dangerous to fly a plane through a large **flock** of birds

WB5 p6

5 **Choose a suitable collective noun for each of these groups.**

swarm litter crowd class team set flock herd

Example: crowd: *a crowd of people*

1 people
2 insects
3 cricketers

4 cows
5 geese
6 kittens

7 students
8 books
9 plates

Here are some collective nouns you should know

a **band** of musicians
a **bunch** of flowers
a **choir** of singers
a **collection** of stamps
a **crowd** of people
a **class** of students
a **colony** of ants
a **crowd** of people
a **crew** of sailors
a **fleet** of ships
a **flock** of birds
a **gang** of thieves
a **herd** of cattle
a **hive** of bees
a **litter** of puppies
a **set** of plates
a **school** of fish
a **swarm** of flies

6 **Find and write the words which cannot be used with the collective nouns.**

Example: litter: puppies birds cubs *birds*

1 **fleet**: boats bikes ships
2 **swarm**: ants insects fish
3 **team**: cards players athletes
4 **set**: tools books trees
5 **flock**: snakes birds sheep
6 **herd**: goats puppies cows

• Let students make their own sentences using collective nouns. Remind them that singular verbs are used with collective nouns.
• **Extension:** Students prepare strategy posters for display in the classroom, illustrating singular and plural nouns and noun types.

WB5 p7

7 **Find and list the abstract nouns in the box.**

Example: *speed (abstract noun)*

> engine speed fuel map emergency ocean
> silence computer kindness airport courage story

> **Abstract nouns**
> name qualities we
> cannot see, hear,
> touch, taste or smell:
> *surprise enjoyment
> honesty*

8 **Choose suitable abstract nouns to complete the sentences.**

> confidence skill pride pleasure truth excitement silence danger

1 There was great *excitement* when the new airport was opened.
2 Experienced pilots try to build the _____ of new pilots.
3 The attendant assured the nervous passenger that there was no _____ .
4 Our teacher insists on _____ while we are working.
5 I get a lot of _____ from finding out how things work.
6 Captain Gordon takes a lot of _____ in her work as a pilot.
7 It takes a lot of _____ to fly a plane.
8 You will get into trouble if you do not tell the _____ .

Word work: Compound nouns

> A **compound noun** is made by putting two separate words together.
> Compound nouns are often written as one word: *run + way* = **runway**
> Sometimes they are written as two separate words: **control tower**
> *The compound nouns on this page all refer to machines or devices in common use.*

WB5 p64

1 **Put together nouns from each oval to make compound nouns.
Write each compound noun as one word.**

Example: motor + cycle *motorcycle*

> ~~motor~~
> air cock head
> lap micro flash
> screw

> craft
> top ~~cycle~~ light
> driver phones pit
> scope

Create a **word bank** to store compound nouns. Write an example sentence for each compound noun.

2 **Now make compound nouns from the words in these ovals. Write the compound nouns as two words.**

> fire
> cell can air
> washing video
> lawn

> machine
> camera mower
> alarm opener phone
> conditioning

- Improve students' reading skills by playing online sight-word games. Select suitable games by using a search engine and typing 'sight word games'.
- **Compound nouns:** Students can create a word bank in a file on their computer or in a vocabulary notebook. Tell them to write a definition and an example sentence for each word they record.

13

Writing: Poster

1 **Design a poster for a display about people who operate machines as part of their work.**

1 Plan the text of your poster. It should contain the following information.
  - The name of the job and the machine s/he operates.
  - Some facts about the work this person does.
  - A picture or photograph of the machine.

2 Plan the layout of your poster.
  Think about the colour of the text and the illustrations you will use. Make sure the text is big enough to read from far away.

3 Draw a rough sketch of your poster.
  Discuss your sketch with another student.

4 Produce a final draft of your poster.
  Ask your teacher to display it in your classroom.

Pilots fly planes.

A pilot must know about
– communication
– navigation
– dealing with emergencies.

2 **Write about a job you would like to do which involves using machines.**

Use the information you discussed in the speaking and listening exercise on page 11.

1 Write notes in word web like the one below.

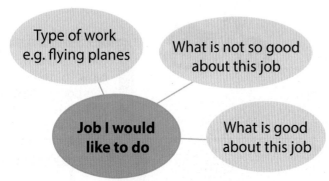

Type of work e.g. flying planes

What is not so good about this job

Job I would like to do

What is good about this job

Look online to find more about the job you chose.

2 Write your first draft.
  - Describe the kind of work you would do.
  - Say what you would like about the job and what you would dislike.

3 Revise what you have written and write a neat copy.

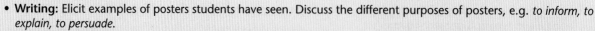
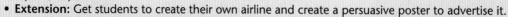

- **Writing:** Elicit examples of posters students have seen. Discuss the different purposes of posters, e.g. *to inform, to explain, to persuade.*
- **Extension:** Get students to create their own airline and create a persuasive poster to advertise it.
- **Digital citizenship:** Take the opportunity to discuss safe online behaviour with students. Remind them never to give personal information to anyone they 'meet' online.

Unit 2

Get ready

**Think of as many different reasons as you can for using computers.
Which other electronic devices do people use regularly?**

Reading

In factual texts like the one below, you often find **text features** which make it easier for
you to find the information you want, e.g. *headings and sub-headings, illustrations*.
You may also find **signal word**s such as *however, in addition*, which help to link different
parts of the text.

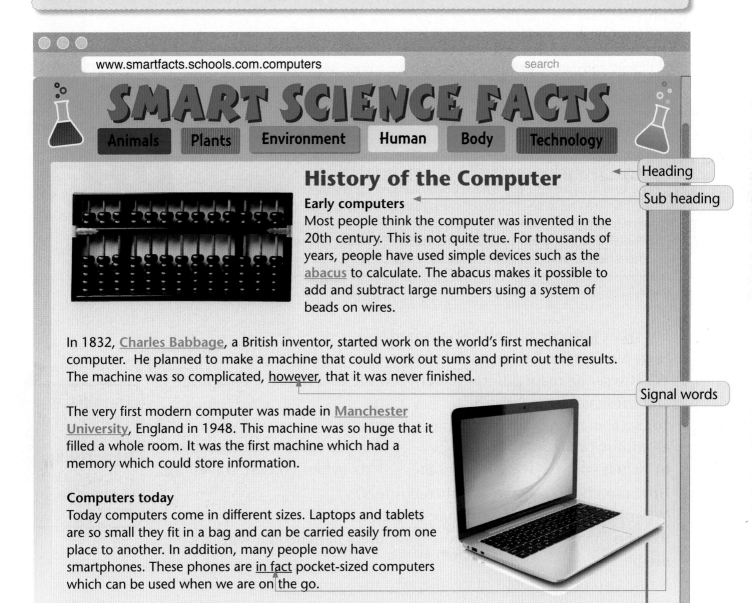

www.smartfacts.schools.com.computers | search

SMART SCIENCE FACTS

Animals | Plants | Environment | Human | Body | Technology

History of the Computer ← Heading

Early computers ← Sub heading

Most people think the computer was invented in the
20th century. This is not quite true. For thousands of
years, people have used simple devices such as the
abacus to calculate. The abacus makes it possible to
add and subtract large numbers using a system of
beads on wires.

In 1832, Charles Babbage, a British inventor, started work on the world's first mechanical
computer. He planned to make a machine that could work out sums and print out the results.
The machine was so complicated, however, that it was never finished.

Signal words

The very first modern computer was made in Manchester
University, England in 1948. This machine was so huge that it
filled a whole room. It was the first machine which had a
memory which could store information.

Computers today

Today computers come in different sizes. Laptops and tablets
are so small they fit in a bag and can be carried easily from one
place to another. In addition, many people now have
smartphones. These phones are in fact pocket-sized computers
which can be used when we are on the go.

- **Get ready:** In the units on Energy and Matter, students discuss and read about machines. Remind them that
  computers are machines.
- **Reading:** Ask students to survey the text by looking at the layout, headings and pictures. Ask *'What is the
  text about? What type of text is it?'* (a story, a letter, a webpage?). Elicit what they know about the history of
  computers and ask them to predict what information the webpage might contain.

Computers play an important role in modern life. We use them in the workplace or during our free time for playing games, watching movies or listening to music. Computers <u>also</u> help us to keep in contact with friends and family who live a long way away. We can send emails and photographs, <u>as well as</u> talk to them on <u>Skype</u>. We can send messages and videos from our phones <u>too</u>, using <u>WhatsApp</u>.

Signal words

Computers make learning fun for children. They can find computer games online which help them with subjects like Mathematics or spelling. In addition, they can use the <u>Internet</u> to find out information for their school projects.

One important use for computers is in factories. In many factories, robots perform tasks once done by humans. The <u>robots</u> are controlled by computers, and are frequently used for difficult and dangerous tasks such as welding, cutting and drilling.

Signal words

Computers are particularly useful in hospitals. <u>For example</u>, doctors use them to carry out tests which them find out what is wrong with their patients. There are now special <u>x-ray machines</u> which use computers to give a picture of the inside of the body. Computers help nurses to monitor their patients and know when they need help.
The lives of disabled people have been changed by computers. Audio programmes have been created which read books to the blind. Wheelchairs have been fitted with mini-computers which enable disabled people to move about. Using the Internet and sending and receiving emails has reduced the isolation felt by many of them.

1 For what purpose was an abacus used?
2 How did Charles Babbage contribute to the development of the modern computer?
3 What was the main difference between the first modern computer and those we have today?
4 To use something 'on the go' means to use it:
   a) all the time.
   c) at home or in the office.
   b) when you are away from home.
   d) when you are travelling.
5 How can children make use of computers?
6 What kind of work is often done by robots?
7 Explain in your own words how computers help people who are disabled.
8 Name two other groups of people who use computers at work.
9 What do you think is the most important use of computers? Why?

The **URL** is the address of the website. **Hyperlinks** will take you to another website.

• **Reading**: Conduct a class *Think Aloud* (see page **184**). Read a paragraph at a time with students and ask questions, e.g. What did this paragraph tell you? Did you learn anything new?
• **DA** According to ability students can continue the *Think Aloud* independently.
• **Comprehension**: Identify different question types. Remind students that they must use their own words in their answers.

Paragraphs

A **paragraph** is a group of sentences about a topic. We use paragraphs to organise material when we write. They have
   a main idea.
   details which develop the main idea.
Each paragraph introduces a new idea.

Read this example of a paragraph.

Main idea → <u>Computers come in different sizes</u>. Laptops and tablets are so small they fit in a bag and can be carried easily from one place to another.

Detail → In addition, many people now have smartphones. These phones are in fact pocket-sized computers which can be used when we are on the go. ← Details

1 **Look at the first two paragraphs of *The History of Computers*. Find:**
   1 the main idea in each paragraph.
   2 details which develop this idea.

2 **Write a paragraph on the following main idea:** *Cell phones have many uses.*

Speaking and listening

These pictures show machines which were invented in the past 200 years.

1 **a)** Describe each machine. Who uses it? What is it used for?
   b) Which of these machines do you think has made the greatest difference to our lives? Why?

2 Choose an important invention. Find out about it and present it to your class.
   a) Find out more about this invention. Make questions to guide your research, e.g. *Who invented it? When? How is it used?*
   b) Make notes for your presentation. Include a picture or a diagram of the invention.
   c) Give your presentation to your class. Remember to:
   • speak slowly and clearly.
   • look at your audience.
   • use your notes to help you, but try not to read.

> Find information about the invention you chose. Use this information to create a portfolio of machines.

• **Speaking and listening**: In large classes, it is difficult for all students to have the opportunity to give their presentations. If there is no time for this, they could present to their groups.
• **Communication protocol**: Remind students to listen respectfully, and not interrupt or call out.
• Groups can create a portfolio of machines with pictures and a short description of their function.

Language

Sentences

A **sentence** is a group of words which contains a **subject** and a **verb** and expresses a complete idea. There are four types of sentences.
Declarative: Makes a statement and ends in a full stop.
Example: *Computers have many different uses.*
Interrogative: Asks a question and ends with a question mark.
Example: *Do you have a computer at home?*
Imperative: Gives an instruction and ends in a full stop.
Example: *Look for information online.*
Exclamatory: Expresses strong feeling and ends with an exclamation mark.
Example: *Well done! What a surprise!*

1 Read these sentences. State which type of sentences they are.

WB5 p49

Example: I received a new tablet for my birthday. *statement*

1 Did you receive my email?
2 My aunt attached a photo to her email.
3 Remember to save your work.
4 Do you often play computer games?
5 Oh dear! The Internet is not working.
6 We often use computers at school.
7 Wait for me in the computer room.
8 Be quiet! I can't hear what the teacher is saying.

2 Copy and punctuate these sentences.

Example: when do you use your computer   *When do you use your computer?*

1 doctors find computers useful
2 hurry up we are going to be late
3 do you have a smartphone
4 don't forget to tell your friends
5 what are you doing on the weekend
6 look out there's a car coming
7 this term we are learning about forces and machines
8 that's an amazing game where did you get it

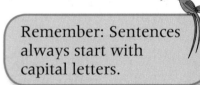

Remember: Sentences always start with capital letters.

3 Use your own ideas to write an example of each type of sentence.
a) declarative   c) imperative
b) interrogative   d) exclamatory

• To help students to engage with the topic, ask them what they already know about sentence types and punctuation before reading the information in the focus box at the top of the page.
• **DA** According to ability allow some students to complete fewer sentences in Exercises 2 and 3.

Subject and predicate

Sentences have two parts.
1 **Subject**: the person or thing which performs the action.
2 **Predicate**: the part of the sentence which contains the verb.

Tara	*has a new computer.*
Tara and her friends	*play computer games.*
↑	↑
subject	**predicate**

Tara is a simple subject.
Tara and her friends is a complete subject.

WB5 p32

1 **Underline the subject in each of these sentences. Is it singular or plural? Is it a simple or a complete subject?**

Example: <u>The students</u> love their computer lessons. *plural – simple*

1 My friend and I often call each other.
2 The Internet is really useful for research.
3 My parents often help me with my work.
4 We all enjoy watching videos online.
5 The computer room is open every day.
6 Marie's mother and sister waited for her.

The simple **predicate** in a sentence is the verb or verb phrase.
The **complete predicate** is the verb + the information related to it.

Jake <u>sent</u> a text to his friend.   *He <u>is waiting</u> for a reply.*
↖   ↗
simple predicates
Sheena <u>saw her friends</u>.   *They <u>were waiting at the bus stop</u>.*
↖   ↗
complete predicates

2 **Circle the simple predicate and underline the complete predicate in these sentences.**

Example: My sister (bought) a new smartphone yesterday.

1 We learnt how to create a website.
2 My brother is using his new tablet.
3 We are waiting for our computer lesson.
4 Brandon has lost his cell phone.
5 Dad's new computer was expensive.
6 The library is open on Saturdays

3 **Write complete predicates for these subjects.**

1 The students in my class
2 Our teacher
3 Smartphones
4 The bus
5 The school library
6 My friends and I

• **Subject and predicate:** Students can identify subject and predicate in the reading text on page 15. When they answer Exercise 5, remind them that the verbs they use in the predicate must agree with the subject.
• **DA** Allow some students to write fewer sentences in Exercise 5.

Word study: Spelling
Syllables

> Dividing words into syllables helps us to read and spell them.

> Words are made up groups of letters called **syllables**. Some words have only one syllable, others have more than one.
> bag = 1 syllable   tab / let = 2 syllables   com / pu / ter = 3 syllables
> The number of vowel sounds in a word equals the number of syllables.

WB5 p32

a) Divide these words into syllables. Write them in a table.

> email   phone   hospital   machine   modern
> inventor   wheelchair   nurse   memory   robot

One syllable	Two syllables	Three syllables
	e / mail	

b) Add three words of your own to each column.

Tricky words

> Some words are difficult to spell. Here are some strategies which may help you.
> Any time you have to divide words into syllables – use space slash space
> 1 Divide long words into syllables: *com / pli / ca/ ted*
> 2 Highlight the difficult part of the word: *beautiful, photograph*
> 3 Sound out words as they are written: *ans-wer, bus-i-ness*
> 4 Find short words inside longer words: *believe* (lie), *separate* (a rat)

**a) Which strategy from the box above would
you use to help you spell these words?**

> Use the **look/ cover/ write/ check** method to help you learn to spell words. Look at the word and learn the spelling. **Cover** the word, then **write** it and **check** you have spelled it correctly.

Example: *geography (2)*

machine	doubt	design
environment	foreign	because
secretary	independence	difficulty
knowledge	necessary	friend

b) Learn the words and test your partner.

- **Syllables:** Get students to sound out words and clap to work out the number of syllables.
- **Tricky words:** Create rhymes and catch phrases with your students to help them spell tricky words.
- **DA** Allow some students to learn fewer words and test them on these.
- You will find more exercises on spelling, including clusters and silent letters, in the Workbook (pages 69–72).

Writing: Report

Write a report about an important invention.

You can write:

- **EITHER** about the invention you described in the Speaking and listening exercise on page 17.
- **OR** about a different invention.

Follow the stages below to write your report.

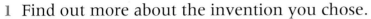

1 Find out more about the invention you chose.

- Decide which information sources you will use, e.g. *encyclopaedias, Internet*.
- Prepare questions to guide your research.
- Carry out your research and make notes about what you find.

2 Plan your report.

   Use an organiser like the one below to help you.

> When you conduct research, you must first decide what you want to find out. Prepare questions using question words like **What? Where? When? Who? Why? How?**

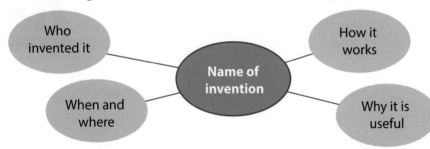

3 Write the first draft of your report.

- Remember to divide your report into paragraphs.
- Each paragraph should have a main idea with details which develop this idea.
- Use signal words like *also, in addition, for example*.

4 Show your first draft to another student. Ask this student to tell you:

- what he/she likes about your report.
- what you could improve.

5 Write or type a neat copy of your report to give to your teacher.

 Activity

Prepare a class folder about important inventions.

- Each of you prepares a page about the invention you chose for your report. Use different fonts and colours.
- Include pictures of the invention you chose.
- Display your folder in your classroom.

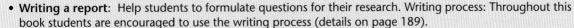

- **Writing a report:** Help students to formulate questions for their research. Writing process: Throughout this book students are encouraged to use the writing process (details on page 189).
- **DA** Allow some students to write just one paragraph for their report.
- Students who are talented artists can help others with their reports.
- **Activity:** Encourage students to be supportive each others' efforts.

Get ready

Think of different machines which make sounds as they work.
What sounds do they make? Are they loud or soft?

Reading

1 **The two poems below were written by British poet, Michael Rosen.**
Look over them to see which text features you can find.

> Poetry: Look for the following text features:
> • Short lines and verses
> • Lines which rhyme
> • Rhythm and repetition

Lubricate the Joints

Lubricate the joints
and the railtrack points
the gears
and the shears
and the clocks
and the locks;
and the drills
and the mills
and the trimmers

and the strimmers
and the rotors
and the motors
keep them whirring
keep them purring
keep them smooth
on the move
in the grooooooooooove
oh yeah!

Beneath my Feet

I stood in the street
and beneath my feet
I felt the purring
and murmuring
of tubes and pipes.

All the people in the houses, shops and factories
switching on and phoning up
washing away and turning off
buttons, taps, levers, controls

and the pipes and tubes hummed
with the flow and current
purring
and murmuring
beneath my feet
in the street.

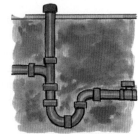

• **Get ready:** Get students to classify the different sounds made by machines, e.g. *machines in the kitchen, in the street, on a construction site.*
• **Reading:** Read the poems aloud so students can appreciate the rhythm and the sounds created.

1 What does 'lubricate' mean?
2 Give an example of a machine which has to be lubricated, e.g. a car engine.
3 Explain why the second poem is called *Beneath My Feet*.
4 What kind of *buttons* and *controls* do you think people might switch on and turn off in their houses?
5 What do you think was the poet's purpose when he wrote these poems?
   a) to inform
   b) to entertain
   c) to persuade
6 Write an example from each poem of two lines which rhyme.
7 Find two examples of onomatopoeia in *Beneath My Feet*.
8 Which poem did you prefer? Why?

> Onomatopoeia **is when the sound of a word imitates its meaning, e.g.** *whirr* imitates the sound made by some machines.

> What did you learn from reading these poems? Complete a 'Reading response' chart (page 183) in your Learning Journal.

2 **Make notes about the poems in a table.**

Title and text type	*Lubricate the Joints: Poem*	*Beneath My Feet*
Topic		
Text features		
Words which were new to me		
What I liked		

3 **Prepare a recitation of both poems.**

> Shall we recite one poem each?

> Good idea. Which one would you like to recite?

> Look for websites with recordings of sounds. Play them for your friends to guess.

1 Plan your recitation.
   • Will you speak *in unison* (together) or separately?
   • Will you recite some lines faster than others?
   • Will you beat out the rhythm or use sound effects?
2 Perform your recitation to your class.

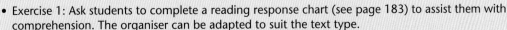

• Exercise 1: Ask students to complete a reading response chart (see page 183) to assist them with comprehension. The organiser can be adapted to suit the text type.
• **ICT** Film machines in action on an electronic device. Play the videos to students and get them to describe what they can see.
• **Learning Journal:** Students can make notes about poems they read using the table from this page.

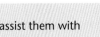

Speaking and listening

1  **Look at the comic strip. Talk about what is happening.**

2 **Work in groups of five or six students. Act out the situation in the comic strip.**

You can add more scenes to your play.

Look online for comic strips. What features do they contain?

Language: Simple present tense

Subject–verb agreement

We use the **simple present tense** for *facts* or for things which happen *regularly*.
The machine makes a lot of noise. (fact)
The students use the computer room on Thursdays. (regular action)
Verbs must agree with their subjects. If the subject is **singular** (one person or thing) we use a singular verb: *Jodie's mother <u>makes</u> dresses on her sewing machine.*
If the subject is **plural**, we use a plural verb: *Dressmakers <u>use</u> sewing machines for their work.*

- Discuss features of comic strips, e.g. speech bubbles, captions, sounds. Get students to create their own comic strips about machines. Suggest titles, e.g. *Machines Rule*.
- Allow students to first use JC when they perform their skits. They can then perform the same skit in SJE.

24

1 **Choose the correct verb forms to complete the paragraph.**

WB5 p23–4

1 Machines *perform* (perform / performs) many tasks.
2 We _____ (has / have) a lot of machines in our streets.
3 We _____ (learns / learn) about machines in our science lessons.
4 My brother sometimes _____ (lets / let) me use his new tablet.
5 I often _____ (stays / stay) after school for Computer Club.
6 My big sister _____ (wants / want) to learn to drive.
7 My sister and I _____ (loves / love) playing computer games.
8 Kymani often _____ (helps / help) his father in the garden.

2 **Select suitable verbs to complete the paragraph. Write the correct endings.**

prefer ~~love~~ watch come ask want switch refuse go

Selena's brother Chris loves watching sports. As soon as he _____ (1) home from school, he _____ (2) on the television and _____ (3) football. Selena and her sister _____ (4) watching movies. They often _____ (5) Chris to change the programme but he always _____ (6). Sometimes Chris _____ (7) out with his friends in the evening. Then Selena and her sister can choose what they _____ (8) to watch.

Verbs ending in '**sh**', '**tch**' and '**x**' add 'es' in the simple present tense, e.g. she *watches*, she *brushes*, she *mixes*
The verbs **go** and **do** also add **es**: she *goes*, she *does*
Verbs ending in '**y**' change '**y**' to '**ies**', e.g. she *carries*

Subject–verb agreement: questions

We use the helping verb do / does + root verb to form questions in the simple present tense.
Does Chris *like* sports?

helping verb   root verb

1 **Complete the questions with *do* or *does*. Circle the root verbs.**

Example: <u>Do</u> you often use machinery?

1 Where _____ you go to school?
2 _____ your school have a computer room?
3 Which subjects _____ you like best?
4 _____ your teacher give you a lot of homework?
5 Which machines _____ builders use?
6 _____ an electric drill make a lot of noise?

• You could point out the pronoun 'I' is singular, and 'you' is singular if we are talking to one person. However, 's' is not added to verbs used with these pronouns.
• **Questions:** The word *interrogative* could be used here instead of question. '**Helping**' verbs are sometimes known as *auxiliary verbs*.

2 **Write questions using each set of words.**

> Example: where / bus / stop *Where does the bus stop?*

1 what games / Max / like playing
2 the girls / work hard / in class
3 your friend / live / near you
4 you / walk to school
5 where / your teacher / live
6 what / your friends / do / on weekends

Subject–verb agreement: negatives

1 **Rewrite the sentences below as negative sentences.**

> Example: Mom needs a robot.
> *Mom does not need a robot.*

1 The children help Mom with the housework.
2 Mom has a lot of equipment in her kitchen.
3 Dara enjoys using a sewing machine.
4 My sister often sends emails to her friends.
5 My brother lets me play games on his computer.
6 My Mom and Dad watch television in the evening.

We also use do / does to form the negative of the simple present tense.
Mom does not want the robot to stay.

helping verb   root verb

The children do not want the robot to go.

2 **What do you do on the weekend? Write sentences as follows:**

* four sentences saying what you do.
* four sentences saying what you do not do.

Subject–verb agreement: collective nouns

1 **Complete the sentences with the correct forms of the verbs in brackets.**

We use **singular verbs** with collective nouns.
*My group often **gives** presentations to the class.* Group is a collective noun.

Not all the subjects of the sentences are collective nouns.

1 Our class sometimes _____ (takes / take) part in competitions.
2 The teachers at my school _____ (gives / give) us a lot of homework.
3 The school choir _____ (is / are) learning some new songs.
4 All the students _____ (enjoys / enjoy) computer lessons.
5 There _____ (is / are) a new set of encyclopaedias in the school library.
6 The band _____ (plays / play) regularly at festivals and competitions.
7 The crowd always _____ (claps / clap) loudly.
8 The school team _____ (wins / win) most of its matches.

---

* Before attempting the exercise on collective nouns, revise the list of collective nouns on page 12. Identify the sentences that have collective nouns as their subjects.
* **DA** Allow some students to write fewer sentences.

Subject–verb agreement: indefinite pronouns

Words like *everybody* and *something* are **indefinite pronouns**. We use singular verbs with them.
Example: *Everybody* **wants** *to have a smartphone. Something* **is** *wrong with my phone.*

Complete the story with the correct verb forms.

Everyone *knows* (knows / know) Davina Phillips, the famous television presenter. Today it _____ (1 is / are) Prize Giving at Paul's school and Davina _____ (2 is / are) going to present the awards. Nobody _____ (3 wants / want) to miss this event, but neither of Paul's parents _____ (4 is / are) able to go. Paul's aunt and cousins _____ (5 is / are) there, however. Every parent in the audience _____ (6 claps / clap) loudly when Davina and the Principal _____ (7 enters / enter) the hall. The choir _____ (8 starts / start) singing. The students _____(9 goes / go) up one at a time to collect their prizes. Each student in the school _____ (10 receives / receive) a signed photograph of Davina.

These words are always used with singular verbs	
everybody	everything
everyone	anyone
someone	somebody
something	anything
somebody	anybody
nobody	no one
nothing	none
neither	either
each	every

Word study: Interjections

WB5 p47

1 **Find the interjections in the following sentences.**

1 Wow! That dog is really fierce.
2 Oh dear! The battery on my phone is flat.
3 Ouch! I pinched my finger in the door.
4 Help! I'm going to fall.
5 Shh! I can't hear what my friend is saying.
6 Great! I've got enough money to buy a tablet.
7 Whew! It's very hot today.
8 Sorry! I didn't mean to break the glass.

2 **Complete these sentences with suitable interjections.**

1 *Hey!* That's not your phone.
2 _____ Don't make so much noise.
3 _____ The holidays start tomorrow.
4 _____ I can't remember my password.
5 _____ You won the competition.
6 _____ I hit my head on the bed.
7 _____ I've can't find your book.
8 _____ That machine is huge.

- **Exercise 8:** You may need to go through this exercise with the whole class before students write answers.
- **DA** Allow some students to write only the subjects with the correct verbs.
- **Interjections:** Students can create cartoons to illustrate different interjections

Onomatopoeia

1 There are onomatopoeic words for sounds made by tools and machines. Think of as many as you can.

Screech!

Whirr!

Click!

Boom!

2 a) Match these words with a suitable phrase below.

crunch whack bang crash clang creak jingle rattle splash drip

1 a heavy object falling into water
2 a bunch of keys
3 a cricket bat hitting a ball
4 someone stepping on broken glass
5 a glass falling to the floor

6 a door slamming
7 water pouring very slowly from a tap
8 windows shaking in the wind
9 trees swaying in the wind
10 a hammer hitting a metal object

b) Use the words in your own sentences.

Example: *The rock fell into the water with a loud splash.*

3 Suggest onomatopoeic words for the sound made by:

1 a clock
2 a cell phone
3 a washing machine

4 the horn of a car
5 an old bus
6 a metal chain

Research onomatopoeia online. Classify the sounds, e.g. sounds made by animals, people or machines.

Writing

Screeching brakes and blaring horn
Crazy dog running across the road
Racing recklessly in front of the bus
Everyone clinging to their seats
Each one thankful he's safe
Cheering the skilful driver
Heading home safely now

In an **acrostic poem** the poet chooses a word and uses the letters to write each line of the poem. Look at the example.

1 Choose two more onomatopoeic words. Create verses with them to add to the acrostic poem above.

2 Write verses in groups. Combine them to make a class acrostic poem.

Screech!

28

• **Onomatopoeia:** Before beginning the exercises, brainstorm examples of onomatopoeia. After completing the exercises, students can look for examples online and classify the sounds they find.
• **Writing:** Students can create a class poem for a wall display or to go on their class blog.
• **Learning Journal:** Students can collect interesting words and phrases to use in their writing.

Unit 4

Get ready

Road users are safe if everyone obeys the rules of the road. Which rules of the road do you know?

Reading

Look at the title of the story and the pictures.

- Predict what the story will be about.
- As you read, compare the story with your predictions.

> **Predicting** means using clues such as pictures, headings and text to think ahead about what might happen in a text.

WB5 p78

In Business

Characters → Clive had built a pushcart. It had not been easy to find a crate the right size and source the wheels from a junk yard. Mr. Taylor from next door had helped him assemble it.

> **PUSHCART RIDE**
> **$1.00**
> 25% discount if you push it back up the hill yourself!

"It's nice to see you making something," he said. "Too many of you boys just sit in front of a screen all day pressing buttons."

Problem 1 → Clive didn't tell Mr. Taylor that he didn't have any buttons to press. There was no flash computer or smart cell phone in his house. In fact, since Mom lost her job, there wasn't much of anything.

Solution 1 → That's why he wanted a pushcart: to help Mom.

Setting → There it was in all its glory, at the top of a hill, painted blue and red with leftover paint. He put up a sign. By midday business was booming. Kids were lining up to exchange their hot dollars for three minutes of the sweetest terror. One after the other, they hurtled down the hill, swerving this way and that, clattering and rattling and squealing at the tops of their voices.

- **Get ready:** Take the opportunity to review road safety rules with your students.
- **Reading:** Talk about different pre-reading strategies, e.g. *surveying, scanning, predicting*. Explain that these will help students when they approach a new text. Tell them to stop from time to time as they read and review their predictions. Is there anything they want to change?

They took no notice of Mrs. Dee who shook her fist and cursed when the pushcart narrowly missed a customer who jumped in fright and knocked over her pile of carefully arranged mangoes. "Look what you have done!" she screamed. "You have ruined my display."

"Why is she shouting at me?" thought Clive. "She should be shouting at her customer."

Then Mr. Taylor came along. He didn't roar or yell. He came close to Clive and whispered in his ear. "This is dangerous Clive. What if a car comes up while these children are going down?"

> **Problem 2**

Clive took notice of Mr. Taylor. "I should have thought about safety," he told himself. Next time the pushcart came back up the hill, he picked up his sign and threw it in the cart. "All done!" he announced to the children still clamouring for a ride; and he strode home with heavy pockets and a light heart.

> **Solution 2**

Tomorrow he'd find another, safer location for his business.

Leonie Bennett

Comprehension:
Read each question carefully. Think about where you will find the answer.
Right there: You will find the information right there in the text.
Think and search: You have to combine information from different parts of the text.
Author and me: You have to work out the answer from clues the author gives you.
On my own: You use your own ideas based on what you have read in the text.

1 Explain in your own words why Clive built a pushcart.
2 How much did children pay for a ride if they pushed the cart up the hill themselves?
3 What do you think Mrs. Dee's occupation is?
4 Was Clive's business successful by midday? How do you know that?
5 '*She* (Mrs. Dee) *should be shouting at her customer*.' Why does Clive think that? Do you agree with him?
6 What does the phrase '*with heavy pockets and a light heart*' tell us about Clive?
7 Think of a word or phrase similar in meaning to '*clamouring*'.
8 Which expressions in the list below best describe Clive?
  lazy   energetic   good at making things   disobedient   inconsiderate   inventive
9 What do you think of Clive's behaviour in this story? Provide evidence from the text to support your answer.
10 What would be an ideal location for Clive's business?

- Discuss QAR (question–answer relationships). Remind students that they will not always find the answer to questions directly in the text. They often need to 'read between the lines' and infer from clues in the text what the writer is telling them.
- **Learning Journal**: Students can complete a 'Reading response' chart (page 183) about the comprehension exercise.

Story elements

The elements of a story include
  Characters: the people or animals in the story.
  Setting: the time and the place where the events take place.
  Conflict: problem faced by the character.
  Resolution: the way the characters solve the problem at the end of the story.

1 **Discuss and complete this story map about 'In Business'.**

In some stories the characters must solve more than one problem.

Title of story	
Characters	
Setting	
Conflict	
Resolution	

2 **Draw a diagram like this to show the second problem and solution in the story 'In Business'.**

Problem 1 Clive's mother had no money.	→	**Solution 1** Clive made a pushcart to earn some money.

Speaking and listening

Look at the diagrams. Explain how to make your own rocket.
You should only make the rocket if you have an adult to supervise you.

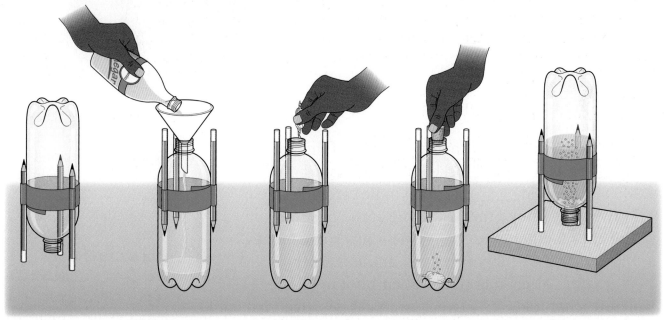

Make 'feet' for your rocket.

Half fill the bottle with vinegar.

Wrap baking soda in paper. Place in bottle.

Seal the bottle with a cork.

Take your rocket outside and launch it.

- **Comprehension**: Point out that the setting of a story is not always described in the first paragraph. Sometimes, as in this story, it becomes clear as the story develops.
- **Speaking and listening**: Emphasise the importance of safety when students make models. An adult should always check that the activity they have chosen is safe, and supervise them when they are working with tools.

Language: Pronouns

Pronouns are words we use to replace nouns. When the noun is the **subject** of the sentence, we use subject pronouns.
Clive made a pushcart.   ~~Clive~~ He painted it with leftover paint.
When the noun is the **object** of the sentence, we use object pronouns.
Mr Taylor spoke to Clive. He told ~~Clive~~ him the road was dangerous.

ICT Activity

Look online to find out how to make a toy vehicle out of waste products such as plastic bottles or cans.
Collect the materials you need and make your vehicle.
Ask an adult to supervise you.
Bring your vehicle to class and explain how you made it.

---

1 **Are the underlined words the subject or object of the verbs in the sentences?**

> The subject of a verb *performs* the action. The object *receives* the action.

1 <u>Clive's friends</u> all wanted a ride in the pushcart.
2 The following day, <u>Clive</u> found a new place for his cart.
3 Did the pushcart overturn <u>the trader's stall</u>?
4 Did <u>Mr. Taylor</u> speak to Clive?
5 <u>Some of the people in the market</u> shouted at Clive.
6 The children paid <u>Clive</u> one dollar for each ride.
7 Mom told <u>my brother and me</u> to be careful.
8 The children did not see <u>the bump in the road</u>.

WB5 p15

2 **Choose the correct pronouns to complete the sentences.**

1 Clive told *them* (they / them) the price of the ride.
2 _____ (I / Me) made a rocket out of a plastic bottle.
3 My teacher told _____ (we / us) to be careful.
4 I saw _____ (they / them) waiting at the bus stop.
5 The girl's mother gave _____ (she / her) some money.
6 Did _____ (they / them) see you at the market?
7 _____ (She / Her) told (they / them) not to be late.
8 Our teacher told _____ (we / us) that _____ (we / us) could go home early.

Subject pronouns	
I	we
you	you
he, she, it	they

Object pronouns	
me	us
you	you
him, her, it	them

- **Pronouns:** Students often find it difficult to use pronouns correctly as they are used differently in JC. Tell them to ask questions to check whether words are the subject or the object of verbs, e.g. *Who wanted a ride? Clive's friends* (subject). *What did the pushcart overturn? The trader's stall* (object).
- **DA** Allow some students to write fewer sentences in each exercise.

3 **Replace the underlined nouns with pronouns.**

The children saw the notice about the pushcart rides. ~~The children~~ *They* told Clive they were bored and wanted to have fun. <u>Clive</u> told <u>the children</u> to wait their turn. Amos became impatient. <u>Amos</u> did not want to wait for his turn. <u>Amos</u> pushed in front of Marissa and Crystal and jumped into the cart. <u>Marissa and Crystal</u> were furious. "Marissa and I were before Amos," Crystal told Clive. "Please let <u>Marissa and me</u> go first." It was too late. Amos raced down the slope and Clive could not stop <u>Amos</u>. The cart hit a bump and Amos fell out. <u>Amos</u> was not hurt, but the cart was damaged. The girls were disappointed. Clive told the girls to go home. <u>Clive</u> promised to repair the cart. Amos offered to help <u>Clive</u>.

> There is no difference between subject and object pronouns in Jamaican Creole.
> **JC:** **Singular**: mi, yu, im, har, it **Plural**: wi, unu, dem

4 **Rewrite these sentences in Standard Jamaican English.**

Example: Mi like har. *I like her.*

1 Wi nuh like dem.
2 Dem no like wi.
3 Im tink dat nuh right.
4 Unu kno betta.
5 Mi see yuh dere.
6 Im say im kno har.
7 Shi tell wi fi wait dere.
8 Im see mi dere las week.

Word study: Word building – root words

WB5 p63

> **Root words** are the main parts of words. We can add endings and word parts like prefixes and suffixes to them. We sometimes need to change the spelling of root words when we add endings and word parts.
> Example: *care* (root word) *cared, caring, careful, carefully, careless, carelessly*

1 **Write root words from which these words are formed.**

Example: dangerous *danger*

1 disagree
2 arrangement
3 sweetest
4 invention
5 building
6 considerate
7 beautiful
8 impatiently
9 construction
10 renewable
11 crowded
12 happiness

> We sometimes change the spelling of root words when we add endings or word parts, e.g. *plan – planned, stop – stopped.*

- Exercise 3 (pronouns): Tell students to read this exercise aloud as it is written. Then they can read it with pronouns replacing the underlined nouns, and observe the difference.
- **DA** Allow some students to write just the pronouns instead of writing out the whole exercise.
- **Extension:** Exercise 1 (root words): Students can name the parts of speech of the root words they find.

2 **Complete the sentences with the correct forms of the root words in brackets.**

> Example: Mr. Taylor told Clive he should be more *careful*. (care)

1 Amos was very _____ when the pushcart was damaged. (help)
2 The children were _____ about the pushcart rides. (excite)
3 Most of them waited _____ for their ride. (patient)
4 Mr. Taylor was _____ about the children's safety. (worry)
5 The cart narrowly avoided hitting a _____ . (build)
6 Clive painted the cart in _____ colours. (attract)

Prefixes

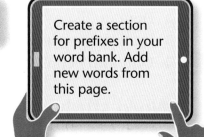

Remember: A prefix is a group of letters added to the beginning of a word to change its meaning.

Here are some prefixes you should know.

bi	*two*	bicycle	im-	*not*	impossible
dis-	*not*	dishonest	mis-	*wrong*	misunderstand
ir-	*not*	irresponsible	multi-	*many*	multi-coloured
in-	*not*	incorrect			

3 **Add prefixes to these words. Add them to the table.**   WB5 p65–6

Use your dictionary to help you.

> legal perfect obedient complete friendly active mature
> possible responsible grateful appear regular logical

Create a section for prefixes in your word bank. Add new words from this page.

dis-	il-	im-
dishonest	*illegible*	*impatient*
in-	ir-	un-
incorrect	*irrelevant*	*unusual*

4 **Choose one word from each section of the table. Write it in a sentence of your own.**

> Example: *The traders thought Clive was irresponsible.*

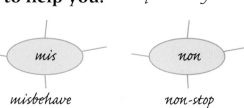

pre

pre-arrange

5 **Add prefixes to these words. Use your dictionary to help you. Use the words to complete the word webs.**

> fiction school place flight manage
> stick paid fortune iron

mis

misbehave

non

non-stop

6 **Choose one word from each web. Write it in a sentence of your own.**

• Extend students' vocabulary by giving them a list of root words and asking them to find as many words made from these words as they can. Students can learn to spell some of the words on this page.
• **ICT** There are several interactive games online which students can use to help them learn about prefixes.

Study skills: Using a dictionary

Study the extract from a dictionary.

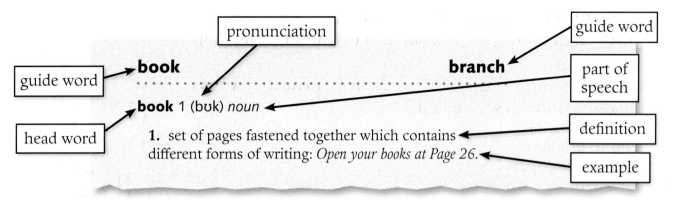

pronunciation

guide word

guide word

head word

book

branch

part of speech

book 1 (bʊk) *noun*

1. set of pages fastened together which contains different forms of writing: *Open your books at Page 26.*

definition

example

1 Underline the words which could be used between the guide words.

Example: book – branch: bay   blood   <u>bookcase</u>   bubble   boat

1	**family – football**	fact	farm	field	forest	fashion
2	**greet – grill**	grasp	grid	ground	grey	grumble
3	**cross – crown**	crush	crow	crop	cry	crowd
4	**middle – might**	midday	midnight	mild	midget	migrate
5	**bathe – battle**	bay	batsman	bathroom	baseball	barrier

2 Write a definition and an example sentence for these words.

Example: *location (noun): place   Clive looked for a new location for his pushcart.*

1 solution (noun)   2 swerve (verb)   3 vehicle (noun)   4 hazardous (adjective)

Writing: Story

1 Write a story beginning with this sentence:
Shanice had invited her friends to go on a picnic, but it was raining.

2 Complete a story plan.

3 Use your own ideas to finish the plan.

Title of story	
Characters	*Shanice, her friends*
Setting	*Shanice's house*
Conflict	*The rain has ruined Shanice's plans.*
Resolution	

- **Using a dictionary**: Model how to use a dictionary to decipher the meanings of words.
- Encourage students to work out the meaning of words from the context before they look in the dictionary.
- **Writing**: Share ideas about possible solutions to Shanice's problem. After students have written their first draft, discuss how they could improve it, e.g. use *interesting adjectives, include some conversation.*

Reading

Grade 5 students carried out a traffic survey on the road outside their school. Study this table of their results and answer the questions.

Type of vehicle	Direction: Going into town centre		Direction: Going away from town centre	
	From 8.00 am to 8.10 am	From 4.00 pm to 4.10 pm	From 8.00 am to 8.10 am	From 4.00 pm to 4.10 pm
Car	42	19	17	37
Truck	7	1	2	5
Van	7	5	3	4
Bus	3	2	1	2
Taxi	1	0	1	3
Motorbike	10	6	5	9

1 How many times a day did the students survey the traffic?

   a) once
   b) twice
   c) three times
   d) four times

2 For how long did the students survey the traffic each time?

   a) an hour
   b) fifteen minutes
   c) ten minutes
   d) twenty minutes

3 Which vehicle was the most frequently counted?

   a) car
   b) bus
   c) motorbike
   d) van

4 Which vehicle was seen least frequently?

   a) van
   b) taxi
   c) truck
   d) car

5 How many cars were counted going away from town in the afternoon?

   a) 17
   b) 19
   c) 42
   d) 37

6 **a)** Do more vehicles go into the town in the morning or in the evening?
   b) Why do you think this might be?

7 Do you think it is good or bad to travel along a busy road? Why/ Why not?

8 In two sentences, summarise the information in the table. Do not give details of different types of vehicles. Begin your sentences like this:

There is more traffic …   *There is less traffic …*

Activity

1 **Conduct your own survey of how students travel to school. Present your results in a table like the one above.**

• Discuss with students the possible reasons for conducting a traffic survey. Ask them to suggest other surveys student groups could conduct.
• **Activity**: Help students to conduct the survey. Show them how to record the results and enter them in a table.

2 **Read this poem about a boy on a bicycle and identify the features of a poem.**

Swooping down the slope
With the wind at my back
My bike wheels whirring
I'm flying through the air
Just like an aeroplane.

Climbing up the hill
My muscles straining
Bike wheels grinding
Moving at a snail's pace
Struggling to the top.

Julia Sander

3 **Answer the questions.**

1 What is the poet doing?
  a) climbing a hill
  b) pretending to be an aeroplane
  c) going for a walk
  d) riding his bicycle

2 Where is he in the first verse of the poem?

3 Find an example of onomatopoeia in the first verse.

4 Why do you think the poet compares himself to an aeroplane?

5 How does the writer feel in the first verse of the poem?
  a) enthusiastic
  b) anxious
  c) exhausted
  d) bored

6 How does his mood change in the second verse?

7 a) Which is the odd one out of these words?

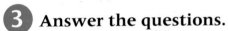

  straining   struggling   swooping   grinding

  b) Explain why the word you chose is the odd one out.

8 Explain why the poet says that he is moving
  '*at a snail's pace*'.

9 Which part of the boy's bicycle ride would you enjoy
  most? Why?

In your Learning Journal,
copy and complete a 'How
did I do?' chart (page 183)
to reflect on your reading
comprehension.

• Encourage students to reflect on their ability as readers. Ask questions to guide their reflections, e.g. *What do you enjoy reading? What do you find difficult? How could you improve?*
• **Learning Journal:** Work with your class to help them complete a *'How did I do?'* chart (page 183).

37

Language
Nouns

1 **Find and write three common nouns and three proper nouns from the poem on the previous page.**

2 **Use the collective nouns in the box to complete the sentences.**

> bunch   group   team   swarm   gang   set   crowd   collection

1 The former student donated a *set* of encyclopaedias to the school library.
2 The _____ of footballers waited impatiently for the rain to stop.
3 The _____ was so big I could not see my friends.
4 'The Illustrated Anancy' is a _____ of stories for children.
5 The police arrested the _____ of thieves who tried to break into the bank.
6 The Caymans are a _____ of islands which are not far from Jamaica.
7 Grandad found a _____ of ants nesting in the roots of the tree.
8 Tara picked a lovely _____ of flowers for her grandmother.

3 **Change these adjectives into abstract nouns.**

> Example: dangerous *danger*

1 proud	3 hopeful	5 strong	7 beautiful
2 excited	4 anxious	6 envious	8 happy

Sentences

1 **Write these sentences with correct punctuation. State which type of sentence they are.**

1 do you know how to ride a bicycle
2 do not run across the road
3 my new bicycle has a puncture
4 look out there's a car coming
5 there is a lot of traffic on the road today
6 have you ever travelled by plane
7 hurry up we're going to be late
8 where are you going today

2 **Write predicates for each of these sentences. Underline each complete predicate and circle each simple predicate.**

> Example: Carl is meeting his friend at the library.

1 The library …
2 My brother and sister …
3 The cars in the road …
4 My friend and I …
5 The footballer …
6 The pilot and the co-pilot …
7 My school …
8 My mother's new car …

- You may wish to revise each grammar point before students complete the exercises.
- **Sentences:** Remind students of the four types of sentence: *declarative, interrogative, imperative and exclamatory.*
- **DA** Work with some students in a group and observe where they have difficulties.

Verbs

1 Identify the subject in each sentence. Is it singular or plural?

Example: The students carried out a traffic survey. *the students – plural*

1 The man is riding a bicycle.
2 His friends are waiting for him in the town centre.
3 His bicycle goes very fast.
4 The children learn about road safety at school.
5 The roads are very dangerous.
6 My brother's car is very old.
7 My friends and I take the bus to school.
8 The bus stops outside our school.

2 Complete these sentences with the correct verb forms.

Example: Machines *perform* a lot of different tasks.   (perform / performs)

1 Computers _____ learning more fun. (make / makes)
2 My brother _____ a lot of time on his computer. (spend / spends)
3 We all _____ watching DVD's. (like / likes)
4 The national football team _____ every day. (trains / train)
5 _____ want to play my new game with me? (do / does)
6 Everyone _____ to keep the classroom tidy. (help / helps)
7 My old phone _____ not work very well. (do / does)
8 Nobody _____ to get into trouble. (want / wants)

Pronouns

Choose the correct pronoun to complete these sentences.

Example: My aunt lives in the USA. (She/Her) is an airline pilot.
She is an airline pilot.

1 My aunt told (we / us) about her work.
2 (I / Me) found it very interesting.
3 (She / Her) promised to take me to the airport.
4 The pilot spoke to us during the flight but we did not see (he / him).
5 My cousins were at the airport. I saw (they / them) waiting for me.
6 My cousins and (I / me) meet every year.
7 (We / Us) often spend time at the beach.
8 I sent (they / them) an email but (they / them) have not responded.

- **Verbs**: Remind students that singular verbs are used with collective nouns and indefinite pronouns.
- **Pronouns**: You may wish to revise subject and object pronouns with students before they complete this exercise.

Word work: Compound nouns

Select the correct words to make compound nouns.

1 Books are stored in a book *case*.
   a) page   b) chapter   c) case   d) review

2 Paul used a screw_____ to tighten the screws on his cycle.
   a) top   b) driver   c) head   d) hammer

3 The guest speaker used a micro_____ to speak to the audience.
   a) wave   b) scope   c) plug   d) phone

4 The stone smashed the head_____ on the truck.
   a) beam   b) light   c) board   d) break

5 You need to wash the wind_____ on your car.
   a) screen   b) wiper   c) pane   d) mirror

6 The students recorded only one motor_____ in their survey.
   a) way   b) horn   c) traffic   d) cycle

Word building

1 **Build as many words as you can from the prefixes and root words in the circles.**

Prefixes:
mis- dis- im- un –

Root words:
appear   place   sure   agree   understand   usual

2 **Choose four of your new words. Write each one in a sentence of your own.**

Onomatopoeia

What sounds do the words below suggest to you? Write them in your own sentences.

You may need to change the words to fit your sentences.

Example: drip *The water dripped slowly from the tap.*

1 crash   3 buzz   5 whistle
2 ring   4 clang   6 whirr

Writing: Paragraphs

1 **Write a paragraph on each of the following topics.**
  • An interesting journey
  • A machine you use at home or at school
  • A member of your family

2 **Create an organiser like this to make notes for your paragraphs.**

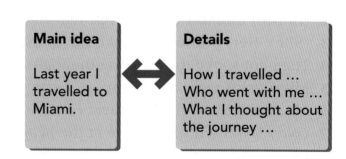

Main idea	Details
Last year I travelled to Miami.	How I travelled … Who went with me … What I thought about the journey …

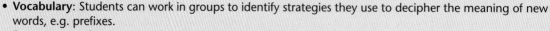
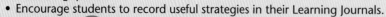

• **Vocabulary:** Students can work in groups to identify strategies they use to decipher the meaning of new words, e.g. prefixes.
• Encourage students to record useful strategies in their Learning Journals.
• **Paragraphs: DA** Allow some students to write a paragraph on one of the topics.

Story

Write a story based on the pictures below.

- Look at the pictures. What story do they tell?
- Imagine you are one of the people in these pictures. Write what happened from the point of view of this person.

1 Plan your story using a story map like the one on page 31.
   - Answer the questions Who? Where? What? Why?
   - Think about how the different characters feel?
2 Write the first draft of your story.
3 Check your first draft carefully.
   - Can you make it sound more exciting? How?
   - Is the punctuation correct?
   - Are the words correctly spelt?
4 Write a neat copy of your story for your teacher.

With a partner, assess your writing skills. What could you improve? Complete a 'How did I do?' chart (Page 183) in your Learning Journal.

Story: Allow students to get into pairs or groups to discuss and roleplay different characters. Brainstorm useful vocabulary and write it on the board.

Self-evaluation: Give students plenty of support as they assess their skills. Complete this as a class exercise until they are able to do it independently.

Unit 5

Get ready

Which areas in Jamaica are mountainous?
What kind of habitat do they provide?

> **habitat:** the natural home of a plant or animal.

Reading

Scan the two texts below.

- In which parishes are the Lower Morass and the Cockpit Country?
- What type of landscape would you find there?

The Lower Morass

Wetlands are very important for the water cycle on our planet, but they now cover only 3% of the world's surface. The Lower Morass in the parish of St Elizabeth is the largest wetland wildlife habitat in the Caribbean. The morass is formed by the Black River and its tributaries, which create a large freshwater swamp. The swamp provides a rich habitat, where many different species of birds, crabs, fish and other creatures thrive. The mangrove trees of the Lower Morass, whose spidery roots extend up to 40 feet into the water, are truly spectacular.

In recent years these wetlands have been threatened by human activity. The varied flora and fauna of the Morass attract many visitors, who love watching the crocodiles swimming in the river. The number of crocodiles in the river is declining, however, due to the draining of the swamp for agriculture and the development of beach areas for tourism. Although the government has taken steps to control the use of the Lower Morass, it will need to monitor human activity in the area carefully.

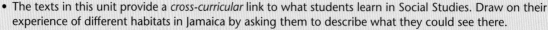

- The texts in this unit provide a *cross-curricular* link to what students learn in Social Studies. Draw on their experience of different habitats in Jamaica by asking them to describe what they could see there.
- Conduct a Think Aloud (see page 184) to help students understand the texts fully.
- Discuss habitats in different parts of Jamaica. What kinds of flora and fauna are found there? What kind of work do people do?

Cockpit Country

Cockpit Country, which lies to the south east of Montego Bay in the parish of Trelawny, is a 500 square mile highland area in the interior of Jamaica. The landscape is made up of hundreds of cone-shaped hills rising up sharply above deep hollows, which resemble the cockpits where cock fighting takes place.

There are few roads in the Cockpit Country, and even today the only way of crossing it directly is on foot. In the past these mountains provided a safe retreat for the Maroons, whose descendants still live there.

The Cockpit Country is home to a number of rare plants and animals which are found nowhere else. It is also a refuge for plants and animals which were once common in Jamaica like the black-billed parrot, but are threatened by human activity such as deforestation. In 2006 there were widespread protests when a bauxite mining company began drilling in the area.

1 What is represented by the following?   Right there
   a) 3%   c) 500 square miles
   b) 40 feet   d) 2006

2 Many different species *thrive* in the Lower Morass means that they
   a) dislike living there.   c) do very well there.
   b) are unhealthy.   d) are very crowded.

 Think and search

3 Why do people visit the Morass?

4 What type of human activity takes place in the Morass? What is the writer's opinion of this activity?   Author and me

5 Explain how the Cockpit Country got its name.

6 Why do you think there are few roads in the Cockpit Country?

7 Deforestation means
   a) planting trees.   c) protecting trees.
   b) damaging trees.   d) cutting down trees.

8 What types of *human activity* are mentioned in the reading passages?

9 Why do you think there were protests when a bauxite company began drilling in the Cockpit Country?

10 Which of the areas described would you most like to visit? Why?   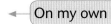 On my own

Remind students of QAR (studied in Unit 4) and help them identify the different question types. Show them how to make deductions using clues in the text, e.g. Question 4. They can work out the answer from the information provided in the first paragraph. The answer to Question 9 can be deduced from the information about threatened species in the last paragraph.

Cause and effect

> The **cause** is the reason why something happens. The **effect** is what happens.
>
> The black-billed parrot is losing its habitat. **EFFECT**
>
> Trees are being cut down in the Cockpit Country. **CAUSE**
>
> Numbers of black-billed parrots are declining. **EFFECT**

1 **Identify the cause and effect in these sentences. Enter them in a table.**

CAUSE	EFFECT
1 The Maroons ran away.	They were in danger.

1 The Maroons were in danger because they had run away from their plantations.
2 The river has been polluted by people dumping garbage in it.
3 Many people protested when a mining company started drilling for bauxite.
4 The swamp has been drained, therefore there are fewer alligators in the river.

2 **Read these sentences. State what the effect might be.**
1 It has not rained for a long time.
2 The bush fire got out of control.
3 A broken bottle was dumped in the forest.
4 There was a strong wind last night.

> **Cause and effect: signal words**
> so…   thus …
> therefore …
> because …
> consequently …
> because of this …
> for this reason …

Speaking and listening: Presentation

1 **Find information for a presentation about ONE of the following habitats.**

> highlands   lowlands   wetland   coastal plains

2 **Make notes in a fact sheet like the one on page 70. Include the following information:**
- physical features, e.g. mountains, rivers, beaches
- where this habitat is found in Jamaica
- flora (plants which grow there)
- fauna (wildlife in the area)

3 **Use the information in your fact sheet to give a presentation.**
Remember to speak loudly and clearly and to look at your audience as you speak.

> Look online to find information about the habitat you chose.

- **Presentation:** Remind students of the guidelines for presentation outlined on page 98. Get them to evaluate each other's presentations based on the information contained and the method of delivery.
- **Learning Journal:** Students can assess their presentations using a 'How did I do?' chart (page 183).
- **Extension:** Students could produce *quick-write* paragraphs based on the cause and effect structure. Give them starter sentences, e.g. *A lot of forests have been cut down in Jamaica.*

Language: Adjectives

> **Adjectives** describe nouns. They tell us more about people, animals, places and events. They can be placed either before or after nouns.
> *The mountains provided a <u>safe</u> retreat for the Maroons.*
> *The mangrove trees are <u>spectacular</u>.*

WB5 p12

1 Find and write four adjectives from the reading texts on pages 42–3.

2 Match the adjectives with suitable nouns.

Example: *high mountain*

Adjectives

> high
> loud   early
> deep   heavy   steep
> rainy   broken
> bright

Nouns

> river
> weather   slope
> sunlight   load
> morning

Adjectival phrases

> **Adjectival phrases** are groups of adjectives which describe nouns. They can go before or after nouns.
> the **tall green** trees   a butterfly **with bright blue wings**

WB5 p14

1 Underline the adjectival phrases. Circle the nouns they describe.

Example: *The (alligator) had <u>sharp pointed</u> teeth.*

1 The parrot made a loud screeching noise
2 The weather yesterday was cool and rainy.
3 The excited young boys raced into the forest.
4 They saw some juicy red fruit hanging from a branch.
5 An exquisite blue butterfly flitted from leaf to leaf.

2 Rewrite this paragraph. Use adjectives and adjectival phrases to add interest.

> Yesterday we went for a walk in the forest. We saw some birds perching in the trees. My friend saw a lizard on a tree root. I sat on a log and drank some water. Some ants crossed the path in front of me. Suddenly a parrot flew past me.

Example: *Yesterday we went for a walk in the cool shady forest.*

- Demonstrate how adjectives can make a difference to sentences. Provide a simple sentence, e.g. *The dog ran down the path.* Add adjectives, e.g. *The fierce dog ran down the rough, stony path.*
- Students can brainstorm adjectives for different situations, e.g. *a forest, mountains, a storm.*
- **DA** Allow some students to work in pairs or groups to complete Exercise 4.

Comparative and superlative

When we compare **two thing**s, we add '**-r**' or '**-er**' to adjectives. When we compare **more than two things** we add '**-st**' or '**-est**'.

    The Rio Minho is **longer** *than the Black River. It is the* **longest** *river in Jamaica.*

Sometimes we change the spelling when we add -er or -est.

    *big – big**ger** – big**gest***   *tidy – ti**dier** – ti**diest***

NOTE: Some adjectives are **irregular**: *good / better / best*   *bad / worse / worst*

WB5 p15–16

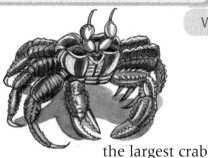

a large crab   a larger crab   the largest crab

1 **Copy and complete these sentences with the correct adjective forms.**

    Example: The Blue Mountains are *higher* than the Cockpit Country.   (high)

1 The sun is _____ at midday than in the early morning.   (hot)

2 The weather is much _____ today than it was yesterday. (good)

3 Dunns River Falls are one of the _____ places in Jamaica. (lovely)

4 In the afternoon the wind was _____ than in the morning.   (strong)

5 Getting lost in the forest was one of the _____ experiences of my life. (bad)

6 The grass is always _____ after it has rained. (green)

7 Living beside the sea was the _____ time in my life. (happy)

2 **Write your own sentences comparing these things.**

    Example: a crab / a shrimp / big   *A crab is bigger than a shrimp.*

1 palm tree / banana tree / tall   4 lions / elephants / fierce

2 mango / banana / juicy   5 snake / lizard / thin

3 hummingbird / crow / pretty   6 bees / butterflies / busy

Longer adjectives use **more** or **most** in front of the adjective.

    The trip up the river was **more exciting** *than the walk in the forest.*

    Seeing the alligators was the **most exciting** *part of the trip.*

3 **Write sentences of your own using the following adjectives.**

1 more beautiful   5 more interesting

2 the most beautiful   6 the most interesting

3 more useful   7 more dangerous

4 the most useful   8 the most dangerous

- Demonstrate comparative and superlative adjectives by making sentences about items or people in the classroom, e.g. *Josh is taller/ smaller than Michael. Ben is the tallest student in the class.*
- Exercises 6 and 7: Remind students that verbs must agree with their subjects (*A mango is…. Lions are…*)

Word study: Locating information

WB5 p110–12

> A **table of contents** tells us which sections a book contains.
> An index lists the contents of a book in alphabetical order.

1 **Use the information in the table of contents to answer the questions.**

1 On what page does the unit about farming begin?
2 In which units would you find information about the following topics?
   • Annual rainfall in the Cayman Islands
   • Volcanoes in the Caribbean
   • Dates when the islands became independent
   • Bauxite Mining

Islands of the Caribbean

Contents

Unit		Page
1	Geography	3
2	Population	11
3	Weather and climate	15
4	History and culture	19
5	Fishing	25
6	Agriculture	31
7	Industry	38

2 **Study this extract from an index.**

A
alligators   46
animals:
    camouflage   50–51
    carnivorous   53
    endangered   66–67
    hunters   46–47
    nocturnal   46

B
bamboo   14
bats   27–28
beetles   13
birds   22–27
breadfruit   56

butterflies   70–73
    colours   70
    eggs   71
    food   72

C
camouflage   50–52
carnivorous plants 53
chameleons   49–50
coneys   66
conservation   68, 69

D/E
deforestation   62–63
endangered species 66

F/G
ferns   18
fish   16–17
flowers   24–25
frogs   19
fruits   58–59
ginger   58
greenhouse effect   65–70

H/I
hummingbirds   25
insects   19
    camouflage   50–52
    carnivorous   52
    pollination   52

1 From what type of book is this index taken?
2 On which pages would you find information about the following?
   a) birds' nests
   b) species which are endangered
   c) what butterflies eat
   d) bullfrogs
   e) parrots
   f) mangoes
3 What different types of animals are listed in the index?
4 What is an *endangered* animal?
5 What do the words *carnivorous* and *camouflage* mean? Use your dictionary to help you.
6 What is a nocturnal animal? Give examples of animals which are nocturnal.

Point out the *table of contents* and *index* in this book. Get students to make up questions about them to ask other students.

Writing: Project

Prepare a group project on different habitats found in Jamaica.

 Research

Decide which habitats you will include in your project. Allocate a different type of habitat to each group member. Conduct research and make notes.

I'll find out about wetland habitats.

I'll look for information about coastal plains.

Look online to find information about the habitat you were allocated.

> **Online research**
> Use a **search engine** like Google and type in the area you wish to research, e.g. *wetlands + Jamaica*.
> Look at the first three or four websites listed. Scan them to see if they contain useful information.
> Choose the best two websites. Read them carefully and make notes.
> Always record the **URL** (the address of the site) for the sites you consulted, e.g. http://nepa.gov.jm/student/resource-material/pdf/Importance_of_Wetlands

2 Writing

1 Write a rough draft of your section of the project.
   Use your own words; do not copy directly from your
      information sources.

> You can use the information you found in the speaking and listening activity on page 44.

2 Discuss your draft with the rest of your group.
   • Does it contain information about the physical features and the flora and fauna found in this habitat?
   • Is all the information relevant?
   • Is the information organised in a logical sequence?

> After completing your project, assess how well you worked as a group.

3 Decide how you will present your project.
   • Which text features such as headings and bullet points will you include?
   • If it is typed, what fonts and colours will you use?
   • Will you include illustrations or diagrams?

4 Each of you prepares a neat copy of your section of the project.
   Then assemble it, and give a presentation copy to your teacher.

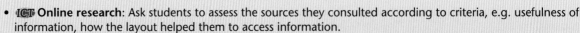

48

- **ICT Online research:** Ask students to assess the sources they consulted according to criteria, e.g. usefulness of information, how the layout helped them to access information.
- **Digital citizenship:** Explain the importance of crediting the sources we use for research. Point out that it is illegal to copy someone else's work. Students must use their own words and use quotation marks with any copied matter.

Unit 6

Get ready

**Which birds and animals are endemic to Jamaica?
What type of habitat do they live in?**

Reading

Skim the text below.

- What kind of text is it? How do you know that?
- Who are the main characters? What is the setting?

> **Skimming** means looking over a text quickly to get a general idea of what it is about.

An Endangered Species

Danielle and Ashani were visiting Hope Zoo. Ashani wanted information for his project on reptiles, so they went to look at the hatchery where iguanas are bred before they are released in the wild.

Behind a glass screen they saw hundreds of tiny lizards scuttling around. One of the officers approached. "I see you are interested in our hatchlings," he said. "They are Jamaican rock iguanas, one of the rarest lizards in the world. For a long time, people thought they were extinct."

"Why was that?" Ashani asked.

"In the 19th century, the Indian Mongoose was introduced to Jamaica to control rats and other pests in the cane fields. Mongooses feed on baby lizards, so the iguana population nearly died out. Then in 1990, a small colony was discovered in the Hellshire Hills. Now we are doing all we can to protect them, but it's not easy. Charcoal burners are felling trees and destroying their habitat. Roads have been built for traffic to and from the bauxite mines as well."

The Jamaican rock iguana is endemic to Jamaica. It is a critically endangered species.

- **Get ready:** Explain to students that an *endemic* species is one that is only found in one place.
- Discuss which species are endemic to Jamaica and why it is important to protect them.
- Help students make a *text-to-self* connections by asking them to talk about birds and animals they have seen. If they have visited a zoo or a nature reserve, they can describe what they saw there.
- Students can make a *text-to-text* connection: compare this text with other texts about Jamaican animals.

Beside the hatchery there was a large cage. Danielle peered into it. She could just make out the shape of a large iguana at the back.

"Why is this one on its own?" she asked the officer.

"Ah, this is Sandy. He has a special history," he told her. "He was not born in captivity like the rest. He was caught in the wild by two foolish boys, who thought it would be fun to have a pet iguana."

"How did he get here?" asked Ashani.

"A couple of boys overheard charcoal burners saying that they sometimes caught sight of iguanas in the forest. The boys followed them to the forest, armed with a net. When they spotted Sandy sunning himself on a tree root, they threw their net over him and he was unable to escape."

"That's terrible!" said Ashani. "What happened then?"

"The boys returned to their village with their prize and tied him to a tree in their yard. Luckily their neighbour noticed what was happening. She could see that Sandy was injured and was not sure what to do. She had heard about our breeding programme, so she contacted us, and Sandy was brought here."

"What will happen to him now?" asked Danielle.

"We are monitoring him, and when he has fully recovered, we will take him back to the Hellshire Hills where he belongs."

1 'Extinct' means that

   a) a species has died out in one part of the world.

   b) a species has died out completely

   c) almost all the members of a species have disappeared

   d) a species needs to be protected

2 Explain what is meant by the term 'a hatchling'.

3 What was the effect of introducing the Indian Mongoose?

4 Why do you think that the iguanas are bred in captivity? ◄ Deducing

5 How is their habitat being destroyed?

6 Where was Sandy born?

7 What can you *infer* about the officer's attitude towards the boys who caught him? ◄ Making inferences

8 What is the 'prize' the boys brought back to the village? Why is it referred to as a 'prize'?

9 What do you think should be done about the boys who captured Sandy?

10 Do you think it is important to protect Jamaica's endemic species? Why?

> **Inferring** means using clues to work out what is not said directly. We can *infer* that Ashani is shocked about the boys' behaviour when he says "That's terrible!"

Research the Jamaican Rock Iguana. Make notes for a fact sheet. There is a sample fact sheet on page 70.

- **Comprehension**: Help students identify the different question types.
- **Inferring**: Use the illustrations on page 49 to help students draw inferences. Ask questions, e.g. *What is happening here? What might have happened already? How do you think the people feel?*
- **Digital citizenship**: Tell students that they must not copy directly from the Internet when they present the results of their research.

Speaking and listening

1 **Retell to another student the story of what happened to Sandy, the Jamaican rock iguana.**

> Sandy lived in the forest in the Hellshire Hills

2 **Dramatise the story. You will need the following characters.**

– the charcoal burners   – the boys' neighbour
– the boys   – the wildlife officer

- Divide your roleplay into scenes.
- Make up names for the characters.
- Think about what each character will say and how he or she will speak.
- Perform your roleplay to another group of students. Ask them to tell you what they liked about your roleplay and what you could improve.

Language: Simple past tense

We use the **simple past** tense for actions which were completed in the past.
To make the simple past tense we usually add **–d** or **-ed** to the root verb:
   *Ashani want**ed** information for his project.*
   *The iguanas nearly di**ed** out.*
Verbs ending in a consonant + vowel, double the consonant and add **–ed**:
   *spot / spotted: The boys **spotted** an iguana on a tree root.*
Verbs ending in a consonant + –y, drop –y and add **–ied**:
   *carry – carr**ied**: They **carried** the iguana home.*

WB5 p25–6

1 **Find five examples of verbs in the simple past tense in the story on pages 49–50.**

2 **Complete these sentences with the simple past tense of the verbs in brackets.**

   Example: The neighbour *decided* to contact the zoo.   (decide)

1 The children _____ the tiny hatchlings.   (watch)
2 The charcoal burners _____ to stop the boys.   (try)
3 Danielle _____ her brother to the reptile cages.   (follow)
4 She _____ when she heard the story about Sandy.   (cry)
5 The officer _____ the hatchlings   (monitor)
6 The boys _____ the iguana to a tree.   (tie)
8 The children _____ up and down in excitement.   (skip)
9 The neighbour _____ about Sandy's injuries.   (worry)
10 Ashani _____ his project on reptiles.   (complete)

- **Roleplay:** Suggest signal words students could use in their play, e.g. *however, after that.*
- Let students perform their roleplays to the class. Record on an electronic device.
- **Simple past tense:** Students studied this tense in Grade 4. To avoid a sense of repetition, let them tell you what they know before revising it. They can imagine they are explaining it to a younger student.
- Get students to stand in circles to retell stories about animals, then answer questions about their stories.

51

Many verbs have **irregular** forms in the simple past tense.
> *go*: Ashani and Danielle **went** to see the hatchery.

3 **Find the simple past of these verbs in the story on pages 49–50.**

> see   think   catch   throw   bring

4 **Complete the paragraph with simple past verbs.**

My class *went* (**go**) on a class visit to the zoo last week. My mom _____ (1 make) me a picnic lunch. I _____ (2 **eat**) it on the way there because I _____ (3 **feel**) hungry. We _____ (4 **speak**) to one of the guides at the zoo and she (5 **tell**) about the different species at they have there. I _____ (6 **find**) the information about reptiles very interesting. After we _____ (7 **leave**) the reptiles we _____ (8 **sit**) in the shade and _____ (9 **have**) a cool drink. Our teacher _____ (10 **take**) a lot of pictures on her cell phone. Before we _____ (11 **leave**) the zoo, some of us _____ (12 **buy**) ice cream. On the way home most of us _____ (13 **sleep**) in the bus. Afterwards I _____ (14 **write**) an account of what we had seen at the zoo.

Irregular past tenses for you to learn	
break	broke
bring	brought
buy	bought
come	came
choose	chose
do	did
eat	ate
feel	felt
find	found
give	gave
go	went
have	had
know	knew
leave	left
make	made
pay	paid
run	ran
say	said
see	saw
sit	sat
sleep	slept
speak	spoke
stand	stood
take	took
tell	told
think	thought
write	wrote

To form questions and negative sentences in the simple past we use the helping verb did + the root of the verb.
> **Did** you **see** any snakes at the zoo?
> We **did not** see **any** snakes, but we saw an iguana.

5 **Rewrite these sentences in the negative form.**

Example: We went to the zoo last week. *We did not go to the zoo last week.*

1 I forgot to take my lunch with me.
2 Danielle saw the birds in the aviary.
3 The guide knew the answer.
4 The bus left the school on time.
5 My friend paid for the ice creams.
6 Grandpa came to the zoo with us.
7 We felt very excited about the trip.
8 I thought the visit was interesting.

9 We made drawings of the animals.
10 We sat on the grass to eat our lunch.

- **Simple past**: To give students extra practice, ask them to write sentences in the simple past about what they did the previous day or on the weekend. They could include some negative sentences.
- **DA** Allow some students to write fewer sentences in Exercise 5, and to write only the verbs in Exercise 4.

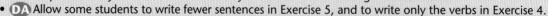

6 **Write these sentences as questions.**

> Example: The boys caught the iguana. *Did the boys catch the iguana?*

1 Ashani wanted to see the lizards.
2 We went to the aviary first.
3 Danielle asked a lot of questions.
4 We had a good time at the zoo.

5 I told everyone about the visit.
6 I felt tired after the visit.
7 The guide looked after the hatchlings.
8 I learnt a lot about reptiles.

7 **Write four questions to ask your friends about a visit they made to a place of interest. Write their answers.**

Word study: Suffixes

> We can add **suffixes** to some *nouns* and *verbs* to change them to *adjectives*.
> **colour** (noun): *The parrot was very colourful.* (adjective)

1 **Add suffixes to these nouns to form adjectives.**

1 fame *famous*
2 beauty
3 anger
4 comfort
5 rest
6 child
7 fun
8 help
9 fury

2 **Add suffixes to the nouns in brackets to form adjectives.**

> Example: It was *peaceful* sitting under the shady trees. (peace)

1 The forest has great _____ beauty. (nature)
2 The weather was _____ on the weekend. (storm)
3 Be _____ when you walk in the forest. (care)
4 I felt very _____ lying in the hammock. (comfort)
5 Everyone was _____ when I slipped on a rock. (help)
6 Dean was rebuked for his _____ behaviour. (self)

Suffixes which form adjectives	
-able / -ible	valuable
	responsible
-al	musical
-ate	fortunate
-ful	peaceful
-ish	foolish
-ive	expensive
-less	careless
-ous	nervous
-y / -ly	windy
	friendly

Suffixes which form nouns	
-ation	examination
-dom	wisdom
-er / -or	painter/ actor
-ence	silence
-ist	tourist
-ment	enjoyment
-ness	kindness
-ion	prediction
-y	jealousy

WB5 p68

> We can add **suffixes** to some *verbs and adjectives* to change them to nouns.
> **silent** (adjective) *The guide asked the students to wait in silence.* (noun)

3 **Add suffixes to these words to form nouns.**

1 attend *attention*
2 decide
3 free
4 art
5 replace
6 obedient
7 enjoy
8 happy
9 reserve
10 govern
11 write
12 conserve

- **Suffixes:** Remind students that suffixes are letters added to the end of words to change their meaning. Tell them to use their dictionaries to check the spelling of words when they add suffixes.
- Students can create a word search using words with suffixes. They can then give it to another student to solve.

4 **Complete the sentences with the correct forms of the words in brackets.**

1 Ashani gave a _____ about reptiles to his class. (present)
2 Tourist _____ has destroyed many wildlife habitats. (develop)
3 The Principal gave us _____ to visit the zoo. (permit)
4 Danielle told the story of Sandy without any _____. (hesitate)
5 _____ have been monitoring the number of iguanas. (science)
6 In the 19th century there was a huge _____ in the number of iguanas. (reduce)

Writing: Story

1 **Reread the story about Sandy, the iguana, on page 50. Plot the elements on a herringbone.**

Who?
Charcoal burners
2 boys, Sandy, neighbour

When?

Where?

What?

Why?

How?

2 **Imagine that you are Sandy. Tell the story of what happened after you returned to the Hellshire Hills.**

- How did you feel about being back in the wild?
- Did you have any more adventures?

1 **Planning:**
   - Brainstorm ideas for your story. Share them with another student ask him / her to comment.
   - Plot the elements of your story on a herringbone.
2 **Drafting:** Write the first draft of your story. Show it to another student and discuss how you could improve it.
3 **Revising:** Use the checklist below to help you revise your story, then write or type a neat copy for your teacher.

Checklist: Revising a story
Have I:
  introduced the characters and described the setting? ☐
  retold the events in the correct sequence? ☐
  edited my first draft to make it more interesting? ☐
  checked the spelling, grammar and punctuation? ☐

Add your completed checklists to your Learning Journal.

- **Writing:** Make it clear to students that they must write their story in the first person, as if they were Sandy. Discuss with them the grammar and punctuation points they should check when they revise their stories, e.g. *capital letters, sentence punctuation, subject–verb agreement*. Ask students to help you create a class checklist.
- **Learning Journal:** Students can include completed checklists in their journals.
- **DA** Some students could write a group story where each group member writes part of the story.

Get ready

Where can you find coral reefs in Jamaica?
What would you expect to see if you went to a coral reef?

Reading

Scan the flyer.

- What is the purpose of the flyer?
- For what audience was it written?

> A **flyer** is a printed advertisement or announcement handed out to people.

OUR REEF IS A NATIONAL TREASURE

Help us to protect it.

DO

✓ Anchor in the sands around the reef, not on the coral itself.

✓ Dive with a recommended diving company.

✓ Dispose responsibly of any garbage you create or find.

✓ Respect the beauty of this fragile natural world.

DO NOT

✗ Stand on or break off pieces of coral.

✗ Help yourself to samples of fish, coral fans or sponges.

✗ Jet-ski over the reefs.

✗ Use a spear-gun for fishing.

Jamaica Marine Conservation

www.watersports.jam.com

- Show students a YouTube clip about text features. Ask them to identify different text features in the poster.
- Students can create a graphic organiser like the one on page 186 to show the causes and effects of damaging coral reefs.

Letters to the Editor

Boat owners are irresponsible

The reef at Negril is one of Jamaica's national treasures; however, we are not doing enough to protect it.

Last week I took my nephew and his children out to the reef in our motorboat. While we were there, we saw several tourist boats drop anchor on the reef itself. One boat owner tried three times to find a place on the reef to secure the anchor and each time a large chunk of coral broke off. The boats stayed there for over an hour, and their owners allowed the tourists to walk all over the reef. Some of them even snapped off bits of coral which they took home with them as souvenirs.

More needs to be done to control the activities of local boat companies. They should understand that the coral reefs are an important natural feature, and that once they have been destroyed, they can never be replaced.

Please publish my letter. I am sure that many of your readers will feel as I do.

Charmaine Phillips

We must protect the reef!

Mrs Phillips is right. Negril's coral reef is an important part of our natural heritage. We should do all we can to preserve it.

I take visitors out to the reef every day in my glass-bottomed boat. They are always amazed by the brightly coloured fish and delicate coral fans they see. If the reef is destroyed, there will be nothing for them to see and I will lose my livelihood.

That is why I am always careful to anchor on the sands around the reef, not on the reef itself. I never allow my customers to walk on the reef or to break off pieces of coral to take home.

Unfortunately, not every boat company is as responsible as mine. I often see other boats dropping anchor on the reef, or letting tourists walk on the coral.

The Negril Coral Reef Preservation Society is trying to stop this kind of behaviour. We should all support their work.

Errol Jackson

- Tell students to skim both letters to find out the main idea.
- Compare and contrast the information in the flyer with the information in the letters. *What is similar? What is different?*
- Point out that letters to the editor printed in a newspaper are usually set out in this way and do not follow the accepted layout for a formal letter.

1 What is the purpose of the flyer on page 55?

2 Which activities mentioned in the flyer are also mentioned in the letters?

3 Which instruction in the flyer is most important in your opinion? Why?

4 Why is the reef popular with tourists?

5 Which statement best summarises the attitude of Mrs. Phillips towards ← Inferring
  the boat owners?

  a) They are only interested in making money.

  b) They are aware of the importance of the reef.

  c) They want tourists to enjoy themselves.

  c) They behave very carelessly.

6 What do you think is Mr. Jackson's reason for writing to the newspaper? ← Deducing

7 The statement 'I will lose my livelihood' means that Mr. Jackson

  a) will have to sell his boat.

  b) will not have any work.

  c) must stop going to the reef.

  d) must be more responsible.

8 Why is the work of the Negril Coral Reef Preservation Society important? ← Deducing

9 Why do you think it is important to preserve coral reefs?

10 What other features of Jamaica's natural heritage should be preserved.

Speaking and listening: Debate

1 **Discuss the importance of tourism in Jamaica.**

* What benefits does it bring?
* What are the disadvantages?

Tourists bring money to Jamaica.

Yes, but tourism sometimes harms the environment.

2 **Make notes in a T-chart like the one below.**

Tourism in Jamaica	
Advantages	Disadvantages
Provides jobs for Jamaicans	*Destroys habitats*

We **make notes** on a discussion or a text we have read to record the key points. You do not need to write in full sentences when you make notes.

3 **Conduct a mini-debate on the following motion.**

We need more tourism in Jamaica.

* Divide your group into two smaller groups. One group prepares a speech in favour of the motion. The other prepares a speech against the motion.
* Choose a student from each group to present the speeches. Then open the discussion to everyone.

---

* **Comprehension**: Help students identify the question types before they answer.
* **Debate**: Students may need support in completing the T-chart and in preparing their speeches. Note that a *motion* for a debate is sometimes known as a *moot*.
* Students could suggest aspects of Jamaican culture which should be promoted to tourists, e.g. music, food, dance.

Language
Direct speech

The words people say are known as **direct speech**. When we write, we put **quotation marks** around the direct speech.
  "*A lot of boat owners are irresponsible.*"
Mrs. Phillips stated.
  "*That's not true!*" *Errol protested.*
We place a punctuation mark (comma, question mark or exclamation mark) *before* the closing quotation marks.

A lot of boat owners are irresponsible.

That's not true!

WB5 p52–3

1 **Underline the direct speech and add quotation marks to these sentences.**
Add sentence punctuation where it is needed.

Example: "*We are not doing enough to protect the reef,*" *said Mrs. Phillips.*

1 I take visitors to the reef everyday said Errol
2 We should respect the natural environment Mrs. Phillips remarked
3 Remember to bring water with you Errol reminded his customers
4 We're looking forward to our trip to the reef the tourists said
5 I hope the sea will be calm said Grandma
6 Do you enjoy diving I asked the boat owner

When the direct speech comes last, put a punctuation mark *inside* the quotation marks.
  "*My uncle has a glass-bottomed boat,*" *Dwayne told his friend.*
When the direct speech comes first, put a comma before the first quotation mark.
  Dwayne's friend said, "*I would love to go out in your uncle's boat.*"
When there is more than one piece of direct speech, put quotation marks around each part. Each new piece of speech begins with a capital letter.
  "*Let me talk to my uncle,*" *said Dwayne.* "*Perhaps we can go together.*"

2 **Rewrite these sentences using quotation marks.**
Add sentence punctuation where it is needed.
1 Errol said Please do not stand up in the boat
2 Is this your first time in Jamaica Errol asked the tourist
3 We come every year the tourist answered we love the sunshine
4 Hurry up my father shouted the boat is about to leave
5 Jayden asked how deep is the water on the reef
6 Sit down my father told me you'll fall in if you're not careful
7 Can you see the fish my sister asked me
8 What is that big fish Janelle asked is it a shark

Study the information in the box above before you write your answers.

• To help students place quotation marks in the correct places, tell them to identify the words which were said.
• Exercise 2: Explain that when the speech comes last, we use normal sentence punctuation before the final quotation mark (full stop, question mark, exclamation mark).
• **DA** Allow some students to complete the first three examples in each exercise.

3 **Rewrite this dialogue. Use quotation marks.**

> Example: *"Why are we getting in a boat?" Shaun asked.*

Shaun: Why are we getting in a boat?
Dad: We're going to see the coral reef.
Shaun: How will we see the coral?
Dad: The boat has a glass bottom. We can see through it.
Shaun: How do we know the glass won't break?
Dad: It's very strong. It won't break.
Shaun: Will Mummy come with us?
Dad: Yes, she will. Now hurry up and get in the boat.

Simple and compound sentences

A **clause** is a group of words which contains a *subject* and a verb and expresses a complete idea. Sentences can have one or more clauses.
> *The tourists wanted to go to the reef.* (one clause)
> *The tourists wanted to go to the reef but the sea was too rough.* (two clauses)
>
>   1st clause   2nd clause

But is a *conjunction* which joins the two clauses.

1 **Copy the sentences with more than one clause. Put brackets round each clause.**

> Example: *(The sea was rough) (and the waves were very high.)*

1 The glass-bottomed boat dropped anchor on the reef.
2 I jumped into the water and swam towards the reef.
3 I love swimming but sometimes the water is too cold.
4 Sometimes dolphins swim right into the bay.
5 It was very hot walking along the beach.
6 We stopped for a while so we could rest in the shade.
7 We wanted to go to the beach but it was raining.
8 The sun was shining and it was very hot.
9 I loved the sound of the waves lapping against the boat.
10 We packed our things away and went home.

> A sentence with one clause is a simple sentence. A sentence with two clauses which are equally important is a compound sentence.

- **Language** Exercise 3: Brainstorm different words of speech, e.g. *respond, shout, complain, whisper*. Encourage students to use different words of speech in their answers.
- **Simple and compound sentences**: Give students practice in extending sentences. Provide them with simple sentences to change into compound sentences, e.g. *I went to the beach yesterday, but….*

2 **Join the sentences with *and, but* or *so*.**

Example: The bus arrived. Everyone got on. *The bus arrived and everyone got on.*

1 I called my friend. I told him about the visit.
2 We enjoyed our trip to the reef. We have never returned.
3 The walk was very tiring. We rested when we got home.
4 A lot of people visit the reef. Not many see an octopus.
5 The boat left the beach. It headed out to sea.
6 It was time to leave. We packed our things.
7 My little brother liked the boat. He was scared of the waves.
8 Mom took a lot of pictures. She mailed them to her sister.

Study skills: Graphs and tables

1 **Study the information in the bar graph. It shows the number of tourists arriving in Jamaica each year.**

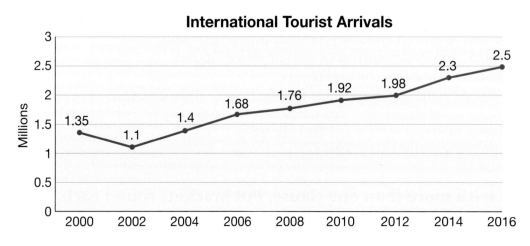

Source: http://data.worldbank.org

1 How many international tourists came to Jamaica in 2000?
2 How many came in 2016?
3 How would you describe the general pattern in tourist arrivals?
   a) falling   b) rising   c) up and down   d) static (*not changing*)
4 Compared to 2000, the number of tourists coming to Jamaica in 2016 was
   a) half as many
   b) twice as many
   c) one and a half times as many
   d) three times as many
5 What benefits might the increase in tourism bring to the island?
6 What problems might it create?

Let students first discuss the information in the *bar graph* and *pie chart* on the next page in pairs, then go through the questions with the whole class. Elicit examples of different types of graphs and discuss why we present information in graphic form, e.g. easy to grasp at a glance.

60

2 **Study the information in the pie chart. Answer the questions.**

1 From which country did the largest number of tourists come in 2015?
2 From which region did the second largest number of tourists come?
3 From which areas did similar numbers come?
4 To which countries might 'other' refer? Why do you think there were so few tourists from these countries?

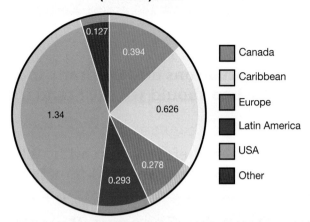

International Tourist Stopovers in Jamaica (millions) 2015

- Canada
- Caribbean
- Europe
- Latin America
- USA
- Other

0.127, 0.394, 0.626, 1.34, 0.278, 0.293

Data retrieved from the Jamaica Tourist Board, May 2017
http://www.jtbonline.org/report-and-statistic

Writing: Letter to the editor

Write the text of an email to a newspaper to express your opinion about plans for a new hotel which is to be built close to a wetland area in Jamaica.

1 **Planning:**
  • Decide the stance you will take. Are you in favour of or against the plans?
  • Note the arguments you will use.

2 **Drafting:** Write in clear, well-organised paragraphs.
  • Introduction: Introduce yourself and say why you are writing.
  • Body of letter: State your opinion about the plans. Give reasons to support your opinion.
  • Conclusion: Say what actions you think should be taken, e.g. *cancel the plans/ build the hotel.*

3 **Revising:** Revise your first draft and prepare a neat copy.

Use ideas from the T-chart you prepared for the debate on tourism (page 57).

Type your email and post it on your class blog.

• **Writing:** Follow the writing process flow chart (page 189).
• **Letters to the editor:** Today these are likely to be sent as emails. Students can therefore write in the style of the letters on page 56 Remind them that they must use correct spelling and punctuation in emails. The formats for informal and formal letters will be practised later in the book.

Get ready

In which situations do Jamaicans speak in Creole? When should we use Standard English?

Reading

Scan the poem before you read it. Which elements of poetry can you identify?

Don' Ride no Coconut Bough Down Dere

1 Papa face serious him say 'dere's no way,
  Ah want any o' yuh to go out and play
  An' mash up me yam hill dem down dey,
  Specially wid unoo coconut bough.'

2 De hill so steep an' slippery,
  We could hear dat hill a-call out to we,
  We could hear it say, 'come slide down me,
  Yuh know yuh want to do it now.'

3 De yam vine twist roun' de hog plum tree,
  Dem turn dem likkle face to we,
  Dem say to Lainey, Bonnie and to me,
  'Memba whey yu fada say.'

4 De coconut bough dem waitin' dere
  Say 'don lissen to dem vine yuh hear,
  Yuh puppa really mean nex' year,
  Him neva mean today.'

5 We fin' some bough, jus' what we need,
  Head big an' solid, perfec' fe speed,
  Me in de middle, Bonnie in de lead,
  We jump pon we coconut bough dem.

6 An' den we all begin to race,
  De breeze like razor pon we face,
  We feget 'bout going slow in case,
  We break off Papa yam stem.

7 De t'ree o' we an de dog, Puppy,
  Fly down de hill pass de pear tree,
  Tear through de cocoa a' coffee,
  We noh memba de yam no more.

8 Up de hill an' down agen,
  Lean de bough into de ben'
  We only see de yam vine dem when
  We stop, 'bout half past four.

9 Dem lyin' lifeless pon de groun'
  De hill dem flat, dem all mash down,
  None o' we could meck a soun',
  We didn' know wha' fe do.

10 De hill so steep an' long an' slippery,
  We could hear dat hill a-call out to we,
  We could hear it a-say, 'come slide down me,'
  An we say, 'no, thank yuh.'

Valerie Bloom

- Revise the elements of poetry (described on pages 22-3) and ask students to identify them in the poem.
- **Discuss the picture**: Ask students to say what they think the poem will be about and to predict how the poem might end.
- Ask students to identify examples of JC in the poem and translate them to SJE.

Devices like **personification** and **similes** are often found in poems.
Personification means writing about things as if they were human. In this poem, the yam vine, the coconut branch and the hill all speak to the children.

> *We could hear dat hill a-call out to we,*
> *We could hear it a-say, 'come slide down me,*
> *Yuh know yuh want to do it now.'*

Similes describe something by comparing it to something else using *like* or *as*, e.g. *De breeze like razor pon we face.*

1 What did the children's father tell them at the beginning of the poem?
2 Where was the yam hill?
3 Why do you think the children ignored what their father said?   ← **Inferring**
4 Describe the branch the children used to slide down the hill.
5 Which words in verse 7 tell us that the children are travelling very fast?
6 Why do you think they forgot about the yam?   ← **Inferring**
7 What is 'lyin' lifeless pon de groun' in verse 9?
8 Explain why none of the children could 'meck a soun'.
9 What do you think the children's father will do when he discovers what has happened?
10 Did you enjoy reading this poem? Why / Why not?

Language awareness

1 **Read out the first three verses of the poem.**
Change them to Standard English. Which version do you prefer? Why?

2 **How would you say these expressions in Standard English?**

1 Don' mash up me yam hill.
2 Dem all mash down.
3 Mi deh leff. Likkle more.
4 Wha gwaan wid yuh todeh?
5 Mi deh yah.

6 Who dat gyal deh ova deh?
7 Mi big up John fi everything him duh.
8 Mi soon come.
9 Mi nuh biznizz.
10 Wha yuh deh pon?

3 **Match these Jamaican proverbs to their meanings.**

1 Cockroach no biznizz inna fowl fight.
2 Tuh much rat nebba dig gud hole
3 If yuh lie wid dawg yuh git up wid fleas.
4 Young bud nuh know storm.
5 Mi old but mi nuh cold.
6 Duppy know who fi frighten.

a) Young people take too many risks.
b) Value what old people can offer.
c) Stay out of things that don't concern you.
d) Bullies pick on those who are weaker.
e) Be careful of bad company.
f) You can't do a good job if there are too many of you.

- **Language awareness:** Play recordings of conversations where JC is used and ask students to translate common expressions into SJE.
- Students can record conversations in different parts of the school, e.g. *the canteen, the schoolyard*, and then comment on the language used.

4 **Read these two poems. They were written by a Jamaican student, Joel McGowan, when he was nine years old.**

Scenery

Scenery can be the very best thing,
Through my eyes, the best scenery is in spring.
Scenery looks good from high or low,
Scenery makes background when you put on a show.
Painters are inventive and also unique,
To paint good pictures is what they seek.
Some uninformed people, destroy nature for their homes,
But nature … should always be left alone.

Habitat

A habitat is where animals and plants live,
It's where they come from, and not something you give.
Plants need sun and water, if not they will dry up,
They need more water than you can fill into a cup.
Animals are a different thing,
They need fruits and meats like birds need wings.
Do not take them from their habitats,
If you do, animals such as birds may fall victims to cats.

Joel McGowan

1 According to the writer, in what way are some people destroying nature?
2 How do you think the writer feels about this? How do you know?
3 Do you agree that 'nature should always be left alone'? Why / Why not?
4 What is needed by both animals and plants?
5 In what way does the writer say that animals are different from plants?
6 Why does the writer say that animals should not be taken from their habitats?

Speaking and listening: Description

1 **Choose a place where you like to be, eg a forest or a beach.**

2 **Close your eyes and imagine you are there. Make notes.**

What things can you see there?	
What can you hear and smell?	
What do you do there?	
How do you feel when you are there?	

• **Speaking and listening:** Discuss different descriptive techniques, e.g. visualising a place or an object and working from left to right, or top to bottom. Another descriptive technique students can use is to observe using different senses, e.g. *hearing, smell.*
• Take students out on a nature walk or walk around a park. Then ask them to complete an observation sheet about how people interact with the environment.

Language: Adverbs

We use **adverbs** describe how actions are done.
> *The children screamed **loudly** as they flew down the hill.*

Here the adverb *loudly* tells us how the children screamed.
Most adverbs are formed by adding **-ly** to adjectives: *loud – loudly*
Remember these tricky spellings:
> Adjectives ending in *-y* change *y* to *i*: *happy – happily*
> Adjectives ending in *l* add *-ly*: *careful – carefully*
> Adjectives ending in *-ic* add *-ally*: *enthusiastic – enthusiastically*

NOTE: Some adjectives and adverbs have the same forms: *hard, fast, straight, early, late*

1 **Change these adjectives into adverbs.**

WB5 p39–40

Example: faithful *faithfully*

1 angry	4 nervous	7 cheerful	10 serious
2 lazy	5 majestic	8 lucky	11 silent
3 envious	6 heavy	9 graceful	12 noisy

2 **Choose a suitable adverb to add to each sentence.**

Example: *The excited children jumped <u>eagerly</u> on to the coconut bough.*

1 The children's father spoke to them when they returned.
2 They promised they would not do it again.
3 The boy picked a mango and ate it.
4 We waited for the bus to arrive.
5 My baby brother plays with his bricks for hours.
6 We all clapped at the end of the performance.
7 It rained all day yesterday.
8 I rewrote my composition.

> sternly   happily   eagerly   heavily
> greedily   enthusiastically   carefully
> impatiently   faithfully

Adverbs have different functions. They tell us **how**, **when** or **where** actions are performed
> *The children **played happily outside all day**.*
> *Happily* is an adverb of **manner**. It tells us **how**.
> *Outside* is an adverb of **place**. It tells us **where**.

All day is an adverb of **time**. It tells us **when**.

• Remind students that some adverbs are irregular, e.g. good – well: *He sang well.*
• **Extension**: Write different actions on the board, e.g. *walk, speak, run*. Ask students to suggest as many different adverbs as they can to describe how these actions might be done.

3 **Choose suitable adverbs of time or place to complete the sentences.**

1 It rained all day so we had to stay *inside.*
2 It will _____ be time to go home.
3 We _____ play in Grandad's garden.
4 We looked _____ but could not find the puppy.
5 It is my sister's birthday _____ .
6 I _____ do my homework on time.
7 Did you travel _____ today?
8 We will have a family picnic _____ .
9 Selena has _____ visited another country.
10 Have you found your friend? Yes, she is _____ .

Adverbs to learn	
Time	**Place**
now	here
then	there
today	inside
tomorrow	outside
yesterday	away
soon	above
often	far
never	nearby
sometimes	everywhere
always	nowhere

4 **Write a paragraph about a game you played with your friends. Use at least two adverbs in each sentence.**

Word work: Similes

1 **Read the poem and find as many similes as you can.**

> **Similes** are used in descriptive language to compare one thing to another using the words *like* or *as*:   *The noise was* **like a thunderbolt**.   *The girl could run* **as fast as the wind**.

Example: *like lace clinging to the shore*

WB5 p74

Lazy Day

Surf, like lace clinging to the shore,
Beads of spray like pearls in the air,
Fish as bright as jewels,
Leap from the sparkling sea.
I hear the sound of the waves
Like the soft beating of a drum.
White sand as soft as a pillow
Cushions me where I lie.
It runs through my fingers
Like a warm waterfall.
The clouds move across the sky
Like lazy sailing ships of old.

2 **Complete the following sentences with a simile of your own.**

Example: The shark's teeth were *like razor blades.*

1 The crab's claws were _____ .
2 The waves were _____ .
3 The leaves of the palm tree were _____ .
4 The coconuts were _____ .

Explain that some modern poets do not use rhyme or rhythm in their poems. You may wish to refer to *similes*, *metaphors* and *personification* as figures of speech or literary devices.

66
• **Learning Journal**: Students can record interesting devices that are used in texts they read and can record devices they create themselves.

Metaphors

> **Metaphors** describe things by saying they are something else. They show how both things are similar, e.g.
> *The clouds were **balls of fluffy cotton wool**.*
> This metaphor compares the clouds to cotton wool.

1 **Copy the sentences and underline the metaphors.**

WB5 p75

Example: *The setting sun was <u>a ball of fire</u>.*

1 The clouds were dark mountains blocking out the sun.
2 The storm was an angry giant striding across the sky.
3 The tree was an umbrella over our heads.
4 The tiny fish were silver arrows in the rock pool.
5 The water in the pool was a mirror reflecting the trees.
6 The trees were an archway over our heads.
7 The lightning was a sharp blade slicing through the sky.

2 **Discuss what each metaphor in Exercise 3 means.**

Example: 1 The clouds were so large they looked like mountains blocking out the sun.

Study skills: Using a thesaurus

A **thesaurus** is a list of **synonyms** (*words with similar meanings*). Using a thesaurus will help you make your descriptions more interesting.

big *adj.* broad, enormous, gigantic, heavy, huge, large, loud, massive, mountainous, tall, towering, vast, wide	**small** *adj.* baby, little, microscopic, minute, narrow, short, slender, thin, tiny

1 **Look at the extracts above from a thesaurus. Use adjectives to replace big and small in these sentences.**

Example: On hearing a ~~big~~ cry, Dad rushed to see what had happened. *loud*

1 At the bottom of the hill, there was a **big** yam vine.
2 From the top of the hill, the yam vine looked **small**.
3 Dad was so strong he could carry **big** sacks of yam up the hill.
4 The puppy was so **small** I could tuck it under my arm.
5 We found a nest with some **small** birds in the tree.
6 A **big** crowd of people gathered on the beach after the storm.
7 They stood on the shore and gazed at the **big** waves.
8 The gap in the trees was too **small** for a man to pass through.

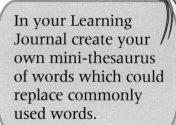

In your Learning Journal create your own mini-thesaurus of words which could replace commonly used words.

2 **Create your own thesaurus for the following word pairs.**

happy / unhappy   nice / nasty   strong / weak   beautiful / ugly

---

• **Study skills** Exercise 2 (thesaurus): Students can use an online thesaurus to find synonyms. Point out that the synonyms found in a thesaurus do not have exactly the same meaning.
• **DA** Allow some students to create thesaurus entries for one or two word pairs only.

Writing: Description

1 **Write a descriptive poem about a rainy day.**

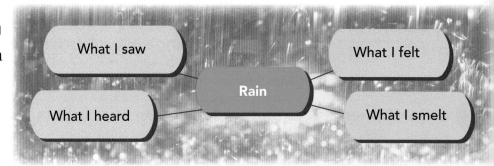

What I saw

What I heard

Rain

What I felt

What I smelt

- Use the organiser above to help you plan your poem.
- Write an opening line, e.g. *The clouds grew dark.*
- Write two or more lines about what you heard.
- Write some lines about what you saw, felt and smelt.
- Try to include at least one simile and one metaphor.
- Write a closing line, e.g. about when the rain stopped.

2 **Write a description of a place where you like to be.**
- You can use the notes you made in the speaking and listening exercise on page 64 to help you plan your description.

1 Use an organiser to help you plan.

What I can see there

What I can hear

Name of place

What I do there

How I feel there

What I can smell

2 Write a first draft of your description. Discuss it with another student. Ask him / her to suggest how you could improve your description.

3 Use the checklist below to help you revise your description.

> **Checklist: Description**
> Have I:
>   described what I observed with different senses? ☐
>   used interesting words and phrases? ☐
>   checked the spelling of difficult words in my dictionary? ☐
>   used correct punctuation? ☐

- In sensory descriptions it is not always possible to include all five senses. Advise students to use those which are appropriate to the situation, e.g. taste and smell when describing a meal, sight, hearing and smell for a market scene.
- **Learning Journal:** Remind students to copy and complete checklists in their Learning Journals.

Reading

1 **Scan the text to find the following information:**
- How much do leatherback sea turtles weigh?
- How many eggs do they lay?

The Leatherback Sea Turtle

Leatherback sea turtles are among the oldest creatures on the planet. They have lived in our oceans for more than 65 million years. At two metres long, they are the largest living turtles and they can weigh over 300 kilograms. They feed on jellyfish and sea plants. Their life span is 40 years or more.

1 Habitat

Leatherbacks spend almost their entire life in the sea and travel for hundreds of miles. However far they may travel, females always return to the beach where they hatched to lay their eggs. They nest on beaches in the West Indies, South America and West Africa.

2 Reproduction

Females emerge from the water at night and crawl slowly up the beach. They dig a hole in the sand with their flippers and lay a clutch of up to 70 eggs. After this, they cover the eggs and return to the sea. It is 60 days before the hatchlings break out of the eggs and find their way down to the water.

3 Threats to Leatherbacks

Leatherbacks are an endangered species. Thirty years ago, it was estimated that there were around 115,000 female leatherbacks. Now there are fewer than 25,000. There have always been natural predators like birds and lizards, which feed on turtle eggs and

- Before students read the text, get them to draw on their prior knowledge. *What do they know about turtles? Where are they found?*
- Tell them to prepare for reading: survey the text by looking at the text features (*photos and headings*), and identify the text type.

hatchlings. The greatest danger to leatherbacks today, however, comes from humans. Poachers steal their eggs or kill them for their meat. Turtles are often caught in fishing nets or choke on garbage dumped at sea. Often people destroy their eggs unintentionally when they walk across beaches.

4 Protecting Leatherbacks

If leatherbacks are not protected, they might become extinct. Conservation groups in Jamaica are taking action to protect the species by organising beach clean-ups. Up to 20 tonnes of potentially harmful garbage is cleared from beaches and rivers each year. In St. Elizabeth, Portland and Westmoreland there are special units where the hatchlings are cared for until they are old enough to survive in the sea.

2 **Answer the questions.**

1 How big are leatherback turtles?

2 How long do they live?

3 What is surprising about the place where females lay their eggs?

4 In which section of the text can you find information about the following?

   a) how long it takes for leatherbacks' eggs to hatch

   b) what leatherbacks eat

   c) the number of leatherbacks in the world today

5 A *predator* is an animal

   a) which is dangerous to humans.   **c)** which is hunted by other animals.

   b) that kills and eats other animals.   **d)** which is endangered.

6 The greatest danger to leatherbacks is caused by

   a) birds.   **b)** fishing nets.   **c)** jellyfish.   **d)** people.

7 *Unintentionally* (section 3) means

   a) on purpose **b)** without meaning to **c)** carelessly   **d)** lazily

8 Explain why turtle conservation groups are organising beach clean-ups.

9 Why do you think it is important to protect turtles?

10 How could you and your fellow students help to protect turtles?

3 **Make notes about leatherbacks in a fact sheet like the one below.**

Name	Leatherback Sea Turtle
Size	
Diet	
Habitat	
Reproduction	

> You do not need to write in full sentences when you make notes.

• **Comprehension:** Remind students to read words in context for Questions 5 and 7.
• **DA** You may need to help some students by reading the text with them and explaining the unfamiliar words.
• **Extension:** Students could add new headings to the fact sheet, e.g. Threats, Protection.

70

Language: Adjectives

1 **Write four adjectives you could use to describe each of the nouns below.**

Example: a tree *tall, shady, green, beautiful*

1 your home   2 your best friend   3 the ocean   4 a bus

2 **Add adjectives to this paragraph to make it more interesting.**

It was a *warm, sunny* day. Jade stood on the beach and watched the fishing boats. The fishermen were holding up fish. A flock of birds was flying over the sea. A man wearing a hat and a woman with a scarf were talking to the fisherman.

3 **Choose the correct forms of the adjectives in brackets to complete the sentences.**

Example: Jamaica is one of the *largest* islands in the Caribbean. (large)

1 The weather is usually _____ in March than in April. (dry)
2 Castleton Gardens is one of the _____ places in Jamaica. (beautiful)
3 Parrots are the _____ birds on the island. (noisy)
4 Leatherbacks are one of the _____ species of turtle. (rare)
5 Sunrise is usually the _____ time of day. (cool)
6 I think you will feel _____ after you have rested. (relaxed)
7 I hope it will be _____ in the afternoon.   (sunny)
8 That was the _____ ice cream I have ever tasted. (delicious)
9 The _____ predators threatening turtles are humans. (dangerous)
10 The beach was much _____ after the clean-up. (safe)

Simple past tense

1 **Write the simple past tense forms of the following verbs.**

Example: give *gave*

1 finish	4 buy	7 protect	10 take
2 think	5 do	8 go	11 listen
3 begin	6 keep	9 see	12 make

- You may find it helpful to revise each grammar point by looking at the information boxes in the relevant units before students attempt the exercises.
- **Simple past tense:** Tell students to make sentences orally for each verb. Saying it in context will help them find the correct form, e.g. *finish:* Yesterday I <u>finished</u> my work early.

2 **Complete the paragraph. Write the simple past of the verbs in brackets.**

Cara *had* (1 **have**) a bad day. She _____ (2 **wake**) up late and _____ (3 **not have**) time for breakfast. She _____ (4 **leave**) her homework in her bedroom. She _____ (5 **miss**) the bus and _____ (6 **get**) to school very late. Her teacher _____ (7 **ask**) for her homework. Cara _____ (8 **tell**) her that her homework _____ (9 **be**) at home. Her teacher _____ (10 **call**) her to the front of the class. Cara _____ (11 **sigh**). She _____ (12 **know**) she would be in trouble.

I had a bad day.

Adverbs

a) Change the adjectives in the box into adverbs.

Example: careless *carelessly*

~~careless~~ angry responsible heavy needless eager noisy painful hungry

b) Complete the sentences with the adverbs you created.

Example: Many boat companies behave *carelessly* when they take tourists to the reef.

Errol's Glass-Bottomed Boats

Daily Trips to the Reef

1 Errol always acts _____ when he takes tourists to the reef.
2 When they got to the reef, the tourists jumped _____ into the water.
3 A flock of chattering birds flew _____ across the beach.
4 It rained _____ during the night.
5 After he cut his foot, Amos limped _____ across the sand.
6 Errol shouted _____ at the boatman dropping anchor on the reef.
7 People who help themselves to coral _____ should be stopped.
8 After their swim, the children ate their picnic _____ .

Sentences

1 **Complete the sentences with *and, but* or *so*.**
1 The turtles come out of the sea at night, _____ lay their eggs on the beach.
2 The turtles crawl up the beach, _____ dig a hole for their eggs.
3 Once there were 115,000 female leatherbacks, _____ now there are only 25,000.
4 We wanted to see turtles, _____ we went to the beach after dark.
5 We waited a long time, _____ we did not see any turtles.
6 It was late, _____ we decided to go home.

• **Adverbs:** Remind students of the spelling rules for changing adjectives to adverbs.
• **DA** Allow some students to complete fewer sentences on this page. Rather than copy out whole sentences, they could supply the missing words.

72

2 Use your own ideas to complete the sentences.

1 James and his friends went to the beach, and _____ .
2 We planned to go to the mountains, but _____ .
3 It was raining yesterday, so _____ .
4 Mom promised to take me shopping, but _____ .
5 I was feeling thirsty, so _____ .
6 Paulette picked up her phone, and _____ .

Quotation marks

Rewrite the conversation using quotation marks.
Use different words of speech, e.g. *stated, asked, replied.*

> Example: *"How was your class visit to Hope Zoo?" Grandma asked.*

Grandma: How was your class visit to Hope Zoo?
Ashani: It was really interesting.
Grandma: Did you have a guided tour?
Ashani: Yes, one of the officers showed us around.
Grandma: What did you see there?
Ashani: We saw an iguana called Sandy. It had been injured.
Grandma: How did that happen?
Ashani: Some boys caught it and tied it to a tree.
Grandma: That's dreadful. They should learn to respect animals.

Word study: Suffixes

1 a) Change these nouns to adjectives by adding suffixes.

1 friend *friendly*
2 surprise
3 energy
4 courage
5 peace
6 accident
7 child
8 fury
9 danger
10 comfort
11 sense
12 fame

b) Choose six of the adjectives you made. Use them in your own sentences.

2 Change these words to nouns by adding the suffixes *-ence*, *-ance* or *-ion*.
You may need to change the spelling of the root word when you add the suffix.

1 silent *silence*
2 decide
3 obedient
4 distant
5 permit
6 invade
7 intelligent
8 elegant
9 explode
10 admit
11 innocent
12 receive

• **Quotation marks:** **DA** If students need more practice in using quotation marks, write the responses in the dialogue on the board for them to add punctuation.
• **Extension:** Some students could add more responses to the conversation.
• **Suffixes:** Allow students to use their dictionaries to check spellings.

3 **Add suffixes to the words in brackets to complete the sentences.**

1 You must be very *careful* when you swim near a reef. (care)

2 We were _____ not to have an accident. (fortune)

3 The _____ of tourism should be carefully controlled. (develop)

4 You should not take _____ items with you on boat trips. (value)

5 We saw an _____ for trips to the reef. (advertise)

6 The students followed the guide's _____ . (instruct)

Writing

1 **Find out more about an animal found in Jamaica.**

1 Make notes in a fact sheet like the one below.

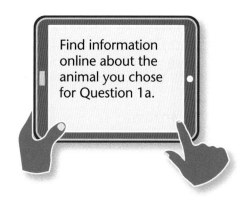

Find information online about the animal you chose for Question 1a.

NAME	
SIZE	
DIET	
HABITAT	
LIFE CYCLE	
OTHER INFORMATION	

2 **Use the information in your fact sheet to write a report.**

• Organise your information in paragraphs.

• Each paragraph must include a main idea and supporting details.

In your Learning Journal use an organiser like the one on page 40 to plan your paragraphs.

2 **Write a story based on the picture below.**

1 **Planning:** Use these questions to help you develop your story.

• Who are the people in the picture?

• Where are they? What are they doing there?

• What problems did they have? What caused the problems?

• How did they solve their problems?

Use an organiser to plan your story, e.g.

• a story map (see page 187)

• a herringbone (see page 187)

2 **Writing:** Write the first draft of your story, then revise it using the checklist for stories on page 54.

• **Writing Task Exercise 1a**: Encourage students to note what they already know about the animal they select before they carry out their research.

• For both writing tasks remind students to follow the *writing process* approach practised in Units 6, 7 and 8.

• **Learning Journal**: Encourage students to reflect on their writing skills by completing a 'How did I do?' chart (page 183).

Get ready

Which types of food do you like?

What is your favourite dish? Describe it to another student.
Explain why you like it.

Reading

1 **Look at the texts on the next two pages. What type of texts are they?**

Jamaica's
Favourite
Biscuits

Aunt Jemima's
Spicy Ginger Snaps

Made in Jamaica

from natural ingredients

350 g

A genuine ginger taste.

Aunt Jemima's Spicy Ginger Snaps Nutrition Facts

Ingredients: *wheat flour, vegetable oil, sugar, fresh ginger, skimmed milk*

Each biscuit contains		% of daily intake*
Calories:	47	2%
Sugars:	3.1 g	3%
Fat:	1.7 g	2%
Salt:	0.1 g	2%

*Recommended daily amount per adult
Best before December 2018

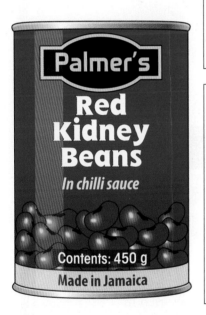

Palmer's
Red Kidney Beans
In chilli sauce

Contents: 450 g
Made in Jamaica

Palmer's Red Kidney Beans Nutrition Facts

Servings per tin: 2
Ingredients: *beans, water, sugar, salt, chilli powder, garlic*

Per serving		% of daily intake
Calories:	168	8%
Carbohydrate:	27.8 g	10%
Protein:	10.7 g	18%
Sugar:	9.9 g	9%
Fat:	1.6 g	2%
Salt:	0.45 g	8%

Once opened, refrigerate and consume within 2 days.

1 What is similar about the information on the front of the biscuit packet and the tin of beans?

2 What do Nutrition Facts tell us about the products?
a) the taste **b)** the cost **c)** the food value **d)** the expiry date

3 Which three nutrients can be found in both products?

4 Compared to one portion of kidney beans the amount of fat in one biscuit is
a) more. **b)** less. **c)** about the same. **d)** not stated.

5 What is another word for consume?

6 Which product do you think is healthier? Why?

- **Get ready:** Discuss the different types of food available in Jamaica. Which are traditional foods? Which have been imported from other countries?
- **Reading:** Discuss special dietary needs, e.g. diabetes. Students can collect food labels and check the ingredients to see which foods are suitable.

2 **Scan the leaflet.**
- What are the six food groups?
- What can you learn from the Food Pyramid?

A Healthy Diet
Why is food so important?

Food contains nutrients which give us energy, keep us healthy and help us to grow. There are six food groups: *staples, fruits, vegetables, legumes, animal products* and *fats, oils and sugar*. A healthy diet includes food from each group in the right amounts every day.

The Food Pyramid

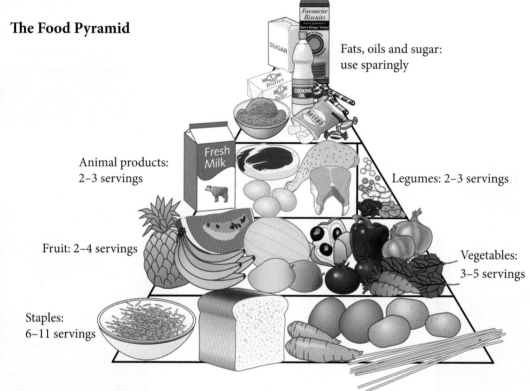

Fats, oils and sugar: use sparingly

Animal products: 2–3 servings

Legumes: 2–3 servings

Fruit: 2–4 servings

Vegetables: 3–5 servings

Staples: 6–11 servings

Go, Grow, Glow!

Staples like rice, potatoes, yam and cereals are **GO** foods. These foods are rich in carbohydrates which give you energy and help to keep you going all day.

Legumes like peas and beans, and animal products like milk, meat and fish are **GROW** foods. They are rich in protein, which builds bone and muscle and makes you grow strong.

Fruit and vegetables are **GLOW** foods. They contain vitamins and minerals which make your skin and hair glow and protect you from disease.

What about fats and sugars?

These foods give you energy but you should only consume them sparingly. Remember that sugar is the number one enemy of healthy teeth.

- Discuss how text features in the leaflet make the information accessible and appealing.
- Select words in the text that are associated with nutrition. Ask students to use context to work out their meaning and then record them in their word bank.
- Watch video clips online about young people and healthy eating.

1 Name one food from each of the six food groups.

2 Which food group should form the biggest proportion of your diet?

3 What type of food might prevent you from catching colds?

4 Which food groups do the following foods belong to?

   a) eggs   **b)** ground provisions   **c)** biscuits   **d)** rice and peas

5 Why is it important to eat protein?

6 The leaflet says that you should consume fats and sugars *sparingly*. This means that you should

   a) eat a lot of them.   **c)** never eat them.

   b) eat small quantities of them.   **d)** save them to eat later.

7 Explain in your own words *sugar is the number one enemy of healthy teeth.*

8 What type of food would you recommend for someone taking part in a football match? Why?

9 Suggest two foods which would provide a healthy snack.

10 Write a menu for a meal which contains food from all six food groups.

A fact states what is true. An **opinion** states what someone believes.
    FACT: Aunt Jemima's Spicy Ginger Snaps are made in Jamaica.
    OPINION: They are 'Jamaica's favourite biscuits'.
Advertisements often include opinions to encourage people to buy products.

3 **Look at the advertisements. Identify three facts and three opinions.**

Choose two or three advertisements from a newspaper or magazine. Find one fact and one opinion in each advertisement and record them in your Learning Journal.

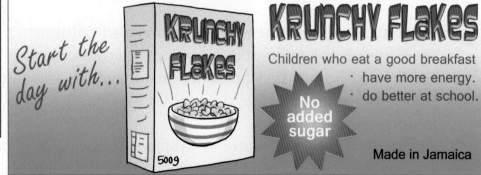

• **Comprehension**: Question 10: Students can write or type their menus for a classroom display.
• **Fact and opinion**: Collect examples of food labels and advertisements, or take pictures on a digital device. Students can study these to identify statements of fact and opinion. They could make their own collection of labels and advertisements.

77

Speaking and listening: Discussion

1 **Study this menu for a school canteen. Change it to provide more healthy food options.**

Which items will you keep? Which will you omit, and which will you add?

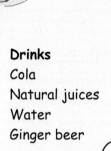

Hillview School Canteen

Main dishes	Snacks	Drinks
Red bean soup	Cheese Crunchies	Cola
Beef or chicken patties	Banana Chips	Natural juices
Hamburgers	Biscuits	Water
Fried chicken, rice and peas	Ice cream	Ginger beer

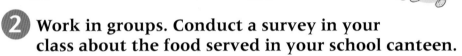

> How often do you buy food in the canteen?

2 **Work in groups. Conduct a survey in your class about the food served in your school canteen.**

a) Prepare some questions, e.g.
  • What do you buy in the school canteen?
  • Does the canteen offer healthy choices? Why / Why not?
  • What would you like to change?

b) Each group member asks your questions to five other students. Note the answers you receive.

c) Share your findings with your group. Choose a group member to report to your class.

Language: Punctuation

WB5 p54

> A **colon** (:) is used to introduce a list. The words before the colon must be a complete sentence.
> Jamaica has many delicious fruits: mangoes, pineapples, guavas and naseberries.
> Put a comma between each item in the list, but do not put a comma before the word **and**.

1 **Punctuate these sentences with colons and commas.**

1 There are a lot of different crops in Jamaica coffee bananas sugar cane and coconuts.

2 The following foods are staples rice bread potatoes and yams.

3 Jamaicans eat many different things for breakfast porridge fried plantain bammy and Johnny cakes

4 Beverages are often flavoured with spices nutmeg ginger vanilla and cinnamon.

5 Gran told me the ingredients for banana cake flour butter sugar eggs and bananas.

• **ICT Speaking and listening**: Record student interviews on an electronic device and play back for students to comment.

• **Alternative to survey**: Organise a *panel discussion* on healthy food choices. Students on panel answer questions from audience. Remind students to observe *communication protocol*.

2 **Complete these sentences with your own list of at least four items.**

1 These are some of my favourite foods …
2 Jamaican ice cream has a lot of different flavours …
3 There are many different shops in town …
4 There are a lot of interesting things to do where I live …
5 Mom checked the items on her shopping list …

> Remember to use correct punctuation in these sentences.

Abbreviations

> **Abbreviations** are a short way of writing words and phrases. They are usually followed by a full stop.
> • a **short form** of the word: *max.* (maximum)
> • the **initials** of the words: *P.T.A.* (Parent Teachers' Association)
> • letters which **sound like** the word: *B.B.Q.* (barbecue)
> **Short forms of Latin words**: *am* ante meridiem (in the morning)
> **Note**: Measurements are *not* usually followed by a full stop: m (metre)

1 **Read the ingredients for banana cake. Write the abbreviations in full.**

WB5 p61–2

Example: *125 grams butter*

125 g butter	2 very ripe bananas, mashed
150 g caster sugar	190 g self-raising flour
1 tsp vanilla extract	60 ml milk
1 egg, beaten	

Abbreviations for you to learn

Full stop		*No full stop*	
Ave.	Avenue	°C	Celsius
N.	north	°F	Fahrenheit
N.W.	north-west	km	kilometre
S.	south	km/h	kilometres per hour
S.E.	south-east	cm	centimetre
Dr.	Doctor	m	metre
Rev.	Reverend	mm	millimetre

• **Abbreviations**: Ask students to suggest places where they might find abbreviations. Get them to note abbreviations they see around them, e.g. in shops and advertisements. See who can produce the longest list. Conventions vary. Explain to students that they may see different punctuation used with abbreviations in some texts.

2 **Match these abbreviations to their meanings**

R.S.V.P   P.S.   etc.   P.T.O.   D.I.Y   U.S.A   e.g.

1 for example
2 and so on
3 Please send an answer.

4 United States of America
5 Please turn over.
6 post scriptum (added at end of letter)

3 **Rewrite the following expressions. Use abbreviations.**

Example: 15 litres *15l.*

1 3 kilograms
2 North East
3 180 degrees Celsius
4 Tuesday, 14th January

5 100 kilometres per hour
6 Ten o'clock in the morning
7 25, Saint Peter's Road
8 2 teaspoonfuls of cinnamon

Word study: Classification

WB5 p115

1 **Underline the odd one out in each group of words.**

Example: bread potatoes <u>milk</u> rice

1	milk	eggs	fish	bananas
2	pineapple	soursop	beans	grapes
3	cake	cheese	chocolate	biscuits
4	rice and peas	tomatoes	callaloo	onions
5	breadfruit	yam	carrots	cassava
6	butter	oil	potatoes	sweets

2 **Classify the following foods according to their food group. Add two more foods to each group.**

bread   curry goat   peppers   yam   naseberry   pumpkin
potatoes   callaloo   kidney beans   coconut oil   ackee
guava   jerk chicken   cho cho   saltfish   papaya   omelette
butter   breadfruit   sweets   gungo peas   mangoes

Create a **word bank** of words linked to nutrition. *Classify* the words in your word bank.

Staples	Fruit	Vegetables	Legumes	Animal Products	Fats, oils, sugars
bread					

3 **Classify different Jamaican dishes.**

a) Brainstorm Jamaican dishes, e.g. rice and peas, ackee and saltfish.
b) Think of what the dishes have in common and put them into categories, e.g. sweet, savoury, spicy.
c) Create a table like the one above.

- **Classification:** Use the *list – group – label* strategy to help students organise their knowledge of vocabulary. After listing words relating to a topic, they think about how to put the words in groups. There may be several ways of doing this. Finally, they suggest titles for each group.

Writing

1 **Study the features of the advertisement on the right.**

Create your own advertisement for a food product. Include:

- the name of the product.
- a slogan to attract customers.
- a description of the product.
- information about the ingredients and contents.

Remember to make your advertisement look appealing.

SPICE UP YOUR LIFE WITH OUR ← slogan

MANGO AND CHILLI RELISH ← name of product

MANGO AND CHILLI RELISH

picture of product

HOT!!!!   HOT!!!!   HOT!!!!

A fruity relish made from mangoes, with a hint of pineapple and a kick of chilli. ← description of product

Delicious with salads and jerk chicken.

Contains only natural ingredients

Made in Jamaica   **Contents: 350g** ← contents

2 **Write a notice for a wall display about foods. Choose your own topic, e.g. healthy foods, seasonal foods.**

1 Gather information for your notice. Make notes.

Foods which are good for you	Foods to avoid
Fruit and vegetables	*Foods which contain a lot of sugar*

2 Plan your notice to make it look eye-catching. You could:
- create a slogan.
- use headings and different coloured fonts.
- include pictures.

3 Prepare the first draft of your notice. Discuss it with another student.
- Is the information clearly presented?
- Will it attract people's attention?
- How could you improve it?

4 Make changes to your first draft and create a final version.

Research healthy and unhealthy foods online.

- Exercise 1: Look at advertisements with students and identify typical features such as slogans, colourful language, illustrations.
- Exercise 2: Organise students to discuss, in groups, the contribution made to the display by each group member.
- **DA** Students can contribute different skills to Exercise 2. Some can create the design, others can create the text.

Get ready

Which different features would you expect to find in a poem?

Reading

Scan the poem. Which typical features of a poem can you observe?

The Party

Deep in the forest
Late at night
Everyone is partying
In the moonlight.
Monkeys are drumming
Hummingbirds are humming,
Slippery snake slithers
Swinging to the sound.
Blushing Miss Mango
Dances the tango,
While nuzzling natty Jackfruit
In his olive-green suit.
Max the Mongoose
Looking most spruce
Flies through the air,
Whirling and twirling
As everyone stares.
Snooty Agouti
And the frog from France
Are boogying together
Into a trance.
Now the party's over,
Dawn is here.
The revellers are leaving,
They all disappear.

Julia Sander

- Students can describe what they see in the picture before reading the poem.
- This poem will benefit from being read aloud. Tell students to look out for *rhythm* and *rhyme* as you read it to them.

1 Which different animals are joining in the dance?

2 Who is providing the music?

3 Which adjectives are used to describe the following?
   a) the mongoose   b) the snake   c) the mango

4 Read the first eight lines aloud, clapping on each beat. How many beats are there in each line?

5 Find and write two examples of rhyming couplets in the poem.

> **rhyming couplets**: pairs of lines in a poem which rhyme with each other.

6 Which different types of dance are mentioned in the poem?

7 In the lines *Max the Mongoose / Looking most spruce*, the word *spruce* means:
   a) strange   c) smart
   b) untidy   d) impressive

8 Agouti and Frog are boogying *into a trance*. This means that:
   a) they are trying to dance better than the other animals.
   b) they are not aware of what is happening around them.
   c) someone has cast a spell on them.
   d) they do not want to dance with the other animals.

9 What do you think is the mood of this poem?
   serious   humorous   sad   surprised   persuasive

10 What do you like best about this poem? Why?

Alliteration

WB5 p76

> **Alliteration** is when we repeat consonant sounds close to one another. It is used to create an effect and make phrases memorable, e.g.
> *Slippery snake slithers*
> *Swinging to the sound.*

1 **Find two more examples of alliteration in the poem.**

2 **Copy the sentences and underline the alliteration.**

Example: *A funny flying fish flew in front of the boat.*

> Record examples of alliteration in your Learning Journal.

1 The slow slimy snail slid down the slope.

2 The hurricane howled around the houses.

3 The river was a raging torrent.

4 The waves were whirling white horses.

- **Comprehension:** Explain that the mood of a poem is the way the poem makes us feel.
- **Learning Journal:** Students can complete a 'Reading response' chart (page 183) about the poem in their journals.

3 **Write a phrase or sentence about each picture using alliteration.**

Speaking and listening

1 **Work in groups. Perform *The Party* to the class.**

1 Plan how you will recite the poem.
  - Will you have any sound effects, e.g. *drumming, clapping*
  - Will some students mime the dancing? What will they do?

2 Practise your recitation.

3 Perform your recitation to the rest of your class.

> Say the lines with **expression**. Emphasise the **rhythm**.

Language

Present continuous tense

> The **present continuous tense** tells us what is happening *now*.
> To form this tense, we use the helping verbs *am / is / are* with the present participle of the main verb.
>
> helping verb   main verb   helping verb   main verb
>
> *Everyone* **is partying**.   *Hummingbirds* **are humming**.

> **Helping verbs** are used with main verbs to **describe actions**.

> WB5 p28

1 **Complete these sentences with *am, is* or *are*.**

1 The animals _____ having a party.
2 They _____ making a lot of noise.
3 Mongoose _____ jumping up and down.
4 Everyone _____ looking at Mongoose.
5 My friends and I _____ sitting outside.
6 A flock of birds _____ flying by.
7 I _____ listening to my friends
8 The sun _____ not shining today.

- **Speaking and listening**: Get students to evaluate other groups' recitations. Agree on a set of criteria, e.g. *Did the students speak clearly? Were the sound effects and the actions effective?*
- **Present continuous**: Students can make sentences about what they can see in the classroom, e.g. *We are listening to our teacher. Carla is sitting next to Cherisse.* Remind students of *subject–verb agreement*.

 84

To form the present participle, we add **-ing** to most verbs: *swing* ⟶ *swinging*
Some verbs drop the final -e: *shake* ⟶ *shaking*
Some verbs double the last letter: *hop* ⟶ *hopping*

2 **Write the present participles of these verbs in a table like the one below.**

make	plan	stroll	sway	dance	shiver	stop	run	trip	travel
prepare	leave	sit	celebrate	laugh	drift	race	grab	escape	get

Add -ing directly	Drop final -e	Double last letter
stroll – strolling	*make – making*	*plan – planning*

3 **Complete these sentences with verbs in the present continuous tense.**

Example: The monkeys _____ (drum). *The monkeys are drumming.*

1 The band _____ (**play**) very loudly.
2 Everyone _____ (**clap**) the band.
3 Mongoose and his friend _____ (**jump**) in the air.
4 Frog _____ (**dance**) with Agouti.
5 They _____ (**celebrate**) Miss Mango's birthday.
6 No one _____ (**dance**) with Snake.
7 It _____ (**get**) late.
8 The animals _____ (**leave**) the forest.

Past continuous tense

We use the **past continuous** to describe what was happening in the past. We use the **helping verbs** *was* and *were* with the **present participle** of the main verb.
  It **was getting** late.   The animals **were getting** tired.

WB5 p29

Complete the paragraph with verbs in the continuous past tense.

At the party Mr. Jackfruit and Miss Mango *were dancing* (1 **dance**) together. The snake _____ (2 **shake**) and the frog _____ (3 **leap**). The monkeys _____ (4 **drum**) and the hummingbirds _____ (5 **hum**). Everyone _____ (6 **swing**). No one _____ (7 **sit**) still. It _____ (8 **rain**) and the wind _____ (9 **blow**) but all the revellers _____ (10 **have**) a good time.

• Get students to look around the classroom and take a mental 'snapshot' of what they see. They can describe what they saw, using the past continuous tense, and compare their observations with those of other students.
• **DA** Put some students in a group and help them form past participles correctly.

Comparative and superlative adverbs

Comparative adverbs compare two actions.
  – Short adverbs: *Frog danced* **faster** *than Miss Mango.*
  – Adverbs ending in **-ly**: *Miss Mango sang* **more sweetly** *than Frog.*
Superlative adverbs compare more than two actions.
  – Short adverbs: *Mongoose danced* **the fastest**.
  – Adverbs ending in **-ly**: *The hummingbirds sang* **the most sweetly**.

1 Complete these sentences with comparative adverbs.

WB5 p41

Example: Tortoise moved *more slowly* than Snake. (slow)

1 Mr. Jackfruit behaved _____ than Frog. (polite)
2 Snake danced _____ than Turtle. (quick)
3 Mongoose danced _____ than Turtle. (good)
4 The monkeys arrived _____ than Mongoose. (early)
5 Tortoise danced _____ than anyone else. (clumsy)
6 Mr. Jackfruit danced _____ than Miss Mango. (bad)
7 Miss Mango dressed _____ than Mr. Potato. (smart)
8 Frog arrived _____ than Mr. Jackfruit. (late)
9 The macaws sang _____ than Snake. (loud)
10 Frog could jump _____ than Agouti. (far)

Irregular adverbs
well – better – best
badly – worse – worst
much – more – most

2 Complete the paragraph with comparative or superlative adverbs.

Miss Mango arrived the *earliest* (**early**) at the party. The other animals arrived _____ (1 **late**) than she did. Miss Mango danced _____ (2 **well**) than the other fruits. Mr. Jackfruit was not a good dancer, but of all the animals, Mr. Turtle danced the _____ (3 **bad**). Snake danced _____ (4 **elegant**) than the other animals. The hummingbirds sang the _____ (5 **tuneful**). As the evening went, on the monkeys drummed more and _____ (6 **noisy**). Soon all the animals began to dance _____ (7 **fast**). At the end, everyone agreed that Mongoose had danced the _____ (8 **well**).

• Exercise 5: Point out that the words in brackets are adjectives. Students must change these into adverbs before writing the comparative forms.
• Exercise 6: Help students to see which adverbs are comparative and which are superlative, e.g. No. 2 compares Miss Mango to the other dancers, No. 3 compares all the dancers.

Word Study: Homographs

A **homograph** is a word that is spelt the same way as another word, but has a different meaning, and is sometimes pronounced differently.

WB5 p60

1 **Write the meanings of the homographs used in these sentences. What parts of speech are they?**

Example: The mongoose seemed to fly in the air.

fly: travel through the air (verb)

1 The potatoes had **bows** on their shirts.
2 The monkeys took a **break** from drumming.
3 It was **light** before everyone stopped dancing.
4 Did you see the mongoose **wave** to his friends?
5 There are some tall trees **close** to our house.
6 Did you remember to **book** the hall for the party?
7 The smallest hummingbirds are really **minute**.
8 Jared watched the ball **roll** away.

2 **Find two different meanings for these homographs. What parts of speech are they?**

Use your dictionaries to help you.

Example: *rock (noun): a stone*
rock (verb): sway backwards and forwards

1 play   3 watch   5 nail
2 rest   4 present   6 store

3 **Use the homographs in Exercise 2 in your own sentences.**

Example: *Frog sat on a rock beside the river.*
We saw him rock to the rhythm of the music.

Homographs you should know
Same pronunciation

bat (n)	sports equipment
	animal
bill (n)	part of bird
	something you pay
book (n)	something to read
book (v)	to arrange to use
break (n)	time for rest
break (v)	to shatter
light (adj.)	not heavy
	opposite of dark
fly (n)	an insect
fly (v)	travel through air
roll (n)	type of bun
roll (v)	e.g. roll down a hill
star (n)	movie star
	star in the sky
trip (n)	journey
trip (v)	to stumble
trunk (n)	part of elephant
	stem of a tree
	part of car
wave (n)	line of water
wave (v)	to greet with hand

Different pronunciation

bow (n)	type of knot
bow (v)	to bend down
close (adj)	near
close (v)	to shut
minute (n)	unit of time
minute (adj)	tiny
tear (n)	drop from the eye
tear (v)	to rip up
wind (n)	movement of air
wind (v)	to twist

- **ICT** Students can look online to find homographs to add to their word banks.
- **Extension:** Students can write example sentences for the homographs they record in their word banks.

Writing

1 **a) Classify the adjectives according to the senses to which they appeal. Suggest fruits and vegetables they could describe.**

> sweet   spicy   bitter   rough   pungent   fresh   cloying   salty   velvety
> sour   savoury   sticky   crunchy   smooth   juicy   mouth-watering   tough   prickly

Taste	Touch	Smell
sweet – mango	*rough*	

b) Choose a fruit or a vegetable. Describe it to another student, using different senses, e.g. *sight, taste, touch* **and** *smell*.

Ask this student to guess the fruit or vegetable you are describing.

c) Write descriptions of three more fruits or vegetables.

2 **Write a poem.**

1 Read the poem about a pineapple.

2 Choose a fruit or vegetable. Write a poem about it.
- Note down adjectives which describe your fruit or vegetable.
- Write a rough draft of your poem, then revise and edit it.
- Draw the shape of your fruit or vegetable on a piece of card.
- Copy your poem on to the card and illustrate it.

> It has a smooth green skin and orange flesh. It has an oval shape. When it is ripe it is juicy and very sweet.

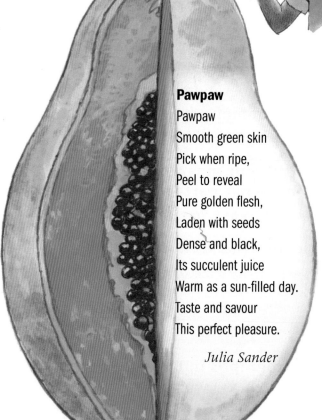

Pawpaw

Pawpaw
Smooth green skin
Pick when ripe,
Peel to reveal
Pure golden flesh,
Laden with seeds
Dense and black,
Its succulent juice
Warm as a sun-filled day.
Taste and savour
This perfect pleasure.

Julia Sander

- **ICT** Students can search online for poems about fruits and vegetables. Ask them to share poems they like with the rest of the class. You could make a collection on the class blog or in a wall display. Remind students that they must always note the name of the poet and the website where they found the poem.
- **Learning Journal**: Ask students to complete a 'How did I do?' chart (page 183) about writing poems.

Get ready

Describe some typical Jamaican foods, e.g. *jerk chicken, curry goat,* **to someone who lives in another country.**

Reading

1 **Skim the story.**

- Who are the people in the story?
- What are they talking about?

It Sounds Delicious!

Gavin's cousin Grace has come to stay for a few days. Grace lives in London, but her parents come from Jamaica. This is her first visit to the island. Gavin's mother is taking the children to a Jerk Fest organised by her church.

"Have you been to a Jerk Fest before?" she asked Grace.

"No, Auntie," Grace replied, "but Mummy sometimes cooks jerk chicken for us at home. What happens at a Jerk Fest?"

"It's an outdoor party where people get together and eat jerk chicken with rice and peas and other traditional Jamaican dishes. There's usually music and dancing as well."

"It sounds a bit like the barbecues we have in England in the summer," said Grace. "It's too cold for us to eat outside in the winter."

"Do you have parties in the winter too?" asked Gavin.

"Yes, of course we do. We have a lot of parties, especially around Christmas time."

"How do people celebrate Christmas in England?" asked Gavin.

"Families get together and give each other presents, just like in Jamaica, but the food we eat is different. On Christmas Day there's a special lunch with roast chicken or turkey, followed by Christmas pudding."

"What's Christmas pudding like?"

"It's a dark colour and very rich. It's made with dried fruits and other ingredients like rum or brandy. The pudding is often made several months before Christmas and stored in a cool place. We serve it warm. Sometimes people pour brandy over it and light it with a match, so it looks as if the pudding is on fire. Daddy told me that in Jamaica you eat fruit cake at Christmas."

- **Get ready**: Discuss with students what Jamaicans eat at special times of the year, e.g. *Christmas, Easter*.
- Study the use of quotation marks in this story. Students can identify statements, questions and exclamations.
  Point out the use of contractions, e.g. *it's, there's*. Ask students to give full forms of these verbs.
- Take the opportunity to discuss traditional Jamaican foods.

"Yes, we do. Mummy makes the best Christmas cake you've ever tasted."

"What do you put in your cake, Auntie?" asked Grace.

"I use a lot of dried fruit like currants, prunes and raisins and soak them in rum for a few days. People say that the longer you soak the fruit, the better the cake tastes. Then I make a cake mix of flour, eggs and butter and add spices like cinnamon. You can store the cake for a few weeks, but in our house, it usually gets eaten very quickly"

"It sounds delicious! I'm going to ask Mummy if I can come back for Christmas."

"Can you bring us a Christmas pudding if you do?" said Gavin.

1 Where do Grace and her parents live?

2 Why do people in England only have barbecues in the summer?

3 What happens at Christmas in England and in Jamaica? What things are the same? What is different?

4 Explain why brandy is sometimes poured over Christmas puddings.

5 Which of these sentences BEST describes Gavin's opinion of his mother's cooking?

  a) He does not like her Christmas cake.

  b) He does not think she is a very good cook.

  c) He is proud of the way she cooks.

  d) He thinks Grace's mother is a better cook.

6 The ingredients of Christmas pudding and Jamaican Christmas cake are

  a) very similar.   b) hard to find.

  c) completely different.   d) exactly the same.

6 Why do you think Christmas cake never lasts long in Gavin's family?

8 Why might Grace want to return to Jamaica for Christmas?

9 What other types of food and drink are eaten at celebrations in Jamaica?

10 Why do you think people eat special foods at Christmas time?

2 **Discuss the meaning of these Jamaican food proverbs.**

1 Pudden cyaa bake widout flah.

2 If yu cyaa tek de heat, get outta di kitchen.

3 When jackass smell corn, 'im gallop.

4 Wha no poison, fatten.

5 Rat belly full, potato have skin.

6 When yu go a fireside an' see food, eat half an' lef half.

> Collect proverbs and sayings associated with food. Use them to create a wall display.

3 **Rewrite the proverbs in Standard Jamaican English.**

Example: Pudden cyaa bake widout flah.

You need the right tools for the job.

- Ask two different students to read the same text out loud to the class, one with and the other without expression. Ask the class to compare and comment on the effect achieved.
- Ask students to suggest proverbs they know either in JC or SJE. Discuss the meaning of each proverb. Think of situations which reflect the proverbs, e.g. *Pudden cyaa bake widout flah: Mom did not have a big enough pan to make soup for everyone.*

Speaking and listening: Perform a skit

1 **Discuss the comic strip. What do you think of Mr. Swanky's behaviour?**
Mrs. Barrett has invited her cousin, Mr. Swanky, to have dinner with her at the Island Grill. The cousin, who lives in New York, is not impressed.

2 **Work in groups. Act out the restaurant scene shown in the comic strip above.**
Use your own ideas to continue the scene. Think about what happened next, e.g. *What did Mr. Swanky eat? What happened at the end of the meal? How did Mrs. Barrett feel?* Perform your scene to another student group.

3 **Make up a skit about a market trader and a difficult customer.**
In which scene would you use Standard English? In which one would you use Jamaican Creole?

> Language awareness

4 **Retell the scene in the restaurant as a story.**
Use a story plan like the one on page 31 to plan your story. Include direct speech in your story. Begin like this:

> Characters

> Direct speech

Mrs. Barrett's cousin, Mr. Swanky, was on a visit from New York. She took him to the Island Grill for dinner. "I reserved a table for two," she told the waitress when they arrived.

> Setting

> Tells story

- Exercise 2: Discuss possible endings for the story with the whole class before groups prepare their skits. Discuss situations where it is appropriate to use JC.
- Exercise 4: Remind students to use quotation marks for direct speech in their stories.
- **DA** Work with some students in a group and help them to write a group story.

Language: Future tense

> The **future tense** tells us about things which have not yet happened. It is formed from *will* or *shall* + a root verb.
>   Grace **will return** to Jamaica for Christmas. I **shall meet** her at the airport.
>   We use *will* for things which will definitely happen. Shall is used for things we plan to do.

WB5 p27

1 **Finish these sentences using suitable verbs in the future tense.**

1 Tariq *will have* a birthday party on the weekend.
2 Dad _____ jerk chicken.
3 Mom _____ a birthday cake.
4 Tariq _____ his friends
5 Tariq's friends _____ at 6 o'clock.
6 Everyone _____ Tariq presents.
7 A band _____ music for us all to dance.
8 The party _____ at midnight.

2 **Write three sentences in the future tense about the following topics:**

- What I will do after school today.
- What I will do on the weekend.
- What I will do for a special festival, e.g. Christmas, Easter, Independence Day.

Reported speech

> **Direct speech** tells us the exact words which people say.
>   *"It's too cold to eat outside in the winter."*
> **Reported speech** reports what people said.
>   *Grace said that it **was** too cold to eat outside in the winter.*
> **Note: Simple present** changes to **simple past** in reported speech.
> Pronouns also change, e.g. I ⟶ he/ she, we ⟶ they

Reported speech is also called **indirect speech**.

It's too cold to eat outside in winter.

1 **Change these sentences from direct to reported speech.**

> Example: "I want to come back at Christmas time," said Grace.
> *Grace said that she wanted to come back at Christmas time.*

1 "I love eating Christmas pudding," said Grace.
2 "Mummy's Christmas cake is delicious," Gavin told Grace.
3 "We have a lot of parties around Christmas time," Grace said.
4 "This food is really delicious," the children said.
5 "I always eat in the best restaurants," said Mr. Swanky.
6 "I don't like jerk chicken," Mr. Swanky told the waiter.
7 "We only serve Jamaican food," said the waiter.
8 "I don't want to eat with my cousin again," Mrs. Barrett said.

- Before attempting the written exercises, get students to practise reporting speech orally. Each student can tell another student three things about him/herself, e.g. *I love eating ice cream.* The other student reports to the class what was said, e.g. *Paul told me that he loved eating ice cream.*
- **DA** Some students may need support when they attempt Exercise 2. Go through the answers orally first before they write.

92

Here are some more changes which take place in reported speech.

Continuous present: *"I **am baking** a cake,"* Gran said.
  *Gran said that she **was baking** a cake.*
Future: *"I **will bake** a cake for Christmas,"* said Gran.
  *Gran said that she **would bake** a cake for Christmas.*

2 **Change these sentences from direct to reported speech.**

Example: "We will all share the cake," said Mummy.

Mummy said that they would all share the cake.

1 "I am learning how to make jerk chicken," Grace told her mother.
2 "We will go to a jerk fest on the weekend," Grace's aunt told her.
3 "Grace is staying for a few days," Gavin told his friends
4 "I will take the cake out of the oven soon," said Gran.
5 "I am planning to cook pancakes," Mummy said.
6 The waiter said, "The food will be ready in a few minutes."

Word study: Compound words for food

WB5 p64

1 **Match the words in the shapes to make the names of items found in a kitchen or dining room.**

Example: *bread + knife = breadknife*

bread dish
sauce tea
table tooth

cloth
spoon pan
cup pick knife
towel pot

2 **Match words from column A with words from column B to make words for foods.**

Example: *bread + fruit = breadfruit*

A				B			
bread	jack	pop	grape	fish	nut	food	bread
cheese	milk	sea	pine	melon	corn	cake	pea
chick	oat	shell	fish	apple	fruit	shake	
fruit	pan	sun		flower	crumb		
ginger	pea	water					

3 **Create a glossary of Jamaican foods. Write entries for different Jamaican foods. Use the internet to help you.**

Glossary of Jamaican Foods	
patties	*pastries containing fillings and spices*
festival	

A **glossary** is a list of unfamiliar or difficult words with an explanation of their meanings. You can find a glossary on page 190 of this book.

• **ICT Compound words:** Students can find a free puzzle-maker site online and create word puzzles using compound words for other students to solve.
• **Glossary:** Get students to use the glossary on page 190 of this book to check the meanings of words used in Language Arts.

Study skills: Diagrams

1 **Work with a partner. Look at the diagram. Give instructions for preparing rice and peas.**

> Use **signal words** when you give a set of instructions: *first, next, after that, then, finally.*

You need:		1 Drain	2 Measure
3 Chop	4 Add	5 Pour	6 Stir
7 Boil	8 Simmer	9 Serve	

2 **Make a list of different ways of cooking food, e.g. fry, bake. List foods which are cooked in these ways.**

Example: *fry: plantain*

- **Diagram**: Remind students that to give instructions we use the root forms of verbs (imperative), e.g. *Drain the kidney beans.*
- **ICT Extension**: Students can look online to find recipes for other dishes. You could produce a classroom recipe book.

Writing: Letter

1 **Study the features of an informal letter. Read the text of the letter.**

Apartment 20/ 36 — Address
Chungking Mansions
Canton

13 March, 2018 — Date

Greeting → Dear Gavin

Opening remarks → Thank you for your letter. I was very interested to hear about your school in Jamaica.

Body → You asked me about what we eat in China. It is a huge country so there are many different styles of cooking. Rice is our staple food, however, and all over China people eat rice at every meal. We serve food in small bowls, not plates, and eat it with chopsticks.

I live in Canton, the southern part of China, and our region is famous for sweet and sour pork. This dish is a blend of sweet and savoury flavours.

Closing remarks → I've heard that there are a lot of Chinese restaurants in Jamaica. Have you ever eaten in one? Could you tell me more about what you eat in Jamaica?

Closing → Your Chinese friend,
Su-Lin

2 **Write a letter to a student in another country. Tell this student about a typical Jamaican dish.**

- Make notes for your letter. Use headings, e.g. *The ingredients for this dish – How it is made – When we eat it*
- Write the first draft of your letter. Use the format for an informal letter shown above.
- Revise your letter using the checklist below.

> **Checklist: Informal letters**
> Have I:
> written the address and date in the top right hand corner? ☐
> used commas in the address and greeting? ☐
> organised the material in paragraphs? ☐
> used a suitable closing? ☐

- Students should be familiar with the format for an informal letter. Ask them to tell you what they remember before studying the letter on this page.
- Conventions vary for punctuating addresses in letters. Explain this to students and tell them what punctuation is correct according to your syllabus.
- **DA** Put some students in a group and help them to organise the material in their letters in paragraphs.

Get ready

Think of different reasons for writing letters.
To whom should you write formal letters? Suggest examples.

Reading

1 **Skim the letter.**
What is the writer's purpose in writing this letter?

Sender's address

St. Saviour's School
Coast Road
Long Bay
30 April, 2018

Date

Recipient's address

The Mayor
Town Hall
Long Bay

Greeting

Dear Sir

Reason for writing

We will be holding a Food Fair at St. Saviour's School on June 5th, and would be honoured if you would conduct the opening ceremony for us.

The purpose of the Fair is to encourage our students to adopt healthy eating habits and to give them the opportunity to sample some traditional Jamaican dishes

Body of letter

Our guest speaker, Mrs. Prudence Williams, is a nutritionist who specialises in diets for young people. Her talk will be followed by a public speaking competition where students will give presentations on the theme of healthy eating. We hope that you will be able to join Mrs. Williams on the judging panel.

Afterwards, some of our students will perform skits and raps they have written themselves about health and nutrition. There will, in addition, be the opportunity to purchase fruit and vegetables grown by our Gardening Club and to sample traditional dishes prepared by some of our parents such as Escovitch fish, Run Down and Cow Foot Soup.

I realise that you have a busy schedule, but it would mean a lot to our students if you could attend our Fair. It will start at 1.00 pm and we will close at 4.00 pm. We hope that you will be able to stay till the end in order to sample the delicious food.

Formal closing

Yours faithfully

Letitia M. Phillips (Principal)

- **Get ready**: Discuss the elements of a formal letter.
- **Reading**: Identify the elements of a formal letter. Point out that the information is organised in paragraphs. Indicate examples of formal language, e.g. *we would be honoured*.

2 **What is the purpose of this flyer and what is the likely audience?**

NOT TO BE MISSED!!!
St. Saviour's School
Food Fair
Friday June 5 2018
1.00 – 4.00 pm
To be opened by
His Worship the Mayor of Long Bay,
Mr. Trevor McFarlane
Guest speaker
Mrs. Prudence Williams
from the Healthy Eating Campaign

◆ *Enjoy the lively entertainment put on by students at the school*

◆ *Purchase delicious fresh garden procuce grown by the school Gardening Club*

◆ *Sample succulent traditional dishes prepared by parents at the school*

Free entry to members of families with students at the school
Visitors: $500 JMD

Our thanks go to the P.T.A of St. Saviour's School for providing refreshments

1 Why is Mrs. Phillips writing to the Mayor?

2 What other request does she make of the Mayor?

3 Which activities at the fair will be provided by students at the school?

4 How are parents at the school contributing to the event?

5 Which words and phrases are used in the poster to make the Food Fair sound appealing?

6 Which word in the poster means the same as 'delicious'?

7 Mrs. Jacobs has a son in Grade 1. She is attending the fair with her older daughter. How much will she pay?

8 Why do you think it would 'mean a lot' to students if the mayor attended?

9 Which activity at the Food Fair would you enjoy the most? Why?

10 Suggest other activities which could be included in a Food Fair.

- Study the layout of the poster. Discuss the text features with students, e.g. headings, bold font, italics, bullet points, snappy phrases, use of colour.
- **Comprehension:** Identify the different types of questions, e.g. Right there, Think and search, Author and me, On my own.

Speaking and listening: Give a presentation

Prepare a presentation about one of these topics

- Jamaican foods
- Foods we eat at special times, e.g. *Christmas, Easter.*

1 **Gather information** for your presentation. Look in a library or online. Use a web like the one on the right to organise your information.

2 **Make notes** for your presentation. Prepare some pictures or diagrams to accompany your presentation.

3 **Practise** giving your presentation to another student. Ask this student to tell you what s/he liked about your presentation and what you could improve. *Use the checklist to help you.*

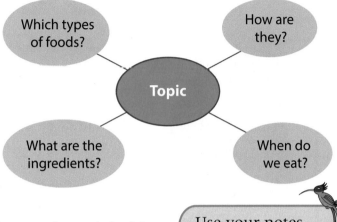

Use your notes. Do not read out your presentation.

Checklist: Presentations

Did the speaker:

present interesting information?	☐
speak clearly and loudly enough for everyone to hear?	☐
use notes and not read out the presentation?	☐
make eye-contact with the audience?	☐

Record your presentation on an electronic device. Play it back and discuss it with another student.

Language: Identify tenses

Read the paragraph. Identify the tenses of the verbs in bold type. Are they

a) simple present?

b) continuous present?

c) simple past?

d) continuous past?

d) future?

The students at St. Saviour's School **were preparing** (1) for their Food Fair. The Principal **wrote** (2) to the Mayor and **invited** (3) him to the fair.

"We **are holding** (4) a food fair on June 5th," she wrote. "We hope you **will come** (5). There **will be** (6) a public speaking competition. The students in the Gardening Club **are growing** (7) vegetables for the fair, and the parents **are preparing** (8) food."

When the mayor **arrived** (9), a group of students **was waiting** (10) to greet him. "Welcome to our school," their leader said. "The students **are sitting** (11) in the hall. The ceremony **will start** (12) in a few minutes."

After the ceremony, the Principal **spoke** (13) to the mayor. "The food **is** (14) ready now," she said

"Good!" the mayor **exclaimed** (15). "I **love** (16) traditional Jamaican food."

- **Presentation:** Before looking at the checklist, discuss with students the guidelines for making a presentation. You might want to add other criteria e.g. *try not to hesitate, don't repeat yourself.* Remind students of communication protocol, e.g. *listen respectfully, don't interrupt.*
- **Learning Journal:** Ask students to complete a 'How did I do?' chart (page 183) about their presentations.

Prepositions of time

> **Prepositions of time**
>
> on   We go to church on Sunday.
> in   We go home in the afternoon.
> at   I got up at five o'clock.
> since   I have lived here since 2015.
> for   We have lived here for ten years.

The fair is on Friday at one o'clock. It lasts for three hours. It will be over by four o'clock.

1 **Select the correct prepositions to complete the sentences.**

1 Mrs. Phillips became Principal of St. Saviour's School five years (ago / from / since).
2 The school has held a Food Fair every year (by / for / since) 2010.
3 The Principal told the students to be ready (by / on / until) midday.
4 They will not go home (by / since / until) everything has been cleared up.
5 The students have been preparing for the fair (on / in / for) the whole term.
6 The mayor will open the fair (at / in / on) one o'clock.
7 The food will be ready (at / in / for) ten minutes.
8 No one will leave (by / before / since) four o'clock.

2 **Complete the paragraph with a suitable prepositional phrase from the list below.**

> at four o'clock   by ten o'clock   for days   until the evening
> ~~on Sunday~~   for several hours   before midnight   in the afternoon

It was my mother's birthday *on Sunday* (1). We had a party for her _____ (2). My sister worked _____ (3) to prepare all the food. Most of the guests arrived _____ (4), but some did not arrive _____ (5). People stayed _____ (6) talking and having a good time, but _____ (7) most of them had left. There was so much clearing up to do, however, that we did not get to bed _____ (8).

Prepositional phrases are groups of words which begin with prepositions, e.g. before midnight, in ten minutes.

3 **Write your own sentences with these prepositional phrases.**

1 until later
2 in 2020
3 since last year
4 before midday
5 for two months
6 by this evening
7 in five minutes
8 on Mondays

- Study the list of prepositions of time and get students to make their own example sentence for each preposition.
- Let students create strategy posters. These should give explanations of prepositions of time and examples used in sentences.
- **DA** Allow some students to complete fewer sentences in Exercises 2 and 4. Give them extra support in completing Exercise 3.

Commas

> We use **commas** to separate pieces of information in sentences, e.g. Items in a list:
> *The gardening group grows tomatoes, onions, beans and yams.*
> (We do not put a comma before *and* in a list.)
> Before *but, and, so,* or *when* they join two clauses:
> *I enjoyed the food, but my friend thought it was too spicy.*
> After some words and phrases if they begin a sentence, e.g. *Well, Oh, Firstly, Later.*
> *Well, that was a surprise.*   *After the fair, we had to clear up.*

1 **Rewrite these sentences using commas where they are needed.**

1 The students performed raps skits and breakdances.
2 Oh dear I think we are going to be late.
3 After the show the guests went outside.
4 You can wait here or you can go inside.
5 Before the show the Principal spoke to the students.
6 Afterwards everyone praised our performance.
7 The Principal chose Paul Marie Chris and Tara to perform their rap.
8 There was a lot to do so it was late when we got home.

> We also use **commas** when we add an extra piece of information to a sentence.
> *Our guest speaker, Mrs. Prudence Williams, specialises in diets for young people.*

WB5 p51

2 **Punctuate the sentences with commas. Underline the information which has been added.**

> Example: *Run Down, a traditional Jamaican dish, is often served with breadfruit.*

1 Ackee Jamaica's national fruit is often served with saltfish.
2 Jerk chicken a spicy chicken dish is cooked on an open grill.
3 Christmas celebrated in December is a time when families get together.
4 The Mayor Mr. Trevor McFarlane performed the opening ceremony.
5 The Principal Mrs. Letitia Phillips welcomed the parents to the school.
6 Carl Thompson the Head Boy of the school gave the vote of thanks.

3 **Add extra information to these sentences.**

> Example: My father grows all our vegetables.
> *My father, a keen gardener, grows all our vegetables.*

1 My mother prepares delicious meals.
2 My friend sings and dances very well.
3 My teacher is always very helpful.
4 Britney never finishes her homework.
5 My favourite book is very exciting.
6 My brother's car often breaks down.

100
- Point out that we use commas in sentences to separate items in order to make the sentences easier to understand. Read out an unpunctuated sentence, then read the same sentence after the commas have been added, so that students can hear the difference.
- Take the opportunity to revise how we use commas in letters.

Word study: Word building

Many words are made up of **root words** + **prefixes** and **suffixes**.

dis / appoint / ment   *un / success / ful*

prefix   root word   suffix   prefix   root word   suffix

Remember: Often the spelling of root words changes when we add suffixes:

beauty – beautiful   please – pleasant

1 **Write the root word for each of the words listed below.**

WB5 pp63, 65–8

1 attraction *attract*	6 uninterested	11 presentation
2 announcement	7 deforestation	12 disastrous
3 dishonest	8 uncommon	13 misplace
4 youngest	9 disagreeable	14 unbelievable
5 encouragement	10 unwanted	15 irregularity

2 **Add prefixes and suffixes from the web below to make two or more new words for each root word.**

Example: connect – *connecting connection disconnect*

Root words:

1 connect	5 serve	9 cycle
2 honest	6 understand	10 comfort
3 please	7 agree	11 serve
4 employ	8 avoid	12 use

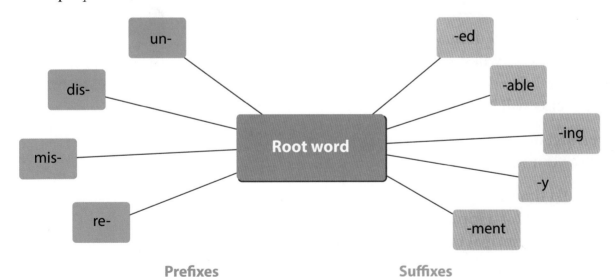

Prefixes   Suffixes

3 **Write your own sentences.**

Choose one new word you made with each prefix and one new word with each suffix in the exercise above. Use them in your own sentences.

- Ask students to identify words composed of a root word, prefix and suffix in texts they read.
- Students can add a section containing root words with prefixes and suffixes to their word banks.
- **DA** Allow some students to complete fewer examples in each exercise on this page.

Writing

1 **Write the words of a short grace to say before a meal.**

Remember to give thanks for the food you are about to eat.

Read your words out to another student.

- Ask him or her to tell you what s/he liked about your grace, and what you could improve.
- Write or type a neat copy of your grace. Decorate it to make it look attractive.

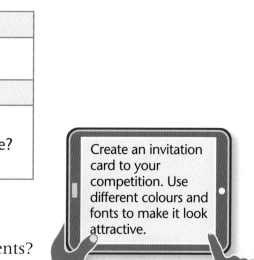

2 **Your class is holding a music and drama competition. Write a letter to your Principal inviting him or her to present the prizes at this event.**

1 Use the RAFTs strategy to help you interpret the task.

Role	Audience
Who are you as the writer?	To whom are you writing?
Format	**Topic + strong verb**
What form will your writing take? (*a letter? a report? a story?*)	What are you writing about?
	Which verb best describes your purpose? (*to invite? to apologise? to complain?*)

> Create an invitation card to your competition. Use different colours and fonts to make it look attractive.

2 Discuss the music and drama competition in groups.
- When and where will it take place?
- Who will be invited? Students from other classes? Parents?
- Which events will be included? What prizes will there be?

3 Use a herringbone structure like the one on page 187 to organise your ideas.

4 Write the first draft of your letter.
- Use the format for a formal letter as shown on page 96.
- Address your Principal by name, e.g. Dear Mr. ... / Mrs. ....
- Close your letter with Yours sincerely, then sign your name.

5 Revise and edit your letter. Use the checklist on page 115 to help you.

- **DA** Look online to find out more about the RAFTs strategy.
- Point out to students that the closing for formal letters is Yours sincerely when we know the name of the recipient. We use *Yours faithfully* with the greeting *Dear Sir or Madam*.
- You could adapt the checklist on page 95 so that it applies to formal letters.

102

Reading

Read the title and look at the pictures.
Predict what the story will be about.

This story is a myth. Myths often explain how something in the natural world began. In many traditional stories or myths, the characters don't have names. They are called 'the old man' or 'the little girl'.

The Tree of Life

A long time ago when people ate only leaves and berries, a young boy found a fabulous tree in the forest. Its branches were laden with every kind of fruit: bananas, mangoes, pawpaws, soursops and many more.

The boy ate greedily. "I won't tell anyone about this tree," he thought to himself. "I will keep the fruit for myself."

He went back to the tree again and again and ate his fill. Soon, his sister noticed that he seemed fatter than before. She became suspicious, and one day when he disappeared in the forest, she followed his trail.

When she saw the tree, she exclaimed, "This is surely the Tree of Life! We can't keep it to ourselves. It is for everyone." Her brother objected, but she ran back to the village to share the good news.

The villagers raced into the forest to find the tree. One after another, they climbed up into its branches. There was plenty for everyone, but, still, they squabbled over the largest and ripest fruit. More and more of them scrambled up the tree to collect the fruit.

Soon, the mighty tree began to creak and the boy's sister cried out, "There are too many of you in the tree. You will kill it."

No one paid any attention to her and within minutes the mighty tree tottered and crashed to the ground. A flash of lightning tore the sky apart and it began to rain furiously. In no time at all, the forest was flooded.

- Before students begin to read, ask them which other myths they know.
- Remind them to pause from time to time as they read, and think about what is happening in the story. Each time they pause, get them to *predict* what might happen next.

The villagers fled to a patch of high ground, and looked miserably at the ruined tree. The fruit which once hung on its branches lay on the ground, completely crushed.

The villagers stayed on the high ground until the floodwater had gone down. They were cold and hungry, and bitterly regretted their selfish behaviour. At last the forest floor reappeared. The tree of life had gone, but all over the forest were hundreds of tiny new trees.

The flood which had destroyed the tree of life had also scattered seeds, and each new tree bore just one kind of fruit.

The villagers had learnt their lesson. From them on, they took only what they needed from the trees, and they taught their children to share.

Retold by Leonie Bennett

1 According to the story, what did people eat *a long time ago*?

2 Why didn't the boy tell anyone about the tree he had found?   ← Inferring

3 His sister became *suspicious*. What does that mean?
   a) She knew her brother had found a special tree.
   b) She thought something strange was going on.
   c) She wanted to go with her brother.
   d) She knew that her brother was doing something wrong.

4 Which words in the story means the same as *quarrelled*?

5 What caused the Tree of Life to fall?   ← Deducing

6 Why do you think that no one paid any attention to the girl?   ← Inferring

7 How were the new trees different from the Tree of Life?

8 Who behaved well in this story? Why do you think that?

9 Who behaved badly? Why do you think that?

10 What lesson do we learn from this story?

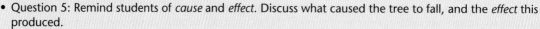

- Question 5: Remind students of *cause* and *effect*. Discuss what caused the tree to fall, and the *effect* this produced.
- Ask students to create posters evaluating their reading, using headings, such as *'What I can do well'*, *'What I need to improve'*, etc.

Language

Identify the verb tenses

Write the verbs from each sentence. What tense are they?

  a) simple present   **c)** simple past   **e)** future

  b) continuous present   **d)** continuous past

1 The boy ate the fruit from the tree.   *ate: simple past*

2 Only one type of fruit grows on the new trees.

3 All the villagers were trying to climb the tree.

4 They learnt an important lesson.

5 New trees are growing on the forest floor.

6 Now the villagers will share the fruit equally.

7 This story teaches us an important lesson.

8 I will always remember this story.

9 The river is flooding the low-lying land.

10 The storm destroyed the tree.

> In pairs, discuss how you identified the tense in each sentence.

Continuous tenses

1 Write sentences in the present continuous tense to describe the picture. Use the verbs in the list below.

  shine   cut   play   water   sit   climb   sleep

  Example: *The sun is shining.*

2 Choose suitable verbs to complete the paragraph. Use the past continuous tense.

  get   shine   load   do   fill   put   feel   cut   sit   help

The sun *was shining* (1) and the whole family _____ (2) ready for a beach party. Everyone except Chris _____ (3) with the preparations. Mom _____ (4) bread to make sandwiches and Gran _____ (5) the water bottles. Adrian and Tavia _____ (6) the car with Dad. Grandpa _____ (7) some folding chairs in the trunk. he two children _____ (8) annoyed with their brother Chris because he _____ not _____ (9) anything to help. He _____ (10) in his room playing with his new computer game.

- **Continuous tenses:** Get students to describe what is happening in the picture in pairs before they write.
- **DA** You may find it helpful to revise how to form the present participle (*running, playing* etc.) with some students before they attempt the exercises.

Reported speech

1 **Change these sentences into reported speech.**

We eat a lot of rice in China.

Su-Lin told me that they eat a lot of rice in China.

1 "I am learning how to cook," Nicardo announced.
2 "My friend is sending me some recipes," said Brandon.
3 "I do not like eating spicy food," Grace told me.
4 "There are many different fruits and vegetables in Jamaica," Tara stated.
5 "My friends are preparing a surprise meal for me," Angelina said.
6 "There will be many tasty dishes at the Food Fair," Mrs. Phillips promised.
7 "We often have beach parties on weekends," Gavin told his cousin.
8 Mom said, "I will teach you how to make rice and peas."

2 **Rewrite these sentences as direct speech.**

Example: Dana told me that she loved the story. *"I love the story," Dana told me.*

1 Mom promised that we would go to the library soon.
2 Rachel said that she liked stories about animals best.
3 My friend told me that he was reading an interesting story.
4 Cheryl and Leanne said that they liked reading about nature.
5 Joel said that he would soon finish writing his story.
6 Our teacher told us that she liked a lot of authors.
7 Mom told me it was time to go to bed.
8 The students said that they were looking forward to the competition.

Punctuation

1 **Punctuate the sentences with commas and colons.**

Example: *Mangoes, pawpaws, bananas and soursop grew on the tree.*

1 The tree was covered in fruits mangoes pawpaws bananas and soursop.
2 The villagers climbed the tree but it could not bear their weight.
3 Anansi the cunning little spider is my favourite story character.
4 My uncle has visited several islands Cuba Trinidad Barbados Grenada.
5 Lisette you must try to read a little faster.
6 On weekends I often see my friends Selena Ashley Alex and Shemarr.
7 My friend Jason Richards lives next door to me.
8 Ah that is my favourite story too.

• Exercise 5: Remind students that they will need to use quotation marks.
• **DA** Help students who find it difficult to convert direct speech to reported speech by going through the exercises orally first.

2 **Use these prepositional phrases of time in your own sentences.**

Example: in five minutes *The bus will be here in five minutes.*

1 before tomorrow
2 after school
3 three years ago
4 until midnight

5 at midday
6 for six months
7 in five years' time
8 on weekends

Word study: Homographs

a) Write two different meanings for these homographs.

1 wave   2 break   3 roll   4 tear   5 trunk   6 light

b) Use each homograph in a sentence of your own.

Example: The boy gave a friendly <u>wave</u>.   The <u>wave</u> crashed onto the beach.

Word building

1 **Add prefixes and suffixes to the root words. Make as many new words as you can.**

Use your dictionary to help you.

Prefixes
mis-   dis-
im-   un-

Root words
appear   agree
understand
comfort

Suffixes
-ance   -able
-ment   -ing

2 **a) Enter the words you make in a chart like the one below.**

New word	Prefix	Root word	Suffix
misunderstanding	mis-	understand	-ing

b) Choose four of the words you made. Write each one in a sentence of your own.

Abbreviations

Write abbreviations for the following expressions.

Example: 2 teaspoonfuls of sugar   *2 tsp. sugar*

1 35 centimetres
2 Doctor Paul Wilkins
3 13 Saint Martin's Road
4 South West Jamaica
5 Wednesday, February 21st

6 50 miles per hour
7 35 kilograms
8 25 degrees Celsius
9 half past eight in the morning
10 two litres

Show students how to use a *semantic analysis* chart like the one in Exercise 3a to indicate how words are constructed by adding affixes to root words. This will help them to spell longer words correctly.

Writing

1 **Write a letter of apology to a family member.**

Your aunt has invited you to stay for a few days during the school holidays but you are unable to go.

Write a letter to your aunt to inform her of the situation. Include the following information:

- Thank your aunt for the invitation.
- Tell her that you will be unable to come, and explain why.
- Give her some news about yourself and your family.

1 Use the RAFTs strategy to help you interpret the task.

Role	Audience
Who are you as the writer?	To whom are you writing?
Format	**Topic + strong verb**
What form will your writing take?	What are you writing about? Which verb best describes your purpose?

2 Write the first draft of your letter.
Read your draft carefully and think how you could improve it.

3 Revise your letter.
Use the checklist on page 95 to help you.

> Type your letter. Revise it using the cut and paste functions.

2 **Write a report about an event where Jamaican dishes were served, e.g. *a Jerk Fest, a Fish Fry, a festival such as Christmas or Easter*.**

1 Plan your report.

- Ask yourself questions beginning with *What? Where? When? Why? How?*
- Use a web to help you organise the information.

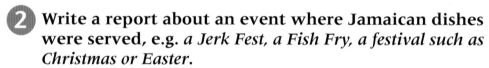
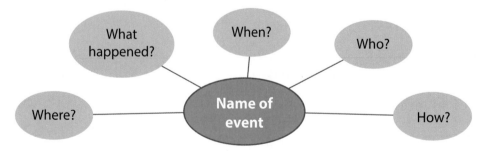

2 Write the first draft of your report.
Remember to organise the information in paragraphs.

3 Revise your report. Write or type a neat copy.

> Use **signal words** in your report, e.g. *first, next, then, after that, finally.*

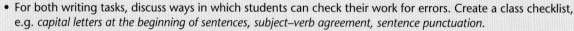

- For both writing tasks, discuss ways in which students can check their work for errors. Create a class checklist, e.g. *capital letters at the beginning of sentences, subject–verb agreement, sentence punctuation.*
- **Learning Journal:** Ask students to complete a 'How did I do?' chart (page 183) to assess how the RAFTs strategy helped them write a letter of apology.

Get ready

In which parish do you live? What is the parish capital?

What type of parish is it: rural or urban?

Which other parishes have you visited? How are they different from your parish?

Reading

1 **What do you know about the work of the Mayor of a parish? What more do you want to know?**

1 Copy the KWL chart and make notes.

The work of the Mayor of the parish		
K	*W*	*L*
What I *K*now	What I *W*ant to know	What I *L*earnt

2 Leave the last column blank. You will complete it after reading the Mayor's speech below.

The Principal of Riverside School, Mr. Frank Thompson, has invited the Mayor of the parish to address the students at Assembly.

An Important Visitor

1 Good morning Mr. Thompson, staff and students of Riverside School. Thank you for inviting me to speak to you today. You may be wondering what a Mayor does. I have a lot of official duties like visiting schools and hospitals in the parish, or opening new buildings and public events like fairs and sports competitions. That is only part of my work, however. I have many other responsibilities, the most important of which is overseeing the work of the municipal corporation.

2 Let me explain the work of the municipal corporation, the new name for the parish council, to you. In Jamaica, every four years each parish elects people to serve as councillors, and one of the councillors is chosen to be mayor. They meet monthly at the parish office to discuss parish business. We make important decisions about the development of the parish. For example, if someone wants to open a new hotel or sports centre in the parish, they must seek permission from the municipal corporation.

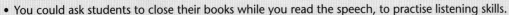

- You could ask students to close their books while you read the speech, to practise listening skills.
- **KWL chart**: Students are probably familiar with this pre-reading strategy. Conduct a class brainstorm to complete the K section of the chart. For the L section, help students to formulate questions to elicit information using question words like *What?* or *How?*
- Make sure that your students are familiar with the role played by a Mayor in the life of a parish.

³ There are many other ways in which the municipal corporation serves the community. We ensure that the roads in the parish are kept in good condition and that there are no fallen trees or other vegetation blocking them. We also provide and maintain street lighting in built-up areas. In addition, we approve plans for new buildings and check that they comply with building regulations.

⁴ One of our most important duties is to make provision for disasters such as fires, floods or hurricanes. We work closely with government agencies such as ODPEM (the Office of Disaster Preparedness and Emergency Management). We coordinate the work of the fire, police and ambulance services and make sure that they are ready to deal with emergencies. We are also responsible for repairing any damage caused during the emergency.

⁵ Of course, the councillors do not do all of this work on their own. We rely on staff in the municipal corporation offices and public institutions such as schools and hospitals to provide essential services to the public.

⁶ As Mayor when I attend official functions like school prize-givings or church services, I wear my robes and chain of office, but I keep this for special occasions. Most of the time as I go about my duties, I am dressed like everyone else.

⁷ I hope you have learnt a little more from my talk about the work of a mayor. Maybe one day in the future one of you will be Mayor of this parish. Thank you for your attention.

2 **After you finish reading, complete the L section of your KWL chart.**

1 What are the two main types of duties performed by the Mayor?

2 How do people become councillors?

3 How often does the Municipal Corporation meet?

4 Why do you think people must get permission from the Municipal Corporation before they build new facilities like hotels and sports centres?

5 Explain in your own words the meaning of the phrase a *built-up area*.

6 What preparations should the Municipal Corporation make when a hurricane is coming?

7 The Mayor says that the Municipal Corporation *coordinates* the work of the emergency services. *Coordinate* means

    a) to carry out by yourself.   **c)** to provide money for.

    b) to get different people to work together.   **d)** to provide help in difficult situations.

8 Which three groups of people provide essential parish services?

9 What do you think is the most important duty of the Municipal Corporation? Why?

10 Would you like to be Mayor of your parish one day? Why/ Why not? Think of questions to guide your research.

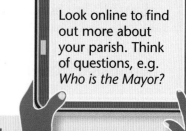

Look online to find out more about your parish. Think of questions, e.g. *Who is the Mayor?*

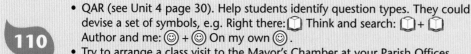

• QAR (see Unit 4 page 30). Help students identify question types. They could devise a set of symbols, e.g. Right there: 📖 Think and search: 📖+📖 Author and me: ☺ + ☺ On my own ☺.

• Try to arrange a class visit to the Mayor's Chamber at your Parish Offices.

Summary

1 **What is the main idea of the first paragraph of the Mayor's speech?**

> A **summary** is a brief account of the main ideas in a speech or piece of writing.

a) The Mayor will talk to the students about the duties of the Municipal Corporation.

b) The Mayor performs official duties and oversees the work of the Municipal Corporation.

c) Mayors go to schools and fairs and perform a lot of official duties.

d) The Mayor works at the Parish Office as head of the Municipal Corporation.

2 **Write the main ideas of paragraphs 2–5. Put them together to make a summary.**

Speaking and listening: Introduction and vote of thanks

Introducing a speaker

When a guest speaker visits your school, you may be asked to introduce him or her to the audience. Here are some tips.

- Welcome the speaker and introduce him or her to the audience.
- Tell the audience one or two interesting facts about the speaker, but be brief.

> Good morning Mr. Thompson, staff and students of Riverside School. It is my pleasure to introduce Mrs. Elaine Walters, Mayor of our parish. Mrs. Walters has been Mayor for two years, and she has done a lot to improve sports facilities for young people. I am sure you are all looking forward to hearing from her, so please join me in welcoming Mrs. Phillips to our school.

Proposing the vote of thanks

At the end of the speech, a member of the audience thanks the speaker.

- Address the speaker using his/her name or title.
- Mention one or two interesting points from his/ her speech.
- Ask the audience to join you in thanking the speaker and start clapping.

> Your Worship, it is my privilege to propose the vote of thanks on behalf of the students of Riverside School. I am sure we have all learnt a lot about the work of the Mayor. I had no idea that a Mayor had so many important duties. Please join me in thanking Mrs. Walters for speaking to us today. (*clap*)

1 **Practise giving the introduction and the vote of thanks above.**

2 **Prepare an introduction and a vote of thanks for a student who is presenting the results of his / her research on municipal corporations.**

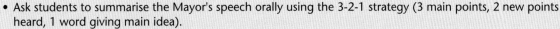

- Ask students to summarise the Mayor's speech orally using the 3-2-1 strategy (3 main points, 2 new points heard, 1 word giving main idea).
- Explain to students that they should address the Mayor as *Your Worship*. Create other situations where students introduce speakers and propose the vote of thanks, e.g. *to resource persons visiting the class.*

Language: Conjunctions

> We use **conjunctions** to join clauses to make longer sentences.
> *[The Mayor visited the school]* **and** *[presented the prizes].*
>
> **first clause   conjunction   second clause**
>
> *[The Mayor works hard]* **because** *[she has many responsibilities.]*
> Conjunctions are sometime placed at the beginning of sentences.
> **Although** *the Mayor works hard, she really enjoys her job.*
> **NOTE**: When the sentence begins with a conjunction, we place a comma between the clauses.

WB5 p45–6

1 **Find six conjunctions in this paragraph.**

The Mayor visited Kim's school recently and spoke to the students. Kim was chosen to propose the vote of thanks because she was good at public speaking. When the Mayor finished speaking, Kim stood up. She spoke in a loud voice so that everyone could hear her. Although her knees were shaking, she sounded confident. Everyone congratulated her after she had spoken.

2 **Join these sentences with** *because, although* **or** *so that.*

> Example: Kim sounded confident. She felt very nervous.
> *Kim sounded confident* <u>*although*</u> *she felt very nervous.*

1 Municipal Corporations are important. They make decisions about the parish.
2 The Mayor often makes official visits. She has other responsibilities.
3 The Mayor wears a chain of office. Everyone can recognise her.
4 Our class will visit the parish capital. We can see the Town Hall.
5 We enjoyed our visit to the parish capital. We saw some interesting buildings.
6 I live in the parish capital. I have never been inside the Courthouse.
7 A guide showed us around. We did not get lost.
8 Greg kept interrupting the guide. Our teacher told him not to.

3 **Use your own ideas to complete the sentences.**

1 I was excited **because** …
2 **Although** it was very late, …
3 We listened carefully **so that** …

4 I enjoyed the visit **although** …
5 I saved money **so that** …
6 Our teacher was pleased **because** …

• You may wish to explain that *and, but, so,* or are coordinating conjunctions. They join clauses which are equally important. *Although, because, so that* are subordinating conjunctions. They join clauses where one clause is more important than the other. Tell students that subordinate means *less important.* Sentences joined with subordinating conjunctions are complex sentences.

4 **Join these sentences with** *after, before, until, when* **or** *while.*

Example: The bus did not leave *until* we were all on board.

1 Our teacher called the roll. The bus left.
2 The bus stopped outside the Town Hall. We all got out.
3 We stayed at the Town Hall. It was time for lunch.
4 We visited the Town Hall. We ate our picnic in the park.
5 Some of us bought ice cream. We ate our picnic lunch.
6 We were in the park. Some of us played football.
7 We put all our garbage in the bin. We left the park.
8 Our visit was over. We went to the bus stop.
9 We waited a long time. The bus arrived.
10 We did not get home. It was nearly dark.

Word work: Spelling

Remember the rule for spelling words with -ie and -ei.

'i' before 'e', when the sound is 'ee', except after c, and the little word 'seize'.

'ie' (sounds like ee)	'ei'	'ei' after 'c'
believe	eight	receive
field		deceive

WB5 p71

1 **Complete these words with ie or ei.**

1 f__ld *field*
2 l__sure
3 perc__ve
4 ch__f
5 conc__ted
6 shr__k
7 r__n
8 for__n
9 br__f
10 gr__f
11 pr__st
12 c__ling

2 **Find and correct the spelling mistakes in these sentences.**
Some sentences may be correct.

1 Dana felt ~~releived~~ when her speech was over. *relieved*
2 Everyone congratulated her on her achievement.
3 Kayla lost the peice of paper with her notes.
4 Have you received my letter?
5 Mom siezed my little brother by the hand.
6 The police succeeded in catching the thieves.
7 I asked the assistant to give me a reciept.
8 There was a large crack across the cieling.

Spellings to learn
eight
height
neighbour
neither
reign
vein
weigh

• Remind students of the spelling strategies practised in Unit 2 page 20, e.g. *dividing words into syllables, Look, Cover, Write, Check.*

It's and **its** are often confused.
Its shows that something belongs to something or someone.
　　We went to the parish church and saw **its** beautiful windows.
It's is short for **it is**.
　　We visited the Town Hall. **It's** in the centre of the town.

3 **Choose *it's* or *its* to complete these sentences.**

　Example: *It's* a long way from my house to the parish capital.

> Read each sentence aloud. Can you say *it is*? If so, the word to choose is **it's**.

1　The County of Cornwall is famous for ____ fine beaches.
2　We plan to visit the parish capital, but _____ a long way from here.
3　If you visit the museum, ____ a good idea to go with a guide.
4　You should go to the Courthouse. _____ history is very interesting.
5　How did the parish of Manchester get ____ name?
6　____ important for us to learn about the history of our parish.
7　If you are looking for the library, ____ on the other side of town.
8　Our school has just celebrated ____ fiftieth anniversary.

WB5 p70

Silent letters

There are many **silent letters** in English. This makes words difficult to spell and pronounce. There are no spelling rules to help you. You just have to *learn* them.

Underline the silent letters. Read these sentences aloud.

　Example: Did you **k**now that the Mayor has resi**g**ned?

1　The Principal wrote a letter and signed it at the end.
2　The students designed a special wreath for Christmas.
3　I was bitten on the wrist by a gnat.
4　The knight knocked with his knuckles on the door.
5　The rat gnawed through the knot in the rope.
6　I always take my knapsack when I travel to foreign lands.
7　After the storm, I knelt and searched through the wreckage.
8　The gnome knelt down and cut the string with a knife.

Invent your own phrases to help you remember how to spell **tricky words**.
　　gnaw: **G**iants **N**ever **A**dvise **W**isely
　　wrist: **W**icked **R**obbers **I**nvent **S**illy **T**hings

Learn to spell these words with silent letters:

Silent k:

knead	design
knack	foreign
knapsack	reign
kneel	resign
knife	sign
knickers	
knight	*Silent w:*
knit	wrap
knock	wreath
knot	wreck
know	wreckage
knowledge	wring
knuckle	wrinkle
	wrist
Silent g:	write
gnash	writer
gnat	wrong
gnaw	wrote
gnome	

• **Silent letters**: Get students to write their own sentences using words with silent letters. They can create *mnemonics* (as in the last information box) to help them remember tricky spellings. You could organise a competition where the class votes for the best mnemonics. Display these in your classroom.

114

Writing: Report

1 **Write a report about the work of someone who works for the emergency services, e.g.** *a fireman, a policeman, an ambulance driver.*

1 Look in the library or online to find out information about:
  * how they train for the job.
  * where they work.
  * the uniform they wear.
  * the kind of work they do.

2 Make notes in an organiser like the one below.

Name of job	
Training	
Uniform	
Place of work	
Type of work	

3 Write the first draft of your report. Organise your information in paragraphs.

4 Revise your first draft and write or type a neat copy.

2 **Write a letter of thanks.**

Imagine that the Mayor of your parish has visited your school and given a talk. You have been asked to write a letter of thanks to the Mayor on behalf of the students at the school.

1 Use the RAFTs strategy practised in Unit 12 to develop your letter.

2 Write the first draft of your letter.
  Use the format for a formal letter found on page 96.
  Write the correct address for your school and your municipal corporation.
  Include the following information:
  * Say that you are writing on behalf of the students at your school.
  * Thank the Mayor for talking to you.
  * Mention two interesting points from the Mayor's speech.

> Look online to find the name of the Mayor of your parish and the address of the parish office.

3 Revise the first draft of your letter using the checklist below.

> **Checklist: Formal letters**
> Have I:
> > written my address and date in the top right hand corner? ☐
> > included the address of the person to whom I am writing? ☐
> > used commas in the address? ☐
> > stated my reason for writing? ☐
> > organised the material in paragraphs? ☐
> > used a suitable closing? ☐

* **Report**: Remind students that each paragraph should consist of a main idea and supporting details.
* After students have revised their first drafts, they should proofread it for errors. Write a list of suggestions on the board of points to check, e.g. *sentence punctuation, subject–verb agreement, spellings.*
* If necessary, tell the students that the correct formal way to address the mayor in writing in the letter address is: His/ Her Worship The Councillor Mayor (Name)

Get ready

Why do people use the parish library?
What types of books would you expect to find there?
What else might you find in a library?

Reading

1 **Skim this account of a visit to the library to find the answers to these questions.**

- Which library did the children visit?
- What is the name of Taylor's friend?
- Who is Mrs. Webster?

Visit to the Parish Library

Taylor and Michelle are very fond of reading, so last week their mother took them to the Hanover Parish Library. When they went in, the children were amazed to see that there were thousands of books on the shelves. They noticed some children choosing books and others sitting quietly at tables reading.

Taylor recognised one of his friends and went over to speak to him. "Hello, Shawn," he whispered. "Do you often come to the library?"

"Yes, I've been a member for two years. Would you like me to show you around?" Shawn offered.

First Shawn showed Taylor and Michelle the fiction section. "This part of the library contains story books, poems, and plays," he told them. "It's simple to find the books you want because the authors' names are in alphabetical order."

Then he took them to the reference section. "This section contains informational books like encyclopaedias and manuals," he said. "I use the books in this section to find information for my school projects. I sometimes use the library computers as well to look things up on the Internet." He pointed out a bank of computers at the other end of the library.

"Do you enjoy coming to the library?" Michelle asked.

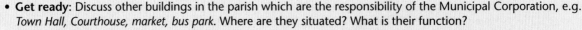

- **Get ready:** Discuss other buildings in the parish which are the responsibility of the Municipal Corporation, e.g. *Town Hall, Courthouse, market, bus park.* Where are they situated? What is their function?
- You could arrange a visit to your parish capital to look at some of these buildings. Students could prepare questions to ask people who work there.

116

"Oh yes. I love spending time here. The thing I like best is Mrs. Webster's library club. Mrs. Webster is one of the librarians. We meet with her once a month to read stories and talk about our favourite books. Mrs. Webster recommends new books to us as well. At the moment we're getting ready for the National Reading Competition next April."

On the way out of the library, Taylor's mother spoke to the librarian. "How can the children join the library?" she asked.

"To join the library they must fill out an application card. Then they will be allowed to take books out."

"Do we have to pay anything?" asked Michelle.

"No, you can borrow one book free of charge for two weeks at a time. If you return the books late you will have to pay a fine."

"How soon can we start borrowing books?" asked Taylor.

"If you fill in the form now, you can start taking books out right away."

1 What surprised Taylor and Michelle when they went into the library?

2 What did they see children doing in the library?

3 In which section of the library would you find a book of fables?

8 Which of these books would you expect to find in the reference section of a library?

  a) mystery stories   **b)** biographies   **c)** a cookery book   **d)** a dictionary

4 Where can you find information for school projects?

5 A librarian is a person who

  a) borrows books from a library.

  b) helps children with their school work.

  c) looks after the books in a library.

  d) shows people how to use computers.

6 Explain how children can borrow books from the library.

7 Do you think Taylor was keen to join the library? How do you know?

9 Why is it important to be quiet in a library?

10 What would you most like to do in a library? Why?

> In your Learning Journal, complete a 'Reading response' chart (page 183) about books you borrow from the library.

> **Fiction** means writing about people who are not real. **Non-fiction** means writing about real events and facts.

2 **Are these books fiction or non-fiction?**

Birds of the Caribbean: Peter Evans
Baba and Mr. Big: C. Everard Palmer
Tales from the West Indies: Philip Sherlock
The Young Warriors: V.S. Reid

Duppy Stories: David Brailsford
Atlas of the Eastern Caribbean
My First Spanish Dictionary
Juice Box and Scandal: Hazel Campbell

Fiction	Non-fiction
Baba and Mr. Big	

- **Classifying books**: Students can use their own ideas to add books to each column.
- Talk about Jamaican authors, e.g. C. Everard Palmer, V.S. Reid, Philip Sherlock , and the contribution they have made to Jamaican culture.

3 **Match the words below to the definitions.**
You can use a dictionary to help you.

> table of contents   index   manual   glossary   fiction   non-fiction
> atlas   ~~directory~~   encyclopaedia   catalogue   thesaurus

> Example: a book which contains a list of addresses or telephone numbers. *directory*

1 list of topics at the back of a book showing on which page they are mentioned
2 a book containing maps
3 books or stories about imaginary events and people
4 list at front of book giving information about the different sections of the book
5 book containing instructions on how to do something
6 book containing lists of words with similar meanings
7 list of items in an exhibition or a library
8 writing that is about real events and people
9 list of difficult words with explanations of their meaning
10 book or set of books which give information about different subjects

4 **Imagine you are a school librarian. Classify these fiction books in alphabetical order** *according to the names of the authors.*

> Example: 1 *The Ring and the Roaring Water: Diane Browne*

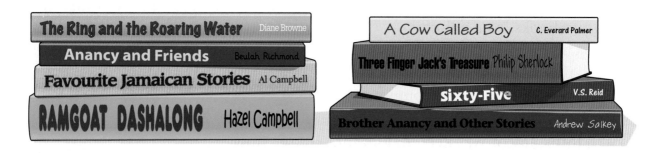

The Ring and the Roaring Water   Diane Browne
Anancy and Friends   Beulah Richmond
Favourite Jamaican Stories   Al Campbell
RAMGOAT DASHALONG   Hazel Campbell

A Cow Called Boy   C. Everard Palmer
Three Finger Jack's Treasure   Philip Sherlock
Sixty-Five   V.S. Reid
Brother Anancy and Other Stories   Andrew Salkey

Speaking and listening: Giving explanations

1 **Work with a partner. Each of you chooses a book you use in class.**
Explain to your partner what each part of the book contains. Use these questions to help you.

• What information can you find on the cover of the book?
• How would you use the Table of Contents?
• What other sections can you find in the book? What kind of information do they contain?

• Discuss the advantages and disadvantages of using books and searching online to find information. Discuss whether books can be replaced by computers.

2 **Roleplay the following situation.**

Student A is a school librarian. He/she explains
to Student B how to find information for a project.
Student A:
- Ask Student B what he/she is looking for.
- Suggest useful sources of information for
  his/her project.
- Explain how to use an index to find information in a
  reference book, e.g. an encyclopaedia.

Student B:
- Ask Student A to help you find information for
  your project.
  Describe your project and tell Student A what kind of information you need.

Language

Possessive adjectives and pronouns

Words like *my, your, his, her* are **possessive adjectives**. We use them to
show who owns something, e.g. *my book, his bag.*
Words like **mine, yours, ours** are **possessive pronouns**. They also show
who owns things, e.g. *That book is mine. These books are yours.*

Adjectives	my	your	his	her	our	their
Pronouns	mine	yours	his	hers	ours	theirs

WB5 p19

1 **Complete the sentences with an adjective from the list below.**

> my   your   his   her   our   their

1 Taylor recognised _____ friend sitting at one of the library tables.
2 Taylor's sister told _____ friends about _____ visit to the library.
3 The children hoped to see _____ friends at the library.
4 I looked for _____ mother but I could not see her in the crowd.
5 Are these _____ books, Ricardo?
6 My sister and I are meeting _____ friends in town.

2 **Complete the paragraph with the pronouns** *mine, yours, his, hers, ours* **or** *theirs.*

Mrs. Webster is sorting out the things the students have left in the library.

> The backpack belongs to Dana. The tablet is _____ too. The ruler is Ben's.
> The notebook is _____ too. These books belong to Javon and Greg. I think the
> pencils are _____ as well. Those are my car keys under the books. The phone
> is _____ too. Who owns this lunch box? Is it _____, Kim?

- **Possessive adjectives and pronouns:** Point out to students that *my, your, his* etc. describe nouns, but *mine,*
  yours etc, are pronouns which stand alone.
- **Digital citizenship:** Tell students that they must make a note of any webpages they consult on the Internet for
  the projects.

3 **Choose the correct words to complete the sentences.**

1 Mrs. Webster told the students to tidy _____ (their / theirs) things.
2 The phone she found was _____ (her / hers).
3 You can borrow my pen as you have lost _____ (your / yours).
4 I don't think that these are _____ (our / ours) books.
5 That is not _____ (your / yours) backpack. It looks like _____ (my / mine)
6 Are these books _____ (their / theirs)?
7 "Have you seen _____ (my / mine) lunch box?" Michelle asked.
8 May we borrow _____ (your / yours) books? We can't find _____ (our / ours).

Possessive nouns

To show that something belongs to someone or something, we add an **apostrophe** to the end of a noun.
Singular nouns add an apostrophe + s:
    Shawn's's book or *This book is Shawn's.*
If the noun ends ends in '**s**'
Either write the apostrophe after the 's': *Mrs. Jones' class   Thomas' book*
Or add another 's': *Mrs. Jones's class, Thomas's book*

1 **Rewrite these sentences correctly using apostrophes.**

> Example: 1 We all liked Keiras story best.
>
> *We all liked Keira's story best.*

1 Nathans mother read him a story about pirates.

For **plural nouns** the apostrophe is placed after the letter 's': *my twin brothers' clothes*
Nouns with their own special plural add '**s**': *the children's posters, the men's books*

2 These paints are Allisons.
3 That is our teachers car.
4 These are Britannys sneakers.
5 Amos story was the winning entry.
6 Janes painting was very neat but her brothers was untidy.
7 The childrens parents were very proud of them.
8 Mrs. Evans class is the noisiest in the school.

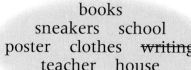

2 **Choose words from each oval and write sentences. Remember to add apostrophes.**

> Example: *Emma's writing is always neat.*

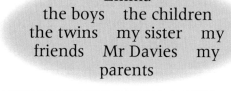

~~Emma~~
the boys   the children
the twins   my sister   my
friends   Mr Davies   my
parents

books
sneakers   school
poster   clothes   ~~writing~~
teacher   house

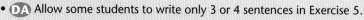

- **Possessive nouns:** You may wish to work through Exercise 4 on the board with students before they attempt the exercise on their own.
- **DA** Allow some students to write only 3 or 4 sentences in Exercise 5.

Get ready

There are legends associated with different parishes in Jamaica. Are there any associated with your parish? What are they?

Which other Jamaican legends do you know?

Reading

What can you *infer* from the picture on this page?

- What do you think has happened?
- What might happen next?

We can use pictures to draw inferences about stories and relationships between people.

Stories from the Parishes

St. Thomas: Yallahs Ponds

One of the strangest features on our island are Yallahs Ponds. The water in these ponds is ten times as salty as the ocean, and it is said that in the past the foul odour could be smelt as far away as Kingston. Channels have been cut from the ponds to the open seas, which has greatly reduced the smell.

No one knows exactly how these ponds were formed, but the most likely explanation is that they were created by a landslide which occurred during the great earthquake of 1692. A legend about the ponds gives a more colourful explanation, however.

According to this legend, there were once two brothers who had both fallen in love with the same woman. She could not make up her mind which one of them to marry. Eventually, the older brother, who was the richer of the two, persuaded the woman to become his bride. The younger brother accepted his fate, but his love for the woman remained as strong as ever.

One day, the older brother had to travel to Kingston on business. He was away for several days, and on his return, he discovered that his wife had betrayed him. She had left their home, and was living with his younger brother.

The older brother was broken-hearted. He began to weep, and once he started weeping, he found that he could not stop. His tears formed two salty puddles which grew deeper and deeper until they drowned his brother and his faithless wife.

- Remember the saying: *A picture tells a thousand words*. Talking about pictures is a good way of helping students draw inferences. Help them to make up a back-story by asking questions: *Who are these people? What is their relationship to one another? What happened before the scene in this picture? How are they feeling now?*
- Legends are an important part of Jamaican culture. Get your students to tell you which ones they know.

St. Elizabeth: Lovers' Leap

Lovers' Leap is a sheer 1,700 foot cliff overhanging the sea in the parish of St. Elizabeth. With its panoramic views of the Caribbean Sea, it is a popular vantage point for visitors. A tragic story is associated with this place, however, which explains why it is known as Lovers' Leap

It is said that in the 18th century two slaves, Mizzy and Tunkey, fell in love. When their master, Mr. Chardley, heard of this, he was furious, for he wanted Mizzy for himself. In a fit of jealousy, he arranged to sell Tunkey to another plantation owner. When Tunkey learnt that he was to be sold, he met Mizzy in secret and the two lovers promised that they would always remain faithful to one another.

The couple realised that the only way they could stay together would be to run away. There was no time to lose, as Tunkey was due to leave the next morning. At dead of night, he tapped gently on Mizzy's door, and the two of them slipped quietly away. They had not reckoned with Mr. Chardley's dog, however, which started barking and woke everyone on the plantation, including Mr. Chardley himself.

Tunkey and Mizzy fled through the forest with Mr. Chardley and his dog hot on their heels. Some hours later, exhausted and trembling, the pair emerged from the forest to find themselves at the top of a precipitous cliff. Sick with fear, they gazed down at the blue waves far below. They looked back towards the forest, and saw Mr. Chardley standing there with a gun levelled at them.

"You will never separate us," cried Tunkey. "Better we die now than return to slavery!" With these words, he grabbed Mizzy by the hand, and together they leapt off the cliff, down to the waters below.

1 Explain in your own words what is strange about Yallahs Ponds.

2 What persuaded the woman in the story to marry the older brother?

3 The words *the younger brother accepted his fate* tell us

  a) he approved of his brother's choice of wife.

  b) he realised he was not destined to marry the woman.

  c) he never gave up hope of marrying the woman.

  d) he did not try to change the situation.

4 Why is the woman described as *faithless*?

5 Which explanation for the existence of the ponds do you believe? Why?

6 Why do people visit Lovers' Leap today?

7 Why did Mr. Chardley sell Tunkey to another plantation owner?

8 Explain in your own words why Mizzy and Tunkey jumped off the cliff.

9 What is the difference between the lovers in the story about Yallahs Ponds and the lovers in the story from St. Elizabeth?

10 Which story do you prefer? Why?

Compare and contrast

> Comprehension strategy

When we **compare and contrast,** we describe the *similarities* and *differences* between two characters, places, things and events.

Copy the diagram. Make notes about the stories as follows.
- Where ovals overlap: things which are similar in both stories
- Left oval: things which are different in the first story
- Right oval: things which are different in the second story

Yallahs Ponds   **Both**   **Lovers' Leap**
                    Two men in love with
                    the same woman

Context clues

Looking at unfamiliar words in context (*the surrounding words and phrases*) helps us understand what they mean.
   *The foul **odour** could be smelt as far away as Kingston.*
Odour means **smell**. The clue is in the verb *smelt*.

Select the correct meaning of the words in bold type. Use context clues to help you.

1 Lovers' Leap has **panoramic** views of the Caribbean Sea.
   a) steep   b) scenic   c) beautiful   d) frightening

2 Its fine views make it a popular **vantage** point for visitors.
   a) resting   b) look-out   c) tourist   d) shelter

3 The two slaves had not **reckoned with** Mr. Chardley's dog.
   a) hidden   b) attacked   c) thought about   d) avoided

4 Mr. Chardley and his dog were **hot on their heels**.
   a) close behind   b) a long way off   c) giving up   d) in difficulty

5 They emerged from the forest to find themselves at the top of a **precipitous** cliff.
   a) low   b) very steep   c) dangerous   d) rocky

6 They saw Mr. Chardley standing there with a gun **levelled** at them.
   a) pointed   b) shooting   c) loaded   d) fired

- **Compare and contrast:** This type of graphic organiser is called a Venn diagram. You may wish to complete it on the board as a class exercise. Use it to compare other well-known Jamaican legends.
- **Context:** Show video clips from YouTube on how to use context to work out the meaning of unfamiliar words.

Speaking and listening: Discuss stories

1 **Work with a partner. Talk about the two stories you read on pages 123–4.**
Make notes in a table like the one below.

Name of story	Yallahs Ponds	Lovers' Leap
Text type		
Characters and setting		
Main events		
Your opinion of the story		
Reason for your opinion		

Look online to find more Jamaican legends. Are there any associated with your parish?

2 **Choose a different Jamaican legend you both know. Make notes using the headings from the table.**

3 **Give a short talk to your group or class about this legend.**

Language: Relative pronouns

> The words **which** and **where** can be used as *relative pronouns* to join two simple sentences.
>
> Yallahs Ponds are deep lakes. They contain salty water.
> Yallahs Ponds are deep lakes **which** contain salty water.
>
> Lovers' Leap is a place on the south coast. The cliffs are very high.
> Lovers' Leap is a place on the south coast **where** the cliffs are very high.

1 **Complete the paragraph with the relative pronouns which or where.**

There is a legend associated with Lovers' Leap *which* (1) tells the story of two lovers. Many visitors come to see the cliff _____ (2) the lovers jumped into the sea. Nowadays, there is a restaurant _____ (3) you can buy refreshments. There is a lighthouse _____ (4) sends signals to warn ships of danger at sea. Near Lovers' Leap is the famous Treasure Beach, _____(5) tourists love to stay. They can visit the Ys Falls _____(6) are not far away, or they can go to Black River _____(7) they can take a river trip. On the way, they drive through Bamboo Avenue _____(8) huge bamboo trees provide a cool, shady area.

• **Relative pronouns:** Point out that when we join sentences with relative pronouns, we often leave out the subject of the second clause, e.g. *Yallahs Ponds are deep lakes which contain salty water.*

• **DA** Allow some students to write only the relative pronouns in Exercise 1.

126

The relative pronoun **who** can also be used to join sentences.
The lovers did not want to be separated. They decided to run away.
*The lovers, **who** did not want to be separated, decided to run away.*
Note: Remember to put commas around the clause beginning with **who**.

2 **Join these sentences with** *who*.

> Example: My aunt lives in Kingston. She promised to take me to Yallahs Ponds.
>
> *My aunt, who lives in Kingston, promised to take me to Yallahs Ponds.*

1 My sister is a tour guide. She takes people to interesting places.
2 The tourists visited Lovers' Leap. They were afraid to go near the cliff.
3 The brothers lived at Yallahs River. They both loved the same woman.
4 My cousins will stay with us in January. They hope to visit Dunn's River Falls.
5 Abigail has been learning Spanish. She hopes to travel abroad.
6 My brother is a fireman. He works for the Jamaica Fire Service.
7 My best friend goes to the same school as me. She knows lots of stories.
8 Mrs. Davis trained as a nurse. She works at our health clinic.

Word work: Sounds

A **consonant blend** is a group of two or more consonants placed together, e.g. *bl, cr, tr*.
Many consonant blends are placed at the beginning of words, e.g.
bl: **bl**ue   **cl**: **cl**ap   **dr**: **dr**ink   **fl**: **fl**y   **st**: **st**art
Others are placed at the end, e.g. **-nd**: ha**nd**   **-ng**: si**ng**

> Words are made up of different sounds. Identifying these sounds will help you read unfamiliar words.

1 **Copy these words and underline the sound blends. For each word, write one more word with the same blend.**

> Example: <u>br</u>eak: *bring, brick*

> Sometimes two consonants are combined to make one sound, e.g. **ch-**, **sh-**, **th-**, **ph**, **wh-**

> break play sand step trip draw creep
> pray snake ring grow

2 **Copy the table. Add three more words to each column.**

ch-	sh-	th-	ph-	wh-
child	*show*	*thing*	*phone*	*whale*

• **Sounds:** Words are made up of *graphemes* (letters or groups of letters which represent sounds). Write words on the board and break them down into sounds, e.g. street: str /ee/t, parish: p/a/r/i/sh, town: t/ow/n.

Some words have clusters of three consonants, e.g.

scr- scream	**shr**: shriek	**spl**: splash
spr: spring	**squ-** squeal	**str**: string
thr: throw	**-tch**: catch	

3 **Some of the words below have missing letters. Complete them with one of the following blends: scr-, spl-, spr-, squ-, str-.**

1 The rock fell into the water with a loud *spl*ash.
2 The wind was very _____ ong yesterday.
3 I slipped on a stone and ____ained my ankle.
4 We could hear the birds _____awking in the trees.
5 We were surprised when the dog ___ ang out of the bushes.
6 Dana ___eamed when she saw the fierce dog.
7 The dog whimpered because it had a ____inter in its paw.
8 The boy ___olled along the beach.
9 I ___eezed my water bottle to get the last drop out.
10 I ____atched my leg on a bush as I walked through the forest.

Word building

As you know, we can form new words by adding **affixes** (*prefixes* and *suffixes*) to root words. Breaking down new words into their different parts will help you understand what they mean.

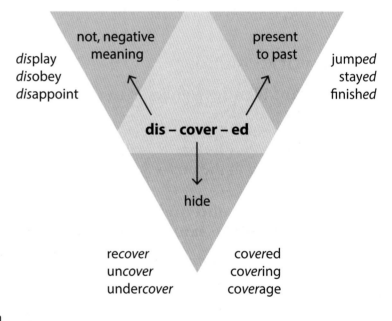

1 **Study the diagram.**

It shows the different parts which make up the word discovered.
* The top corners show the meaning of the prefix and suffix.
* The bottom corner tells us the meaning of the root word, cover.
* Around the triangle are examples of words which can be made from the prefix, suffix and root word.

2 **Draw diagrams like the one above for the following words.**

Try to list three examples of words which can be made from each prefix, root word and suffix.

   a) returned   **b)** misunderstanding   **c)** unfortunate   **d)** transported

* **Word building**: The word parts in the triangle are often known as *morphemes*. Morphemes are small segments of language which have meaning and cannot be divided.
* You may prefer to complete the morpheme triangles as a class exercise on the board.

3 **Find the meanings of the following word parts.**

Example: auto = self

a) tele   b) sub   c) micro   d) scope   e) vision

4 **Make as many words as you can using word parts from the grid below.**

Example: *auto + mobile = automobile*

mobile	vision	micro	wave
scope	auto	way	biography
phone	sub	graph	tele

Writing: Narrative

Imagine that you are one of the characters in a Jamaican legend.

• **EITHER** choose a character from the stories about Yallahs Ponds or Lovers' Leap.

• **OR** choose a character from another Jamaican legend.

Retell the story from this character's point of view.

Which character are you?

I am Mizzy. I was a slave on a plantation a long time ago.

1 Work in pairs. Roleplay interviews with your characters.

• Student A plays the role of the character s/he chose.

• Student B asks questions, e.g. *Who are you? What happened to you? How did you feel about it?*

After your first interview, change roles, so Student A interviews Student B.

2 Use a story map or a herringbone to plan your story.

3 Write a rough draft of your story. Revise it using the checklist on page 54.

4 Write a neat copy of your story. Proofread it using the checklist below.

> Proofreading means checking the grammar, punctuation and spelling in a piece of writing.

Checklist: Proofreading

Have I:
- begun each sentence with a capital letter   ☐
- used correct sentence punctuation?   ☐
- made each verb agree with its subject?   ☐
- used quotation marks with direct speech?   ☐
- checked the spelling of difficult words?   ☐

• Sample graphic organisers for stories can be found on page 187.

• **Proofreading**: When students proofread their work, it is helpful to read through it checking for one point at a time. Students can collaborate to identify the most common errors found in their work and produce a class checklist. This could be uploaded to the class blog and displayed in class.

Unit 16

Get ready

Is there a playground or a park near where you live?

Do you think these facilities are important? Why? Why not?

Reading

A donor has given money to the Municipal Corporation to provide facilities for young people. The Mayor has asked primary schools for their suggestions. The Principal of Riverside School has organised a debate on the topic.

Skim Luke's speech.

- What is the main point?
- What is Luke's first argument?

> An argument in a debate is a statement for or against the idea being discussed.

Luke's Speech

States viewpoint

Mr. Thompson, members of the audience, I propose that the Municipal Corporation should build a skateboarding park. This would provide a place where young people could have a lot of fun, and stop them from skateboarding on the roads.

Arguments for

Why do I suggest a skateboarding park? Firstly, it encourages young people to play outside instead of sitting over their computers hour after hour. We all know that exercise is good for us; skateboarding exercises all your muscles and helps to develop your balance and coordination.

My next point is that skateboarding helps you make friends. You can practise jumps and turns together, and if you are new to the sport, you can learn from others. Besides, once you have your own skateboard, it doesn't cost anything.

My final point is that a skateboard park would reduce accidents. At the moment, if we want to use our skateboards, we have to go on the road. Everyone knows that is really risky. Having a safe place will encourage more young people to take up this sport.

Arguments against

I know that some people think that skateboarding is dangerous. They say we should not encourage young people to do it. I do not agree. In my opinion, skateboarding is no more dangerous than riding a bike. If we have a safe place to practise, there will be no problems.

Conclusion

To sum up, I believe that a skateboarding park would be the best choice for the Municipal Corporation. Members of the audience, I call on you to support my suggestion.

- **Before reading:** Ask students to think of arguments for and against having a skateboard park.
- Indicate the use of signal words in Luke's speech: *firstly, my next point, besides, my final point, to sum up.*
- Point out that Luke includes an argument against the skateboard park, which he *rebuts.*

1 Why does Luke think it is a good idea for children to play outside?
2 What is the main idea of the third paragraph?
3 How might a skateboarding park reduce the number of accidents?
4 Why are some people opposed to skateboard parks?
5 Do you agree that skateboarding is no more dangerous than riding a bike? Why/ Why not?
6 Do you think a skateboard park would be the best choice? Why/ Why not?

Amy's speech

Mr. Thompson, members of the audience, you have all heard Luke's suggestion. I cannot support what he proposed.

Rebuts Luke's arguments

My main reason is that only a few people can use the skateboard park. It is not safe to have more than four or five people skateboarding at the same time. Indeed, skateboards are expensive, and not everyone can afford to buy one. In addition, I think the skateboard park would be more popular with boys than with girls.

At the moment, there is nowhere in our town where young people can play safely or meet their friends. I think that the Municipal Corporation should create a park, where we can all relax and enjoy ourselves. There would be plenty of space there for children to play. If there are enough funds, the Municipal Corporation could provide a playground with swings and slides.

Arguments for

I think the whole community would benefit from the park. There could be seats for people to sit and chat, and a café to buy snacks and drinks.

Have any of you visited Emancipation Park in Kingston? It is a lovely space where people can get away from the hustle and bustle of the city.

Argument against

They enjoy the flowers and trees and shady places to sit. Wouldn't it be wonderful to have a park like this in our town?

I know that creating a park would be expensive. If the Municipal Corporation does not have enough money, it could ask people in the community to contribute.

Conclusion

Members of the audience, only a few people like skateboarding. A park is for everyone. I ask you, therefore, to support my suggestion.

- Study the persuasive devices used in each speech e.g. rhetorical questions, short sentences for impact (*I do not agree. A park is for everyone.*)
- Ensure that students understand key vocabulary for debates: *propose, oppose, argument, rebut.*

7 What arguments does Amy give against the skateboard park?

8 What is the main idea of the third paragraph of her speech?

   a) The Municipal Corporation is not doing enough for young people.

   b) There needs to be a park for young people to relax and have fun.

   c) Young people need playgrounds with swings and slides.

   d) There is no safe space for children to play.

9 What is meant by the phrase *hustle and bustle*?

10 Explain how the whole community might benefit from the park.

11 What might be the disadvantage of creating a park?

12 Which proposal would you support? Why?

Persuasive writing

The purpose of **persuasive speaking** and **writing** is to persuade someone to do something, or to change his or her mind about something. A persuasive speech or composition has the following elements:
Introduction: The speaker or writer states his or her opinion clearly.
Development: S/he makes a number of points to justify his or her opinion.
Conclusion: S/he sums up what has been said and states his/her opinion again.

Look at Luke's and Amy's speeches.

WB5 p100–103

1 Identify the introduction, development and conclusion in each speech.

2 Which main points do they make in their speeches?

Speaking and listening: For and against

Discuss the two speeches.

- Find the points for and against Luke's and Amy's suggestions.
- Write them in a table like the one below.
- Add some points of your own to the table.

We need a skateboard park.	
FOR: *It will stop young people skateboarding on the roads.*	**AGAINST:** *Skateboarding is dangerous.*
The Municipal Corporation should provide a park.	
FOR:	**AGAINST:**

132

- **Speaking and listening:** You could get students to roleplay a radio call-in show where people suggest facilities the Municipal Corporation should provide for the community. The host should use SJE, but the callers can use JC. Translate the JC sections into SJE and repeat the roleplay using SJE.
- **Learning Journal:** Ask students to reflect on their performance in the debate by completing a 'How did I do?' chart (page 183).

Language: Conditional sentences

In a **conditional sentence** one action depends on another.

*If we **have** a skateboarding park, more people **will take up** the sport.*

    ↑   ↑

present   *future*

This sentence tells us what will happen as the **result** of a certain action.

1 **Complete the sentences with the correct verb forms.**

1 If we *go* to the park, we *will have* a lot of fun. (go / have)

2 We _____ our kites if the weather _____ windy. (fly / be)

3 If I _____ enough money, I _____ ice cream. (have / buy)

4 We _____ to our friends if we _____ them in the park. (chat / see)

5 If it _____, we _____ at home (rain / stay)

6 I _____ a drink if I _____ thirsty (buy / feel)

2 **Use your own ideas to complete these conditional sentences.**

1 If we go to the park, we will _____.

2 If I have time, _____.

3 If it is sunny tomorrow, _____.

4 If we help other people, _____ .

This conditional sentence tells us what **might** happen as the result of a certain action.

*If I **had** enough money, I **would buy** a skateboard.*

    ↑   ↑

simple past   *would + root verb*

3 **Match the sentences.**

1 If I wanted buy a skateboard   A if it rained.

2 I would not go to the park   B if she had a day off school.

3 If I had a bicycle   C I would buy a bicycle

4 I would be really pleased   D I would save money for it.

5 Kim would go out with her friends   E I would ride it around the park.

6 If I had enough money   F if I we had swings and slides in the park.

• **Conditional sentences:** Explain to students that we use different verb tenses to indicate whether the sentence tells us what will or what might happen.

• **Exercise 2:** Practise this type of conditional sentence by asking students questions, e.g. *Where would you go if you had a day off school? If you could meet a famous person, who would it be?*

4 **Complete each sentence with the correct verb forms.**

1 If I wanted to ride my bicycle, I *would choose* (choose) a safe place.
2 We _____ (be) very happy if we had a playground in our town.
3 I would be really nervous if I _____ (give) a speech to my class
4 If I _____ (have) time, I would ride my bicycle every day.
5 If the weather was windy we _____ (fly) our kites.
6 I would go to the park every day if I _____ (live) close enough.
7 My friends would help me if I _____ (not know) what to do.
8 If I won a lot of money, I _____ (take) my family on holiday.

Semi-colons

> We can use **semi-colons** instead of a conjunction or full stop between two sentences which are closely connected.
> *I told the boy to be more careful **but** he paid no attention.*
> *I told the boy to be more careful; he paid no attention.*

1 **Rewrite the sentences which need semi-colons.**
Not all the sentences need semi-colons.

1 I can do turns on my skateboard now I want to do jumps.
2 It was getting late so we decided to leave the park.
3 I felt nervous I had never ridden a bicycle before.
4 Kim took a deep breath she jumped into the water.
5 Josh let go of his kite it flew up into the tree.
6 He tried to catch the kite but it was too late.

> **Therefore** and **however** are signal words we can use to join sentences. We use a semi-colon at the end of the first part of the sentence, and a comma after the signal word.
> *Therefore* shows that the second part of the sentence is the result of the first part.
> *Children need space to play; **therefore**, the council should provide a park.*
> *However* shows contrast between two parts of sentences.
> *We would like to have a playground; **however**, it will cost a lot of money.*

2 **Complete these sentences with *however* or *therefore*.**

1 I usually play football on Fridays; *however*, the match was cancelled.
2 The park was closed; _____ we were unable to play there.
3 I looked for my friends; _____ I could not see them there.
4 Most people love swimming; _____ some people do not like it.
5 The grass has just been planted; _____ you should not step on it.
6 The paths are slippery after the rain; _____ you should walk carefully.
7 We hoped to go to the concert; _____ all the tickets had been sold.
8 The students liked Amy's suggestion best; _____ they all voted for her.

- **DA** You may need to go through Exercise 4 (conditional sentences) with some students before they write answers, to ensure they use the correct tense.
- **Semi-colons:** Explain that each part of the sentence must contain a verb.
- **However, therefore:** These words are sometimes called transition words.

Word work: Silent letters

Learn how to spell these words.

Silent b	Silent l	Silent n	Silent t
climb	calf	autumn	castle
comb	half	column	fasten
limb	folk	solemn	rustle
dumb	calm	condemn	listen
thumb	stalk	hymn	nestle

Complete the missing words. They all have silent letters.

1 In the park you can get away from the hus_le and bus_le of the city.
2 A colum_ of ants crawled up the sta_ks of the plants.
3 The leaves rus_led in the autum_ winds.
4 The boy clim_ed up the pa_m tree to get a coconut.
5 When the whis_le blew the footballers wa_ked on to the pitch.
6 We sing hym_s and psa_ms when we go to church.
7 The students waited ca_mly and solem_ly for the service to begin.
8 No dou_t many people will lis_en to the show.

Study skills: Fill out a form

The Municipal Corporation is organising an activity day for primary school students.

Study the form. Write the information you would provide, e.g. for point 1 write your name (family name first).

> Always give correct information when you fill out forms, and follow the instructions carefully.

ACTIVITY DAY FOR STUDENTS

1 NAME _____   _____
        Last   First

2 AGE _____ years   **3** GRADE: _____

4 NAME OF CLASS TEACHER: _____

5 SELECT AND TICK TWO ACTIVITIES YOU WOULD LIKE TO DO.

Cycling	Painting
Swimming	Kite flying
Skateboarding	Football

6 CHOOSE WHAT YOU WOULD LIKE TO EAT FOR LUNCH.

Beef Patties	$200
Stew Chicken	$300
Fried Fish	$350

LUNCH ORDER _____
        Write your lunch order in full.

Please bring your lunch money with you to the Activity Day.

• **Silent letters:** After students have completed the sentences, ask them to read each sentence aloud. Check that they do not pronounce the silent letters.

Writing: Persuasive composition

A local businesswoman has donated money to your school. The Principal has asked the students for their views on how the money should be spent.

Choose ONE of the following options

- Sports equipment for the school football team.
- A play area with swings and slides

Write a persuasive composition in support of the option you chose.

We need new football equipment.

Everyone would like a play area.

 1 **Brainstorm arguments for and against your chosen option.**
Make notes in an organiser like the one below.

Option:	
FOR:	AGAINST:

2 **Plan your composition.**

Introduction	State your opinion clearly: *I believe that the money should be used to …*
Part 1	Arguments in favour of your chosen option:
Part 2	Rebut arguments against the option you chose:
Conclusion	Sum up the points you made and state your opinion again:

3 **Write the first draft of your composition.**
Write in paragraphs.
Each paragraph should have a main idea and supporting details in each paragraph.

Use signal words in your composition, e.g. therefore, however, firstly, in addition, for example.

4 **Revise your composition. Use the checklist below to help you.**

Checklist: A persuasive composition
Have I:
  introduced the topic and stated my opinion clearly? ☐
  included one main idea for each paragraph? ☐
  provided reasons and examples to support my opinion? ☐
  used signal words? ☐

Type your composition. Upload it on to your class blog for your fellow students to read.

- Before students start preparing their compositions, lead a class discussion about how the school facilities could be improved. Encourage them to think of arguments in favour of and against any suggestions they make. For Part 1, of their composition, they may need to write more than one paragraph.
- **DA** Allow some students to provide one argument in favour of their chosen option and one against.

Reading

**Compare the photographs. In which parishes do you think they were taken?
Scan the two texts.**

Are they *fiction* or *non-fiction*? How do you know that?

Jamaica's Parishes

The parish of **Kingston** is located in the
county of Surrey, and has an area of 16 square
kilometres, making it the smallest parish in
Jamaica. It is situated on the flat ground of the
Liguanea Plain on the south side of the island,
at the foot of the Blue Mountains. Kingston is
almost completely surrounded by the parish
of St. Andrew. The combined population of
these two parishes is over 670,000, the highest of any parish on the island.

As Jamaica's capital, Kingston is an important administrative, commercial and
manufacturing centre producing goods for sale at home and abroad. People visit
the city to do business, and also to attend major sporting and cultural events
which are held there. Many people move to Kingston from rural areas to find
employment or to study at one of the many schools, or at the University of
the West Indies. With its busy port and international airport, it is an important
transport hub.

The parish of **Trelawny** is 875 square
kilometres, around twice the size of the parishes
of Kingston and St. Andrew. Its population of
76,000 is more than ten times smaller, however.
It is situated on mainly flat land on the north of
the island, but the highland area of the Cockpit
Country rises in the south of the parish.

The main sources of employment in Trelawny
are agriculture, manufacturing and tourism.
Among the crops grown are bananas, yam, coffee
and coconut. There are rum and sugar factories in Trelawny, and small factories
producing clothing as well. The parish has fine beaches, and tourism makes a
significant contribution to Trelawny's economy. A large number of people are
employed in hotels and restaurants, or work as drivers or guides. In addition, the
parish capital, Falmouth, is an important port for cruise ship passengers.

- Use the photos to discuss the differences between rural and urban parishes. Compare the two parishes
  described here with the parish where students live.
- Talk about the differences between the parishes in Jamaica. Find out which parishes students have visited.

1 How many more people live in Kingston and St. Andrew than in Trelawny?

2 Why do you think the population of Trelawny is much smaller than that of Kingston and St. Andrew?

3 What is similar about the areas where Kingston and Trelawny are situated? What is different?

4 In the sentence *Kingston is a manufacturing centre producing goods for sale at home and abroad,* 'manufacturing' means
   a) selling goods to the public.
   b) making goods by hand or by machine.
   c) inventing new products.
   d) purchasing goods in shops and markets.

5 How is employment in Trelawny different from employment in Kingston?

6 Why do you think Trelawny is popular with tourists?

7 What are the main reasons why some people leave rural areas to live in Kingston?

8 Why do you think some people choose to stay in rural areas like Trelawny?

Compare and contrast

Note the similarities and differences between Kingston and Trelawny in an organiser like the one on page 185.

For and against

Student Essay Competition

Many people claim that it is better to live in a town. I disagree. Which would you prefer, breathing fresh, clean country air, or choking on exhaust gases from cars and vans; waking to the sound of the wind in the trees or to the roar of traffic on the main road?

There are some advantages to living in a town. It is not so far to go to school, and there are plenty of shops to buy what you want. Some towns have shopping malls selling goods which come from all over the world. There are often sports grounds where you can play sports on weekends and during the holidays.

- **Comprehension:** Remind students to use QAR to identify the different question types.
- **The competition:** Tell students to read the first sentence of each paragraph. This will help them to get a general idea of what it is about.

There are many disadvantages, however. With all the heavy traffic passing through, the air in towns is often polluted. This is harmful for our health. Often city dwellers live in apartments or small houses with no gardens. Many children in the city have no space to play, and spend their free time inside.

There are not so many shops in the country, and you cannot buy expensive imported goods there. We do not need them. People grow lots of delicious fruits and vegetables in their gardens, however, and there are always fresh eggs and milk.

There are no special sports facilities in the country either, but who needs them when there is ample space to play games in the open air? I would rather pass my time outside having fun with my friends than spend the day inside playing computer games or watching television.

Life in the country is simple, but it has many advantages. I know that many people will disagree with me, but I for one, plan to stay in the country for the rest of my life.

Lisette Turner

1 Summarise the advantages of town life described by Lisette in her composition.

2 Why does she believe that city life is unhealthy?

3 According to Lisette, which facilities are there in towns but not in the country?

4 What is Lisette's opinion of expensive imported goods?

5 Which word means the same as *ample*? (Paragraph 5)

   a) limited   **b)** special   **c)** plentiful   **d)** spare

6 Which advantages of living in the country does Lisette mention?

7 Which of the following statements best summarises Lisette's views on city life?

   a) There are more advantages than disadvantages.

   b) There are more disadvantages than advantages.

   c) She would like to live in a city one day.

   d) She would have more fun if she lived in a city.

8 Do you agree with Lisette's views? Why? Why not?

How would you respond to the statement *I would rather live in the town than in the country*? Copy and complete the table with your own ideas.

Living in the town	FOR:
	AGAINST:
Living in the country	FOR:
	AGAINST:

- Help students to find the main idea of each paragraph in Lisette's composition. Discuss with them whether they think she has put forward convincing arguments.
- Students could use the notes they make in the table to write their own persuasive composition.

Language: Possessive nouns

Rewrite each phrase using an apostrophe.

> Example: the new bicycle owned by Frank   *Frank's new bicycle*

1 the report written by James
2 the class Mrs. Mackenzie teaches
3 the favourite stories of the boys
4 the house where the girls live

5 the capital of Cuba
6 the toys which belong to the children
7 the Prime Minister of Jamaica
8 The books owned by the students

Relative pronouns

1 **Complete the sentences with who, which or where.**

> Example: There are many beaches in Trelawny *where* tourists like to swim.

1 Leo, _____ lives in St. Elizabeth, is a tour guide.
2 Trelawny is a parish _____ is very popular with tourists.
3 My father took me to the village _____ he lived as a boy.
4 The Cockpit Country is a highland area _____ there are many rare species.
5 Many cruise ships dock at Falmouth _____ is on the north coast.
6 The Mayor, _____ oversees the Municipal Corporation, is a busy person.

2 **Use your own ideas to complete the sentences.**

1 I live in a house which …
2 Do you know the person who …
3 The Town Hall is the place where …

4 I went to the river where …
5 There is a shop in the town which …
6 I like people who …

Punctuation

1 **Name these punctuation marks. Match them to the definitions below.**

   ?   ,   :   !   ;   " "

1 used to show surprise or shock
2 placed around the words people say
3 used before we write a list

4 written after a question
5 connects two closely related sentences
6 used when we add extra information

2 **Rewrite each sentence using correct punctuation.**
One punctuation mark is missing in each sentence.

1 "Do you live in a city" Lisette asked.
2 Brandon who lives in a town, does not like the country.
3 There are many important buildings the Town Hall, the Library and the hospital.
4 There was no sign of the bus it must have left.
5 "Help" the girls shouted loudly.
6 "The winner's name will be announced tomorrow, the Principal told us.

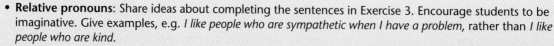

- **Relative pronouns:** Share ideas about completing the sentences in Exercise 3. Encourage students to be imaginative. Give examples, e.g. *I like people who are sympathetic when I have a problem*, rather than *I like people who are kind.*
- **Punctuation:** Write more sentences with missing punctuation on the board for students to correct.

Conjunctions

1 **Choose the correct conjunctions to complete the sentences.**

> Example: We enjoyed going to the park (although / <u>because</u> / so that) we flew our kites.

1 We planned to go to the park (although / because / and) the weather was cold.
2 Many people move to Kingston (before / because / until) they hope to find work.
3 We waited under the trees (so that / until / while) the rain had stopped.
4 The rain did not stop (because / if / so) we all got wet.
5 Amy set out early (although / since / so that) she would not be late.
6 My uncle has not returned to Jamaica (before / since / while) he was a boy.
7 We visited him (but / or / while) he was living in the USA.
8 We waited a long time (although / before / so) our friends arrived.

2 **Use suitable conjunctions to join the sentences in this paragraph.**

Although it was raining, my little brother went to play outside. He was getting wet _____ (1) Mummy told him to come back inside. My little brother pretended not to hear her _____ (2) he was having a lot of fun. He jumped higher and higher _____ (3) soon he slipped over in the mud. He was not really hurt _____ (4) he started crying. _____ (5) she heard him, Mummy ran outside. She picked him up _____ (6) carried him into the house. He stopped crying _____ (7) she gave him a sweet. Mummy told him not to go outside again _____ (8) it had stopped raining.

Word work: Spelling

Find and correct the spelling mistakes in these sentences.
Some sentences may be correct.

> Example: Its important to learn about the parish where we live. *It's*

1 My freinds and I went to the Parish Library.
2 Do you know the proverb "Never judge a book by it's cover?"
3 Did you recieve many presents for your birthday?
4 Tarik desined a poster for the competition.
5 The stray dog could not find its owner.
6 Ashley became very concieted after she won the prize.
7 Chris looked very solem after his teacher rebuked him.
8 Many foriegn tourists come to Jamaica each year.
9 The Mayor of our parish has just resined.
10 The referee blew his whisle to start the match.

> Note spellings of tricky words and write example sentences in your Learning Journal.

- **Conjunctions** Exercise 6: If students are not sure which conjunctions to use, advise them to try reading out the sentences using different conjunctions to see which fits best.
- **DA** Allow some students to complete fewer examples on this page.

Writing

1 **Friendly letter**

Your cousin, who lives in another part of Jamaica, is coming to stay with you. Write a letter to him or her in which you describe your parish.

1 **Planning:** Use the **RAFTs** strategy on page 186 to develop your letter. Make notes for the content of your letter in an organiser.

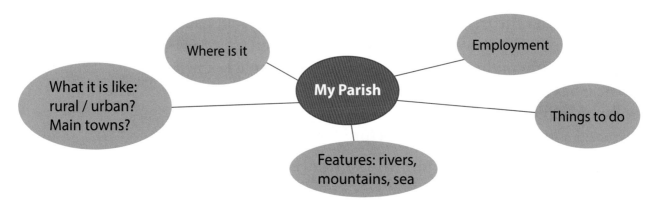

2 **Drafting**: Write the first draft of your letter. Use the format for a friendly letter shown on page 95.

Write a paragraph for each section of your letter.

Remember to tell your cousin you are looking forward to his /her visit.

3 **Revising:** Revise your letter using the checklist on page 95.

Write a neat copy and proofread it.

Persuasive writing

2 Imagine that you are the Mayor of your parish. Describe two or more improvements you would like to make in the parish. State why you think these improvements are important.

1 Make notes about the improvements you want to make.

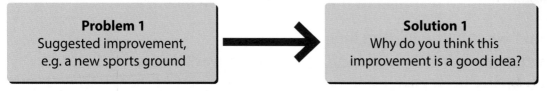

2 Write the first draft of your composition.

• Write an introduction. Begin like this:

If I were Mayor of ____ (name of your parish), I would …

• Write the main part of your composition. Remember to write in paragraphs.

• Write a conclusion to sum up your ideas.

3 Revise your composition. Write or type a neat copy.

142

• Revise the different stages of the writing process before students do the writing exercises on this page. Go through the writing process flow chart on page 189 with them.

• Students could write a letter to a friend in another country about the role of their Municipal Corporation and what they like/ dislike about their parish.

Get ready

Are the roads busy near where you live?

What are the advantages and disadvantages of going everywhere by car?

Reading

Scan the letter.

- What is the writer's *purpose*?
- What is the *audience* for his letter?

Valley Road
Waterloo Park P.O.
3 April, 2018

Traffic Division
14–18 Prospect Road
Spanish Town

Dear Sir or Madam

The centre of our town has become an unpleasant place to shop or to walk, as it is jammed with cars which pollute the environment with their noise and fumes. I believe, therefore, that cars should be prohibited from entering this area. **[Introduction: writer states opinion]**

It is true that the Municipal Corporation has provided car parks, but car drivers appear to be unwilling to use them. I have seen them parking on the sidewalks, on driveways and even on roundabouts. Congestion is so bad that vehicles travel at a snail's pace, polluting the environment with toxic fumes. **[Arguments for a ban]**

There is evidence that traffic fumes have a serious effect on people's health. Cars and other vehicles emit toxic gases such as carbon monoxide. Inhaling these gases irritates the respiratory system, and causes lung disease. They are particularly harmful to young people, whose lungs are still developing. It is not surprising that we have seen an alarming rise in the number of cases of asthma among children recently. **[Facts to support opinion]**

I believe that in future, traffic in the town centre should be restricted to buses and emergency vehicles. Car drivers should be required to park their vehicles in the car parks provided. This will lead to a significant reduction in air pollution. **[Solution]** Furthermore traffic will flow more freely. Buses will run on time, and emergency vehicles will be able to put out fires and take people to hospital without delay. In conclusion, there should be a public debate on this topic, because we all deserve to live in a cleaner, healthier city.

Yours faithfully

Mr. P. Starkey

- Identify the features of a formal letter. Ask students to complete a **RAFTs** chart for this letter. (See page 186).
- Ask students to summarise the letter using the 3-2-1 strategy introduced on page 111.

1 What is the writer's main point?
   a) Cars should be banned from the whole city.
   b) Cars should be banned from part of the city.
   c) All motor vehicles should be banned from the city.
   d) Cars should be banned at certain times of the day.
2 Which two things pollute the city according to Mr. Starkey?
3 Vehicles travel *at a snail's pace*. What does this phrase mean?
4 Why do you think that car drivers are unwilling to use car parks?
5 What effect would banning cars from the city centre have on people's health? Why?
6 Which vehicles would Mr. Starkey allow into the city centre?
7 Why do you think that these vehicles should be allowed into the city centre?
8 What is meant by *a public debate*?
9 On which issues is a public debate needed in your community?
10 How would you deal with traffic problems in your area?

WB5 p56–7

Synonyms

Find words in the letter on the previous page which are similar in meaning to the words in bold.

1 The air is many of our cities is **poisoned** by exhaust gases from vehicles.
2 The number of cars on the road causes **traffic jams**.
3 Cars should be **banned** from driving into the city centre.
4 **Breathing in** exhaust gases is harmful for our lungs.
5 Exhaust gases from vehicles are extremely **poisonous**.
6 Air pollution can cause significant **breathing** problems.
7 Vehicles **give off** gases which pollute the atmosphere.
8 Traffic in the town centre should be **limited** to essential vehicles.

> Add words relating to air pollution to your **word bank**.

Cause and effect

 Discuss Mr. Starkey's letter. Complete an organiser showing cause and effect.

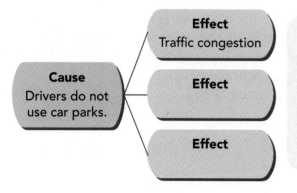

Cause
Drivers do not use car parks.

Effect
Traffic congestion

Effect

Effect

Cause and effect: signal words

so	because
therefore	as a result
consequently	thus
the reason why	

• Discuss signal words that are likely to be used with synonyms and antonyms, e.g. *however, similarly*. Ask students to use these words in sentences of their own.

 144

• **Cause and effect**: Point out that an event or situation might produce several different effects. Give them an everyday example, e.g. *getting up late will affect the rest of the day (miss the bus, late for school, get into trouble)*.

Summary

WB5 p132–3

> **Remember**: A **summary** is a brief account of the main ideas in a speech or written piece. To help you do this:
> * Note the *main point* of each paragraph.
> * Scan the text for *key words*.

> **Key words** are words which help you to understand the meaning of a sentence or group of sentences.

1 **a)** **Which of these words are key words in the first paragraph of the letter?**

> centre   become   unpleasant   cars   jammed   pollute
> therefore   should   banned

b) **Write six key words from paragraph 2 and from paragraph 3.**

2 **What is the main point of each paragraph?**

3 **Summarise the contents of Mr. Starkey's letter in three sentences.**

* You will not be able to include all the points he makes. Choose those you think are the most important.
* Use signal words like therefore, as a result, so, consequently, the reason why.

> Look online for videos for young people about air pollution. Summarise what you learn from them.

Speaking and listening: Debate

> A **motion**, or **moot**, is a statement which provides a topic for a debate.

1 **Make notes for a debate on the following motion:**
All vehicles should be banned from the city centre.

FOR:	AGAINST:
They cause air pollution.	

2 **Choose two speakers from your group.**
* One speaker should speak in favour of the motion.
* The other should speak against it.

> Speakers can use the notes prepared by their group to help them.

3 **After they make their speeches, each speaker should rebut the arguments put forward by the other speaker.**

---

* **Speaking and listening:** Remind speakers of the guidelines in Unit 12 for giving presentations. Everyone participating in the debate should follow correct communication protocol.
* **Extension:** Arrange a *hat debate*. Write different motions on slips of paper, e.g. *All cyclists should take a test before they ride on the road*. Put them in a hat. Students take one out and speak for or against the motion.

Language: Present perfect tense

WB5 p31

> The **present perfect** tells us about something which happened in the past, and affects what is happening now. It does not tell us *when* it happened.
> It is formed from the helping verb has/ have + past participle.
>
> > The centre of town **has become** an unpleasant place to shop or walk.
>
> helping verb   past participle
>
> Most verbs form the past participle by adding **-ed** (*finished, moved*), but there are many irregular verbs.

1 **Find three more examples of verbs in the present perfect in the letter on page 143.**

2 **Complete these sentences with *have* or *has*.**

1 The bus _____ left the town.

2 The passengers _____ paid their fares.

3 The man _____ parked his car in front of the house.

4 We _____ said goodbye to our friends.

5 The bus _____ stopped beside the road.

6 group of students _____ got off the bus.

7 Everyone _____ collected his or her luggage.

8 It _____ been a long time since we left home.

3 **Complete these sentences with verbs in the present perfect.**

> Example: The traffic *has stopped* moving. (stop)

1 The average speed _____ down to 10 m.p.h. (go)

2 Many people _____ about the traffic (protest)

3 The air _____ polluted. (become)

4 The level of asthma _____ . (increase)

5 It _____ noisier. (get)

6 People _____ coming to the town centre. (give up)

7 Emergency vehicles _____ it impossible to get to fires. (find)

8 Mr. Starkey _____ a letter to the Traffic Division. (write)

9 The Traffic Division _____ his letter. (receive)

10 The Municipal Corporation _____ a new car park. (build)

Irregular past participles you should know	
be	been
break	broken
build	built
come	came
drive	driven
eat	eaten
find	found
get	got
give	given
go	went
have	had
hear	heard
hold	held
keep	kept
know	known
pay	paid
run	run
see	seen
send	sent
sit	sat
speak	spoken
spend	spent
stand	stood
take	taken
wear	worn
win	won

- **Present perfect**: Remind students of subject–verb agreement: singular helping verbs with singular subjects and collective nouns.
- Put some students in a group and work through Exercise 3 with them orally before they write.

> To form the **negative** of the present perfect, use *has/ have not + past participle*.
> *The Traffic Division* **has not replied** *to Mr. Starkey's letter.*
> To make a **question**, use *have/ has + noun/ pronoun + past participle*.
> **Has** *Mr. Starkey* **received** *a reply?* **Have** *you* **noticed** *a difference in the traffic?*

4 **When Mr. Starkey wrote his letter, he hoped there would be some changes, but nothing has happened. Write negative sentences in the present perfect.**

Example: The Council / not take / notice *The Council has not taken any notice.*

1 The Council / not / spend money
2 They / not / build / car parks
3 They / not / hold public debate
4 People / not / hear about problem
5 They / not / improve public transport
6 The newspapers / not / discuss issue
7 Air pollution / not / decrease
8 Cars / not / stop coming into town

5 **a) In pairs ask and answer questions based on the table.**

Has Nalina ridden a motorbike?

Yes, she has.

Person	Ride motorbike	Travel by plane	Ride a horse	Drive a car
Nalina	✔	✔		
Dana		✔	✔	✔
Noah	✔			✔

b) Write five sentences about things you have done. Use the present perfect tense.

Word work: Antonyms

WB5 p58

> An **antonym** is a word which means the opposite of another word.
> *big – small*   *cold – hot*   *young – old*   *noisy – quiet*
> Antonyms are often formed by adding *prefixes* and *suffixes* to root words:
> *agree – **dis**agree*   *careful – care**less***

Antonyms you should know

allow	ban	arrive	depart	bitter	sweet
break	repair	cheap	expensive	forbid	permit
lenient	strict	offer	refuse	powerful	weak
ancient	modern	attack	defend	borrow	lend
bright	dull	defeat	victory	guilty	innocent
maximum	minimum	often	seldom	together	apart

• **Antonyms:** Write the prefixes un-, dis-, im- on the board. Ask students to make as many opposite pairs as they can.
• **Exercise 5:** Students can make their own questions to find out what their fellow students have / have not done. You could ask them to find the most unusual/ exciting things people in the class have done.

Find antonyms for the words in bold type.

Example: The town centre is often very noisy. *quiet*

1 My father **often** drives into the town centre.
2 Parking near the town centre is quite **expensive**.
3 The Municipal Corporation should **ban** parking in the town centre.
4 The bus driver **offered** to drop me off at my house.
5 The headlights on our car have been **repaired**.
6 It is **dangerous** to cross the road at the bus station.
7 The cars were travelling quite **slowly** through the town.
8 The amount of traffic in the town has **increased** recently.
9 It is quite **common** for students to ride bicycles to school.
10 There are many **ancient** buildings in the town centre

Study skills: Graphical information

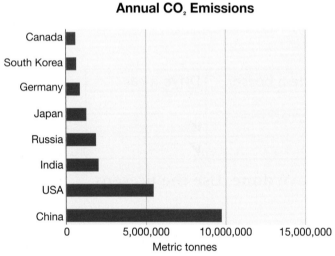

Data retrieved from http://edgar.jrc.ec.europa.eu/
world-population/population-

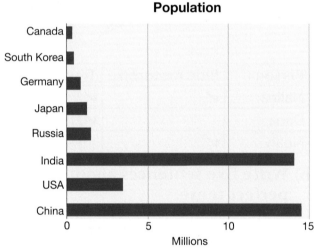

Data retrieved from http://www.worldometers.info/
by-country/

1 **Compare the information in the graphs.**

CO_2 = *carbon dioxide*

1 Which two countries emit the most CO_2 annually?
2 Which countries emit similar amounts of CO_2?
3 Which two countries have the biggest population?
4 Which country do you think produces the greatest amount of CO_2 per head of population?
5 Suggest reasons why China produces much more CO_2 than India.

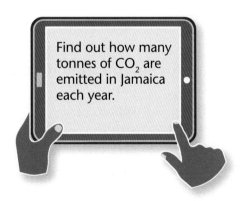

Find out how many tonnes of CO_2 are emitted in Jamaica each year.

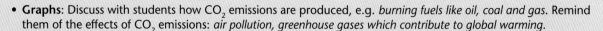

• **Graphs:** Discuss with students how CO_2 emissions are produced, e.g. *burning fuels like oil, coal and gas.* Remind them of the effects of CO_2 emissions: *air pollution, greenhouse gases which contribute to global warming.*

2 **Compare the information about air pollution shown below.**

The major cities shown correspond to the countries shown in the charts on the previous page, e.g. Beijing: China

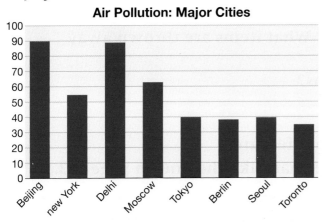

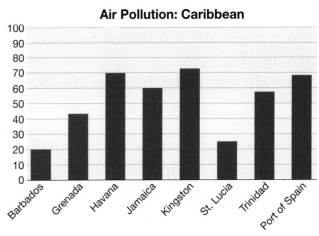

Statistics for 2016 retrieved from https://www.numbeo.com/pollution/

1 Which major world cities have the highest levels of air pollution?
2 In which cities is the level of air pollution fairly low?
3 Why might the level of air pollution be higher in Kingston than in the rest of Jamaica?
4 Which major world cities have lower levels of air pollution than Kingston?
5 Which Caribbean islands have the lowest levels of air pollution?

Writing: Letter

Write a letter to your teacher in which you suggest how students and staff at your school could help to reduce air pollution in your community.

Include the following information in your letter:

- a description of the problems caused by traffic.
- suggestions for what your school could do, e.g.
  - raise awareness of the problem.
  - encourage staff and students to walk or use public transport.

> Use the 6+1 traits of writing strategy shown on page 188 to help you write your letter.

1 Write the first draft of your letter.
  - Use the format for a formal letter shown on page 96.
  - Remember to give reasons and evidence to support your arguments.

2 Revise and edit your letter.
  - Proofread your letter for spelling and punctuation.
  - Type it or write it neatly and give it to your teacher.

> Exchange letters with another student by email. Suggest how the letters could be improved.

- **Graphs:** Pairs of students could make questions about the graphs to ask other student pairs. After answering questions, get students to summarise the information in the graphs orally or in writing.
- **Writing:** The *6+1 traits of writing* strategy shown on page 188 will help students to focus on different aspects of their compositions, e.g. *ideas, planning, word choice.*

Get ready

What items do you throw away at home? What items are thrown away at school?

What do you think happens to these items?

Reading

Survey the text below and identify the text features.

As you read, complete a reading response chart like the one on page 183.

heading

sub-heading

caption

illustration

Caring for the Environment

Waste

Every day people dispose of things they do not need as waste. Substances like paper, plastic and cans take a long time to decay. Did you know that it can take 100 years for common items like plastic bags to rot away?

Rates of decay for household waste

Plastic bottles: up to 1,000 years

Batteries: 100 years

Tin cans: 50 years

Newspaper: 6 months

Fruit and vegetable peel: up to 1 year

Plastic bags: up to 100 years

Glass jars: more than 2,000 years

- Ask students to suggest an appropriate pre-reading strategy to approach thie text.
- Draw on students' prior knowledge of the subject of waste. You could get them to predict the amount of time it takes everyday items to rot away, then check their predictions.

Why is waste a problem?

We live in a throwaway society where waste has become a huge problem. Much of what we throw away will not rot away completely for a hundred years or more. Soon there will be no more room for it on landfill sites. When these sites are full, the only solution is to burn some of the waste, but this releases toxic gases into the air, adding to the level of air pollution. Frequently garbage is dumped in the streets, creating an eyesore in our towns and villages. This is an unhealthy practice as flies breed on rotting waste and spread disease. Many people burn waste in their backyards, releasing toxic fumes which blow right into their houses and those of their neighbours.

DO NOT DUMP RUBBISH HERE BY ORDER

What can we do?

The only way to solve the problem of waste is to reduce the amount we create. This can be done in three main ways:

(bullet points)

- **Reduce:** Create less waste by using less paper and buying fewer throwaway items.
- **Reuse:** Many items we throw away can be reused, e.g. plastic bags and bottles, glass jars.
- **Recycle:** Newspaper and cardboard can be recycled and vegetable and fruit peelings can be made into compost for our gardens.

(bold type)

LET'S ALL WORK TOGETHER TO MAKE OUR TOWNS AND VILLAGES HEALTHIER PLACES TO LIVE!

1 Which items decay quickly?

2 Which take more than 100 years to decay?

3 What exactly is a landfill site?

4 Explain in your own words the meaning of the phrase *a throwaway society*.

5 An eyesore is something that
   a) harms the eyes.
   b) looks extremely unpleasant.
   c) causes a lot of problems.
   d) blocks the streets.

6 How might waste increase air pollution?

7 In which two ways do people sometimes deal with waste instead of sending it to a landfill site?

8 Is it preferable to send waste to a landfill site? Why? Why not?

9 Why is it important to reduce the amount of waste we produce?

10 How could you reduce waste at school?

- Discuss with students how the text features help them to access information in this text.
- Help students to formulate questions (see page 21) to extract information from expository texts.
- Pick out topic specific vocabulary, e.g. *dispose, decay, landfill.* Students can write definitions and add them to their word bank.

Problem and solution

Complete an organiser to show the problem caused by waste and possible solutions.

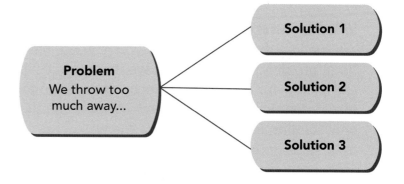

Problem We throw too much away...	Solution 1
	Solution 2
	Solution 3

Speaking and listening

There are different government agencies in Jamaica which are responsible for protecting the environment, dealing with waste and responding to emergencies such as hurricanes. They are:

- NSWMA: National Solid Waste Management Authority
- NEPA: National Environment and Planning Agency
- ODPEM: Office of Disaster Preparedness and Emergency Management

1 **Find information online about ONE of the above agencies.**
- Share your information with the rest of your group.
- Choose a member of your group to represent the agency you chose in a panel discussion.

Some of these agencies have web pages for young people on their websites.

2 **Formulate questions to ask panellists about the agencies they represent.**

Use question words: What? When? Where? Why? How? e.g.
- *What* do you do when there is a hurricane warning?
- *Where* do you dispose of waste?

3 **Form a panel of students representing the government agencies.**

The panel answer questions from the class about its work.

- **ICT** Explain to students that they will take part in a panel discussion similar to those they see on television. Divide the class into groups. Allocate one agency (NSWMA, NEPA or ODPEM) for each group to research online. Depending on the size of your group, two or more groups can research each agency.
- Choose a student to host the discussion. He/she will introduce the speakers and invite questions from the class.

Language: Passive voice

We can use many verbs either in the **active** voice or in the **passive** voice.

Waste collectors **remove** *waste from homes and places of work.* **(Active)**
In the active voice the subject (waste collectors) performs the action (remove).

Waste is **removed** *by waste collectors from homes and places of work.* **(Passive)**
In the passive voice, the subject (*waste*) <u>receives</u> the action.

WB5 p35–6

1 **Underline the verbs in these sentences. Which are** *active*? **Which are** *passive*?

Example: *Often garbage <u>is dumped</u> in the streets. passive*

1 People throw away items they do not need.
2 Waste is taken to landfill sites.
3 Landfill sites are expanding to cope with the waste.
4 A lot of waste is burnt on backyard fires.
5 The air is polluted by fumes from the fires.
6 Disease is spread by flies breeding on rotting garbage.
7 Rotting garbage smells revolting.
8 Paper and plastic bottles are recycled at my school.

Passive verbs are made up of *the verb be + past participle*.
The passive voice can be used in the **past**, **present** and **future**.

Past: *The waste* **was collected** *yesterday.*
Present: *It* **is collected** *every week.*
Future: *It* **will be collected** *again next week.*

2 **Complete the sentences with verbs in the present passive.**

Example: Used paper *is placed* in the recycling bin   (place)

1 A lot of items _____ away every day.   (throw)
2 Landfill sites _____ to deal with waste.   (provide)
3 Waste _____ on landfill sites.   (bury)
4 Instructions on dealing with waste _____ by NSWMA.   (give)
5 Residents _____ not to dump garbage.   (tell)
6 The streets _____ regularly.   (clean)
7 Toxic gases from waste _____ into the atmosphere.   (release)
8 Bottle and glass jars _____ to save waste.   (reuse)
9 Vegetable peelings _____ to make compost.   (use)
10 Our classroom floor _____ every day.   (sweep)

- **Passive voice:** Give the students plenty of examples of active and passive voice so they hear clearly the difference between them, e.g. *We reused the bottles. / The bottles were reused.*
- **Past, present and future:** Explain that to form the past passive we use *was/ were + past participle*, for the present passive we use *is / are + past participle* and for the future we use *will be + past participle*.
- **DA** Put some students in a group and work through the exercises with them.

3 **Read the list of classroom duties. Write sentences in the past passive about what the students did.**

Example: *The used paper was collected by Alex and Tom.*

Classroom Duties	Person
Collect used paper	Alex, Tom
Put bottles and cans in bin	Kim, Maria
Save newspaper	Zack
Clean blackboard	Nathan
Take waste to recycling bin	Jason, Kayla
Sweep classroom floor	Lisette, Shelly
Return books to library	Sam, Xavier
Tidy desks	Everyone!

4 **Some Grade 5 students have written a recycling policy. Write what they plan to do, using the future passive.**

Example: *All waste will be put in the bins provided.*

CLASS RECYCLING POLICY

★ Put all waste in the bins provided.

★ Wash and reuse glass bottles.

★ Use both sides of paper for writing.

★ Place newspapers in the recycling bins.

★ Save card for art projects.

★ Keep plastic bags for reuse.

★ Make compost from fruit peelings.

★ Tell everyone to obey the policy.

Sentences

In the first sentence below, two sentences are joined without using punctuation. In the second sentence, two sentences have been joined with a comma.

Dumping garbage is unhealthy flies breed on it. ✗
Paul collected the bottles, he put them in the recycling bin. ✗

We can either use a **conjunction** to join sentences e.g.
Dumping garbage is unhealthy <u>because</u> flies breed on it. ✔

Or use a **semi-colon**, e.g.
Paul collected the bottles; he put them in the recycling bin. ✔

• Explain to students that we use the passive voice is more formal than the active voice. It is often used in formal reports, e.g. *accounts of science experiments.*

154 • You may wish to tell students that sentences joined without conjunctions are *fused* or *run-on* sentences, and a *comma splice* occurs when two sentences are joined with a comma.

Some sentences below have incorrect punctuation. Rewrite them correctly.

> Example: People dump garbage they know it is unhealthy.
> *People dump garbage although they know it is unhealthy.*

1 There was a lot of waste in the yard, the students organised a clean-up day.
2 You should not throw away plastic bags they take a long time to decay.
3 We asked our neighbours not to burn waste, but they took no notice,
4 An officer from NSWMA visited the school she told the students about waste.
5 We should bring drinks in reusable bottles because plastic bottles create waste.
6 The students prepared a recycling police, their teacher was pleased with them.
7 I try to recycle all my waste there are some items I cannot recycle.

Word work: Homophones

> **Homophones** are words which sound the same but have different spellings and meanings.
> *Waste can be recycled. / I wear a belt round my waist.*

1 **Choose the correct homophones to complete the sentences.**

> Example: The recycling bins were emptied last
> *week.* (weak / week)

1 A landfill site is a _____ ground where waste is stored. (peace / piece)
2 We are not _____ to put plastic bags in the recycling bin. (aloud / allowed)
3 The landfill site was on a _____ outside the town. (plane / plain)
4 The pile of garbage in the street was not a pleasant _____ . (sight / site)
5 The _____ of the bin made it too heavy for me to lift. (wait / weight)
6 After waiting over an hour for his friends, Ajani began to feel _____ . (board / bored)

2 **Write sentences using different homophones.**

> Example: *We should not dump garbage in the sea.*

1 see / sea   3 flower / flour
2 tail / tale   4 wait / weight

Here are some homophones you should know

aloud	you can hear it
allowed	permitted
break	damage
brake	stop a car
board	piece of wood
bored	not interested
flour	used to make bread
flower	part of a plant
peace	calm, quiet time
piece	part of something
plain	flat land
plane	aircraft
right	correct
write	put words on paper
sail	cloth fixed to boat
sale	selling goods
sight	something you see
site	a place
tale	a story
tail	part of animal
toe	part of foot
tow	pull along
wait	stay in one place
weight	how heavy something is
waste	things we throw away
waist	middle part of body
weak	not strong
week	period of 7 days

- **Homophones** Exercise 1: Students can make their own sentences using the homophones they did not select for the gapped sentences.
- Watch video clips about homophones on YouTube.

False homophones

> **False homophones** are words which look similar to speakers of Jamaican Creole, but are pronounced differently in Standard Jamaican English, e.g. *taught / thought*.
> Our teacher **taught** us about pollution.
> She **thought** it was important for us to learn about it.

1 **Choose the correct words to complete the sentences.**

1 _____ of my friends helped me write a recycling policy.   (boat / both)
2 The _____ in cities is more polluted than in rural areas.   (air / hair)
3 Many items made of _____ can be recycled.   (thin / tin)
4 The garbage gave off an unpleasant smell in the _____ .   (eat / heat)
5 The students were told _____ should clean the classroom.   (day / they)
6 You should _____ better than to drop paper on the floor.   (now / know)

2 **Select the correct homophone for each clue below.**

> doze / those   ear / hear   boat / both   at / hot   and / hand
> add / had   think / sink   eat / heat

1 This is what you do with your ears.
2 a light, short sleep
3 You have five fingers on each of these.
4 We do this at mealtimes.

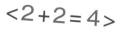

5 When we _____ two and two we get four.
6 It is very _____ in the midday sun.
7 This is where we wash the dishes.
8 We use this to travel on the water.

Writing: Project

Prepare a group project on the theme of pollution.

1 **Research:** Decide which topics you will include in your project, e.g. *air pollution, waste, water pollution*. Allocate these topics to group members. Conduct research and make notes.

2 **Drafting:**
  • Write a rough draft of your section of the project. Do not copy directly from the sources you used. Use your own words.
  • Discuss your draft with members of your group.
    • Is all the material relevant?
    • Does it follow a logical order?

> Remember to produce a **bibliography** (a list of the sources of information you consulted for your project).

3 **Publishing:**
  • Decide which text features your project will contain.
  • Each group member writes his/ her section of the project.
  • Assemble the different sections of the project and give it to your teacher.

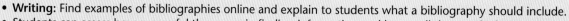

• **Writing:** Find examples of bibliographies online and explain to students what a bibliography should include.
• Students can assess how successful they were in finding information and how well they worked as a group to complete the project.

Get ready

Which is healthier, living in the city or in the country?
Why might this be?

Reading

Survey the title and pictures. Predict what the text will be about.
Read to the end of this page and review your predictions.

- What was similar? What was different?
- What might happen next?

Out of Breath

Crystal stopped for a moment to catch her breath. It was still a long way to the finishing line. She forced herself to go on, but it was no use. Her legs refused to obey her. There was nothing for it but to drop out of the race.

Later as she sat in the classroom, Crystal's friends tried to comfort her. "I don't understand what happened," Crystal told them tearfully. "I was 400 metre champion at my last school. Ever since we moved to Kingston, my running times have got slower. Now I can't even finish the race."

The next morning, Crystal woke feeling really unwell. Her eyes and throat were sore and she was short of breath. "I don't think I can go to school today," she wheezed.

Her mother looked closely at her. "Your eyes are red, and I don't like the sound of that cough. I'll see if I can get you an appointment with the doctor."

A couple of hours later, Crystal and her mother were sitting in the doctor's office. The doctor took Crystal's temperature and listened to her chest with her stethoscope. "Your temperature is normal," she told Crystal, "so we can rule out any infection. However, it's obvious that you are short of breath. I think you have asthma."

"How is that possible?" asked Crystal's mother. "Crystal has always had excellent health. In fact she was a champion runner at her last school."

- Use the DRTA strategy to approach this text. **D**irect: direct students to use an appropriate pre-reading strategy.
  Read: tell students to read up to a certain point in the story. **T**hink: they think about what they have read.
  What has the writer told them so far? Does it fit in with their predictions? What might happen next? **A**fter:
  After they finish reading the text, students review what they have read.

157

"I see that you moved to Kingston quite recently. The level of air pollution is much higher in the city than in other parts of Jamaica. This might be affecting Crystal's breathing. Is there anything else you can think of that might have caused her problem?"

"Not really," said Crystal's mother. "Crystal eats well and exercises every day."

"What about when our neighbours burn garbage in their yard, Mummy?" said Crystal. "My eyes really smart when that happens, and the fumes make me cough."

"What kind of garbage do they burn?" the doctor asked.

"Mainly paper and card," Crystal's mother told the doctor, "but sometimes they burn plastic bottles and tyres."

"That could account for Crystal's problems," the doctor said. "Burning tyres emits really toxic fumes. Don't worry, Crystal. I'm going to give you an inhaler to help you breathe. It won't stop you from competing in races. In fact, many of the world's top athletes suffer from asthma. It doesn't stop them from winning; they just learn to manage their condition. But your mother must talk to your neighbours about their yard fires."

"Thank you, doctor. I'm sure the inhaler will help. I'll go round to our neighbour's house as soon as we get back home," Crystal's mother declared.

1 Why did Crystal drop out of the race?

2 Explain the meaning of the sentence:
   Her legs refused to obey her.

3 We learn that Crystal feels unwell. What exactly are her symptoms?

> After you finish reading the story, review your predictions. How did the story end? Was this what you expected? What was similar? What was different?

4 Why is Crystal's mother surprised that her daughter has asthma?

5 What might have caused Crystal's asthma?

6 Crystal says that her eyes *smart* when the neighbours burn garbage. This means that
   a) her eyes run.
   b) she starts to cry.
   c) her eyes sting.
   d) she cannot see.

7 What does the doctor prescribe for Crystal? Why?

8 How does the doctor try to reassure Crystal?

9 Do you think that Crystal feels happy about moving to Kingston? Find evidence in the text to support your answer.

10 What should be done about people who pollute the environment by dumping or burning garbage?

• Practise phrased cued reading with students. This technique helps students know where to pause so that the passage makes sense. Write a section of the passage on the board with // at the end of each sentence. Mark commas and pauses in the sentences with / e.g. *My eyes really smart when that happens / and the fumes make me cough.//* Ask students to mark pauses in other sections of the story.

Speaking and listening: Telling a story

1 👥 **Discuss the story in pairs or groups.**

- What problems did Crystal face when she moved house?
- Have you or one of your friends ever moved house or gone to a new school?
- How did you or your friend feel about this? What was difficult?

2 **Complete a story map like the one on page 187 for the story about Crystal.**

3 **Retell the story to your group.**

Use the notes in your story map to help you.

> Record your response to the story in a 'Reading response' chart like the one on page 183.

> The story is about a girl called Crystal.

> Crystal was good at running, but when she moved to Kingston, things changed.

> Work with other students and divide the story between you. Each of you tells a different part of the story.

Telling a story is similar in some ways to giving a presentation. You should
- speak clearly and slowly so that everyone can hear.
- use your notes, but don't read them out.
- make eye contact with your audience.

Storytellers must also appeal to their listener's imagination and make them want to hear more. To do this
- pause from time to time to create suspense.
- vary the speed at which you speak, sometimes slow, sometimes faster.
- include conversation and use different voices.

Language

WB5 p37–8

Contractions

Contractions are short forms of verbs. We often use them in speech or in informal writing.

> *I do not* ⟶ *I* **don't** *think I can go to school today.*
> *I will* ⟶ **I'll** *see if I can get an appointment with the doctor.*

We use an *apostrophe* in contractions to show that letters have been left out.

1 **Find five more contractions in the story on pages 157–8. What are the full verb forms?**

- **Research:** Ask students to find out about the pyramid plot structure. Encourage them to practise plotting a story they know well using this structure.
- **Speaking and listening:** If students do not know anyone who has moved house, they can imagine how they might feel about it themselves if they had to move. Record them on an electronic device when they tell the story and play back for comment. They could retell other stories they know or have read.

2 **Write the following contractions as full verbs.**

1 I've *I have*
2 they'll
3 you won't
4 she doesn't

5 they're
6 he can't
7 it isn't
8 I didn't

9 you don't
10 we wouldn't
11 we've
12 she hasn't

3 **Write what Crystal told her mother. Use contractions to replace the full verbs.**

There's

~~There is~~ going to be an athletics competition at school and I have signed up for the 400 metre race. I did not want to go in for it at first, but I am feeling much better now. I do not think I will win but there are not many other competitors. My friends wanted me to enter and they have all wished me luck. I am not sure how well I will do. I know I will not win this time, but I will do my best.

4 **Rewrite this letter using full form verbs.**

We should not use contractions in formal writing.

LETTER TO THE EDITOR

I am writing

~~I'm writing~~ to complain about the amount of waste in town.
You can't walk down the street without tripping over garbage. It's a real eyesore. We shouldn't have to put up with this situation. The Council doesn't do anything about it so we're going to take action ourselves. There'll be a clean-up day on Sunday. You're all welcome to take part.

We'll meet outside the Town Hall at 9:00 am You'll need to bring bags for the garbage. You shouldn't pick it up with your bare hands, so don't forget to bring gloves.
We're hoping to see a lot of people there, so please tell all your friends about this. Let's make our town a cleaner and healthier place.

• **DA** Allow some students to write only the full form verbs in Exercise 4 instead of copying out the whole letter.

Prepositions of place

Prepositions are usually placed before a *noun* or *pronoun*. They tell us how the noun or pronoun a related to the rest of the sentence.
Crystal sat **in** *the classroom. She moved* **to** *Kingston recently.*

prepositions

WB5 p42–3

① **Underline the prepositions in the following paragraph.**

Mrs. Gomez walked <u>to</u> her neighbour's house. She saw her neighbour walk across the yard. She was holding a tyre in her hand. There was a pile of garbage beside the gate. The neighbour walked towards the pile and put the tyre on it. She stood beside the pile for a moment. She took a box of matches out of her pocket.
"Wait a minute," cried Mrs. Gomez cried. She ran through the gate into the yard.

② **Choose the correct prepositions to complete the paragraph.**

There was an athletics match (at / in / to) our school last week. The competitors came from schools which are (above / near to / up) ours. The match was held (in / on / under) the school playing field. Our parents sat (across / beside / between) the field to watch us. At the end there was a relay race where the teams ran (around / to / with) a baton. We all cheered when the runner from our team was first (across / into / towards) the finishing line. After the match we had a picnic (in / on / under) the trees and then we went (to / from / by) the beach for a swim.

③ **Use suitable prepositions to complete the sentences.**

Common prepositions of place	
about	near
above	of
across	off
around	on
at	out / out of
below	over
beside	past
between	through
by	towards
down	under
from	up
in/ into	with / without

    by between around through beside up past inside

1 We went to the competition _____ bus.
2 The bus climbed slowly _____ the steep hill.
3 It crossed the bridge _____ the river.
4 We travelled _____ the centre of town.
5 We drove _____ the Town Hall.
6 Crystal ran _____ the track in record time.
7 I sat _____ my two friends.
8 It was very hot, so we went _____ the house.

• Tell students that some prepositions of time consist of more than one word, e.g. *out of.*
• You may wish to point out that a noun or pronoun which follows a preposition are the object of the preposition.

4 **Draw a diagram to show where you are sitting in relation to other students. Write sentences using the prepositional phrases below to describe where you are sitting.**

> Remember: Prepositional phrases are prepositions which are made up of more than one word, e.g. *in front of   next to*

Example: *I am sitting next to Dwayne.*

> next to   on the other side of   on the right of
> in front of   at the side of

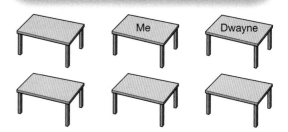

Phrasal verbs

> **Phrasal verbs** are phrases consisting of a *verb + preposition* which have a special meaning, e.g. **drop + out of**:
> *Crystal decided to drop out of the race.*
> *Drop out of* means to stop taking part in something.

1 **Complete these sentences with the prepositions off, on, or up.**
1 I had to get _____ early to get to the match on time.
2 I get ____ very well with the other members of the team.
3 My mother looked _____ the times of the buses on the internet.
4 When I got _____ the bus, my friends were waiting for me.
5 I tried _____ my new sneakers the day before the match.
6 Mom asked me to turn_____ the radio because she had a headache.

2 **Write one sentence of your own for each phrasal verb below.**

> get in   get off   get over something   get on with someone

Word work: Spelling

> Some words have similar spellings and are *easily confused*. Often these words are different parts of speech.
> **advice** (noun): *Crystal listened to the doctor's **advice**.*
> **advise** (verb): *I **advise** you to use the inhaler when you are short of breath.*

1 **What parts of speech are the following words? Use your dictionaries to help you.**

Example: *accept (verb)   except (preposition)*

1 accept / except
2 breath / breathe
3 loose / lose
4 passed / past
5 practice / practise
6 affect / effect

• **Spelling:** Students can add the words in Exercise 1 to their word banks. Tell them to write the part of speech for each word, and an example sentence.

2 **Select the correct words to complete the sentences.**

1 Everyone (accept / except) Crystal herself thought she would win the race.
2 After the match I was so tired I went to (lay / lie) down.
3 I found it difficult to (breath / breathe) because of the smoke.
4 I tried not to let the fumes (affect / effect) me.
5 tried not to (loose / lose) sight of my friend as he raced ahead.
6 We started the race together but my friend soon (passed / past) me.
7 Malik needed to (practice / practise) every day for the race.
8 The other competitors ran (to / too) fast for me to catch them.

Writing: Journal entry

1 **Read these extracts from Crystal's journal.**

WB5 p142

We can use a **journal** to record what we do and how we think and feel. Try keeping a journal for a month. Write in it every day.

Dates of entries

Tuesday, November 21st
I couldn't go to school today as my eyes were sore and I kept on wheezing. Mummy took me to the doctor, who said I had asthma. She gave me an inhaler to help me breathe. She explained that I had probably been affected by the fumes from the neighbours burning garbage in their yard.

Account of events

I was upset when I learnt about the asthma, as I thought it would stop me from competing in track sports; however, the doctor was really kind. She told me that a lot of athletes suffer from asthma, but they learn to cope with it.

How she feels

Wednesday, November 22nd
I feel a lot better today. The inhaler is really helping me to breathe. Mummy went to see the neighbours and told them that the fumes from their fire were making me sick. They apologised to her, and promised to take their waste to the landfill site in future.

Account of events

I'll be able to return to school tomorrow. I'm looking forward to practising my running – and seeing my friends too.

How she feels

2 **Write three or more journal entries.**

EITHER continue Crystal's journal.
OR write about an event in your own life, for example:

- A difficult journey
- A time when you were ill
- Moving house.

You can describe either real or imaginary events.

Include the date of each journal entry and an account of the events which occurred. Remember to describe how you and other people felt.

- Encourage students to keep a regular journal to record the events in their lives and how they feel about them. They can post extracts from their journal on your class blog.
- Organise a Young Writers' Day to showcase students' writing done during the year.

Unit 20

Get ready

Share what you know about the causes of pollution.

Why is pollution harmful? What can we do to reduce it?

Reading

Skim the poem.

- What types of pollution are mentioned?
- Which animals and plants are affected?

Poisoned Talk

Who killed Cock Robin?
I, said the worm,
I did him great harm,
He died on the branch of a withered tree
From the acid that poisoned me.

Who killed the heron?
I, mouthed the fish,
With my tainted flesh
I killed, tern, duck and drake,
All the birds of the lake.

Who killed the lake?
I, boasted Industry,
I poisoned with mercury
Fish, plant and weed
To pamper men's greed.

Who killed the flowers?
I, moaned the wind,
I prowl unconfined
Blowing acid rain
Over field, flood and fen.

Who killed the forest?
I ensured that it died,
Said sulphur dioxide.
And all life within it,
From earthworm to linnet.

Raymond Wilson

robin: a small bird

tainted: poisoned

pamper: satisfy

unconfined: unrestricted

acid rain: rain polluted by chemicals

fen: swamp

sulphur dioxide: a poisonous chemical

linnet: a bird

robin

linnet

- **Get ready**: Discuss the different forms of pollution studied in this unit, and in science lessons to make a cross-curricular link.

164

- **Reading**: There is some unfamiliar vocabulary in this poem which you may wish to explain before reading it. Remind students of the elements of poetry observed in earlier units of this book. Read the poem aloud so the students get a sense of the rhythm.

The poet has based his poem on a nursery rhyme.

> Who killed Cock Robin?
> *I*, said the Sparrow
> *With my bow and arrow,*
> *I killed Cock Robin.*

1 Which of these text features can you find in the poem?

a) verses c) repetition

b) rhymes d) rhythm

2 Which of these devices can you find? Give examples.

a) alliteration c) similes

b) onomatopoeia d) personification

Add examples of devices, like similes, to your Learning Journals.

3 Copy and complete the table.

What was killed?	Who or what killed it?	How was it killed?
Verse 1: Cock Robin	*A worm*	*The robin ate a worm which had eaten poisoned earth.*

4 What message does the poet want to give to his readers?

Dreamer

I dreamt I was an ocean
and no one polluted me.

I dreamt I was a whale
and no hunters chased after me.

I dreamt I was the air
and nothing blackened me.

I dreamt I was a stream
and nobody poisoned me.

I dreamt I was an elephant
and nobody stole my ivory.

I dreamt I was a rainforest
and no one cut down my trees.

I dreamt I painted a smile
on the face of the Earth
for all to see.

Brian Moses

- There is a clear contrast between the two visions of the future portrayed in these poems. Encourage students to think positively about what they can do to help the 'dreamer's' vision become reality.
- Explain that whales are hunted for their meat, and elephants for their ivory tusks.
- Students can use a Venn diagram to compare and contrast the two poems in this unit. They can also compare them with the other texts on air pollution included in this theme.

5 Which text features of poetry listed in questions 1 and 2 can you find in 'Dreamer'?

6 Which natural features does the poet describe in this poem?

7 What kind of future does he dream about?

8 What does he mean by saying that he dreamt that *he painted a smile on the face of the earth?*

    a) His dream would make everyone laugh.

    b) His dream would make the earth a happier place.

    c) He would paint the earth in bright colours.

    d) No one would believe in his dream.

9 How do the themes of the two poems differ?

10 Which poem did you enjoy more? Why?

> The *theme* of a poem is the main idea it expresses.

Speaking and listening: Messages

> There are several different ways of **communicating messages** to the public, e.g. *posters, pictures, notices, advertisements*. These messages can be passed on *visually* or through the media, e.g. *radio, television, the internet*.

1 **What is the message of these posters?**

2 **Share examples of posters, notices, advertisements and jingles you have seen or heard which pass on a message.**

3 **Think of a message you would like to communicate about pollution.**

- Decide how you will communicate your message: a poster, an advertisement, a picture, a jingle, mime?
- Prepare your message so you can present it to your class.

> A jingle is a short song with a catchy tune used to advertise something or pass on a message.

• Speaking and listening: When students discuss the posters, point out that we do not always need words to communicate messages. Help groups to formulate their messages clearly before they design their posters or create their jingles or mimes. When they are ready, each group can present its message to the class. Record on an electronic device and play back for comment.

Language: Helping verbs

Helping verbs are used with main verbs to describe actions.
*The students **have planted** trees in their school garden.*

helping verb   main verb

Note: Helping verbs are sometimes called *auxiliary* verbs.

1 **Copy the sentences. Underline the helping verbs. Circle the main verb.**

Example: *I was dreaming of a world with no pollution.*

1 The trees were swaying in the breeze.
2 Did you see the rainbow in the sky?
3 The water in the rivers will be clean.
4 New trees are growing in the garden.
5 The birds have made their nests in the trees.
6 Air pollution has decreased.
7 People do not dump garbage any more.
8 I am enjoying my walk through the forest.

2 **Choose helping verbs to complete the sentences.**

> am   did   have   has   will   does   are   were

1 We _____ cleared up the garbage in our yard.
2 Dad _____ put the garbage in the bin.
3 We _____ clean our classroom tomorrow.
4 My sister _____ not go to school yesterday.
5 My friends and I _____ organising a beach clean-up.
6 I _____ designing a poster for the clean-up.
7 My little brother _____ not keep his room tidy.
8 When I got home, my brother and sister _____ helping to collect the leaves.

3 **Write your own sentences using the helping verbs in Exercise 2.**

The verbs below are **modal verbs**. They are *helping verbs* used with main verbs to show ability or to say that something is certain, probable or possible.

Can / could show ability: *We **can breathe** clean air in the countryside.*
May / might show possibility: *Don't drink the water. It **might be** polluted.*
Would also shows possibility: *We **would** all be healthier if we breathed clean air.*
Should is used for advice: *We **should recycle** used paper.*
Must tells us that something is necessary: *We **must plant** more trees.*

- **Helping verbs**: Write a list of helping verbs on the board and a list of main verbs. Get students to make sentences. Remind them that they may need to change the main verb to fit the helping verb, e.g. *is + say = is saying*. To make this more exciting, organise a team competition to find which team can make the most sentences.

4 **Identify the modal verb and the main verb in these sentences. Copy and complete the table.**

1 People should walk instead of using cars.
2 We could recycle more items.
3 We must all help to protect the environment.
4 It might rain later on today.
5 Fumes from vehicles may affect your breathing,
6 Everyone can do more to reduce air pollution.
7 Our towns would be cleaner if no one dumped garbage.
8 Industry should not pollute the air we breathe.

	Modal	Main verb
1	should	walk
2		

5 **Write your own sentences using modal verbs.**

Example: *I would love to live beside the sea.*

1 can + try
2 should + remember
3 must + tell
4 might + be

5 could + do
6 may + see
7 would + prefer
8 should + stop

Subject–verb agreement review

Remember: We use *singular* verbs with *singular* subjects and *plural* verbs with *plural* subjects.

  *Paul **is** designing a poster.*   *Tara and Amy **have** created a jingle.*

  subject   singular verb   subject   plural verb

Sometimes the subject of the sentence is separated from the verb by additional information.

  *Mr. and Mrs. Cook, Paul's parents, **have** helped him with his poster.*

    subject   plural verb

1 **Complete each sentence with the correct verb form.**

1 Mrs. Cook, our class teacher, _____ (has / have) displayed our posters.
2 In my class we all _____ (loves / love) writing jingles.
3 All the students in my group _____ (is / are) singing our jingle.
4 Our jingle, which was written by Dana, _____ (is / are) quite short.
5 My best friend and I _____ (was / were) hoping our poster would be best.
6 Ajani, who was absent from school yesterday, _____ (does / do) not know what to do.
7 Aunt Cherisse, my mother's sister, _____ (lives / live) in Miami.
8 The house where she lives _____ (is / are) close to the sea.

• **Subject–verb agreement**: Remind students that many sentences have a complete subject, e.g. *Chris and all his friends.* They must look at the complete subject to find out whether it is singular or plural. Where additional information has been added, students must look further back in the sentence to find the subject.

Remember: We use singular verbs with collective nouns (see page 12) and with indefinite pronouns (see page 27)
*Our group **was** first to present our poster.*

collective noun singular verb
*Everyone **has** enjoyed singing.*

indefinite pronoun singular verb

2 **Complete the paragraph with the correct verb forms.**

Our class often *prepares* (prepares / prepare) posters for wall displays. Sometimes we _____ (1 writes / write) jingles too. Everyone _____ (2 enjoys / enjoy) it when their group _____ (3 performs / perform) their jingle. All the students _____ (4 takes / take) part in their group's performance. No one _____ (5 is / are) ever left out, even if he or she _____ (6 is / are) not able to sing very well. It is the same when we have team games or competitions. Each team _____ (7 takes / take) part. Our teachers always _____ (8 tells / tell) us that it doesn't matter if your team _____ (9 does / do) not win, but of course, everyone _____ (10 is / are) disappointed to be in the losing team.

Word work: Signal words review

We use **signal words** to link ideas when we speak or when we write. They have different functions, e.g. a*dding ideas, introducing new ideas*. You have practised identifying and using signal words throughout this book.

Using the signal words as a guide, complete each sentence in your own words.

1 My mother wants to buy a new car; however, …
2 People often burn garbage; as a result, …
3 We should try to save paper; also, …
4 Dumping garbage creates an eyesore; besides, …
5 Trees are the lungs of our planet; therefore, …
6 Many everyday items can be recycled; for example, …
7 My sister suffers from asthma; nevertheless, …
8 There are many ways of protecting the environment; firstly, …

Signal words for you to use
Introducing ideas and information
firstly	for example
such as	including

Adding ideas and information
also	as well as
besides	in addition
furthermore	too

Contrast
although	nevertheless
however	on the other hand

Cause and effect
as a result	because of
therefore	the reason why

• **Signal words**: Examples of signal words and their uses can be found in the section on graphic organisers (page 186).
• Point out that signal words are often preceded by a semi-colon and followed by a comma.
• **ICT** Get students to look online to find more examples of signal words. They are sometimes called *transition* words.

Writing: Design a poster

1 **Design a poster for your class noticeboard to encourage students to care for the school environment.**

1 Plan the contents of your poster.
   - Create a slogan, e.g.

     Take Pride in Your School
   - Write three or four points for your poster, e.g.

     Keep your classroom clean. Look after your books.

2 Plan the layout of your poster. Think about:
   - How to set out the text on the page.
   - The colours and the illustrations.

3 Make a rough sketch of your poster.
   Discuss it with another student. How could you improve it?

4 Make a presentation copy of your poster.
   Either produce it by hand or use a computer.

Explore fonts, colours and clip art to create your poster.

2 **Write a haiku.**

> A haiku is a short poem which originated in Japan. It usually has 17 syllables divided into three lines like this:
> First line: 5 syllables   Second line: 7 syllables   Third line: 5 syllables

1 Read this haiku.

Forests with tall trees
Swaying gently in the breeze
Birds perch on branches.

2 Write your own haiku about a natural scene, e.g. a river, a beach, a mountain.
   - Write a list of words you could use to write your haiku.
   - Arrange the words to fit the form of a haiku. Try to include some alliteration.

- **Poster**: Allow students to produce posters individually or in pairs. Create a wall display with their posters.
- **Haiku**: Ask students to divide the haiku into syllables, e.g. *For/ests with tall trees Sway/ing gent/ly in the breeze*. Before they create their haikus, get them to imagine different scenes in their mind's eye. Students can copy their haikus on to a piece of paper or card and illustrate them.

Reading

Skim the text below.

- What kind of text is it? How do you know that?
- What is the main idea?

Positive Results for NEPA Campaign

The earth's atmosphere is surrounded by the ozone layer, which acts as an umbrella, protecting us from harmful rays from the sun. Exposure to these rays can cause rashes, sunburn or skin cancer. It can, in addition, cause damage to the eyes and make the body less able to fight disease.

In the second half of the 20th century, scientists observed a huge hole in the ozone layer caused by the widespread use of CFCs (chlorofluorocarbons). These are chemicals used in refrigerators, air-conditioning units and aerosol sprays. As a result, there has been a significant increase in cases of skin cancer and eye diseases around the world.

Fortunately, due to worldwide campaigns aimed at reducing the use of CFCs, the ozone layer is showing signs of recovery, and the gaping hole created by our use of these pollutants is shrinking.

In Jamaica, the National Environment and Planning Agency (NEPA) has created an Ozone Unit, which is campaigning to reduce the use of CFCs on the island. Recently, this unit has conducted an education campaign to raise public awareness. Posters have been displayed in public places and in places of work, advising Jamaicans to check their air-conditioning units and repair any leaks which

You can play your part!
Did you know?
CFCs used in A/C units are creating a hole in the ozone layer.

Check the A/C unit in your car and at home, and get any leaks repaired.

Buying a new car?
Make sure you ask for a CFC free vehicle.

might release CFCs into the atmosphere. In fact, the Ozone Unit recommends replacing all old refrigerators and air-conditioning units with units which comply with modern regulations.

Although CFC levels in the atmosphere have decreased as a result of NEPA's campaign, there are some people who refuse to replace out-dated equipment with new environmentally friendly units. They either do not see the necessity, or lack the funds to do so. New cars and air-conditioning units imported to the island now use ozone-friendly substances, however, so in time, units using CFCs will be phased out.

- Students may need some background knowledge to understand this topic, but let them first read the text to find out as much as they can. Make a text-to-self connection by talking about familiar items such as air-conditioning units, fridges and spray cans. The danger with old units is that they use CFCs which may leak into the atmosphere and affect the ozone layer.

1 Why is the ozone layer described as an *umbrella*?

2 What has created the hole in the ozone layer?

3 What effects are caused by this hole in the ozone layer?

4 Why is the hole shrinking in size?

5 For what purpose has NEPA created an Ozone Unit?

6 How can Jamaicans help to reduce the size of the hole in the ozone layer?

7 Why do some people not follow the advice given by the Ozone Unit?

8 An *ozone-friendly substance* is:

  a) a substance which creates ozone.

  b) a substance which damages the ozone layer.

  c) a substance which makes people more healthy.

  d) a substance which does not harm the ozone layer.

> Find signal words used in the article, e.g. *in addition*.

9 What else do you think NEPA could do to limit the use of CFCs in Jamaica?

10 What other environmental problems are caused by human activity?

Vocabulary

Select the options which are closest in meaning to the words in bold.

1 **Exposure to** harmful rays from the sun from the hole in the ozone layer can cause health problems.

  a) suffering from   **c)** hiding from

  b) lack of protection from   **d)** protection from

> Remember to use clues in the context to help you understand unfamiliar words.

2 A **significant** increase in cases of skin cancer has been observed since the hole was identified.

  a) gradual   **b)** slight   **c)** noticeable   **d)** worrying

3 The widespread use of CFCs in refrigerators and A/C units has created a **gaping** hole in the ozone layer.

  a) quite small   **b)** very large   **c)** unimportant   **d)** permanent

4 The Ozone Unit has attempted to raise public **awareness** of the problems caused by CFCs.

  a) reaction   **c)** anger

  b) sympathy   **d)** understanding

5 New A/C units must all **comply** with modern regulations.

  a) ignore   **c)** complete

  b) obey   **d)** give up

> Look online to find out more about the ozone layer. Find out what is being done to protect it.

6 As new A/C units are imported, units emitting CFCs will gradually **be phased out**.

  a) disappear   **c)** increase

  b) be banned   **d)** continue.

- **Comprehension**: Remind students to use QAR to identify different question types, so that they know where to look for the answers.
- **Vocabulary**: Show students a YouTube clip on how to use context clues to unlock meaning.

172

Language: Present perfect tense

1 Complete the table with the simple past and past participles of the verbs listed.

Verb	Simple past	Past participle	Verb	Simple past	Past participle
begin	began	begun	give		
break			know		
catch			speak		
do			think		
fly			write		

2 Complete the sentences with the present perfect forms of the verbs in brackets.

> Example: The hole in the ozone layer *has decreased* in size. (decrease)

1 NEPA _____ a campaign to reduce the use of CFCs. (conduct)

2 They _____ posters to raise public awareness. (put up)

3 My mother _____ just _____ a new car. (buy)

4 We _____ about air pollution at school this term. (learn)

5 The government _____ a lot to reduce air pollution. (do)

6 Marie _____ a report about her class Clean-Up Day. (write)

7 _____ you _____ that pile of garbage under the tree? (see)

8 My brother _____ the garbage to the landfill site. (take)

Active and passive voice

1 Underline the verbs. Which are in the active voice? Which are in the passive voice?

> Example: The air was polluted with fumes from the traffic. *passive*

1 The garbage is collected every day.

2 The students collected all the used paper.

3 All the glass jars will be saved for reuse.

4 Mummy told me to clear up the yard.

5 A lot of garbage was left in the streets.

6 Too many bottles and cans are dumped.

7 Our class created a recycling policy.

8 Our teacher put a list of rules on the notice board.

- **Present perfect**: Give students more verbs to add to the table. Remind students to use *has* with a singular subject and *have* with plural subjects.
- **Passive voice**: Remind students that the passive voice is formed from the past participle with the appropriate tense of the verb be.

2 **Rewrite these sentences in the passive voice.**

Example: Brad helps Grandpa in the garden. *Grandpa is helped by Brad in the garden.*

1 He cleared all the garbage last week.
2 He sweeps the yard in the morning.
3 He will weed the garden today.
4 We water the plants at sunset every day.
5 Dasheens and yams grow in Grandpa's garden.
6 Grandpa will plant a new tree to give shade.
7 He picked the breadfruit yesterday.
8 Grandma collects the eggs from the henhouse every day.

Contractions

Rewrite the following conversation using contractions.

I've just had an email from my cousin in Mandeville.

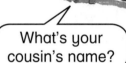

What's your cousin's name?

Kyle:	I have just had an email from my cousin in Mandeville.
Tiffany:	What is your cousin's name?
Kyle:	She is called Tasha. She has written to me about her town.
Tiffany:	I do not know Mandeville. What is it like?
Kyle:	It is in the hills. I have been there quite a few times.
Tiffany:	I would love to go there one day.
Kyle:	I will ask if you can come with us next time we go there.
Tiffany:	I do not know if my mother will let me go.
Kyle:	That should not be a problem. I will ask my mother to invite you.
Tiffany:	I cannot wait to go.

Prepositions

Choose the correct prepositions to complete the sentences.

1 Last week Kyle's mother took him **to / on / by** a visit to his cousins in Mandeville.
2 Tiffany went **by / for / with** them.
3 They travelled to Mandeville **by / on / with** coach.
4 Tiffany sat **above / below / beside** Kyle on the coach.
5 The road to Mandeville goes **across / at / through** May Pen.
6 Our teacher was vexed **at / with / for** us for dropping paper in the classroom.
7 She told us to stay **after / before / until** school and clear up.
8 Kiandra wrote a report **of / with / about** air pollution.

• Exercise 4: You may need to help students to identify the verb and the tense used in each sentence.
• **DA** You may need to work through the exercises orally with some students before they begin to write.

Word work: Antonyms

Match the antonyms in the circles.

first
love push sweet
break lose sell forbid
modern slow wealthy
sunset near

pull
distant fast bitter
ancient sunrise mend
purchase permit detest
last poor win

Homophones

Find and correct the homophones which have been used wrongly.

Example: The ~~breaks~~ *brakes* on my brother's car need to be repaired.

1 We are not aloud to dump garbage in the schoolyard.
2 My brother's car broke down so my father had to toe it home.
3 The clearing up took a long time and everyone was board.
4 It is not polite to stair at people we do not know.
5 The students had a cake sail to raise money for recycling bins.
6 My grandfather has a peace of land where he grows vegetable.
7 After his illness Grandpa was too week to work in his garden.
8 The nurse recorded the wait of each student in the class.

Synonyms

1 Select synonyms to replace the words in bold type.

1 We were all **alarmed** when the yard fire spread to the trees.
   a) surprised   **b)** worried   **c)** delighted   **d)** furious
2 The ruined building was **demolished** as it was thought to be unsafe.
   a) painted   **b)** repaired   **c)** sold   **d)** destroyed
3 Accidents happen when safety checks are **overlooked**.
   a) completed   **b)** ignored   **c)** prevented   **d)** refused
4 There was nothing Angelina **loathed** more than the smell from rotting garbage.
   a) enjoyed   **b)** hated   **c)** preferred   **d)** avoided
5 No one can **foretell** what will happen in ten years from now.
   a) understand   **b)** announce   **c)** predict   **d)** remember
6 Amos was **infuriated** by his brother's thoughtless behaviour.
   a) annoyed   **b)** satisfied   **c)** disappointed   **d)** puzzled

2 Think of synonyms for the words happy and sad. Use them to make word webs.

• **Homophones:** Ask students to write their own sentences using the homophones in this exercise correctly.
• Students could create word searches that include homophones, which they can then give to other students to solve.
• **Learning Journal:** Students can complete a 'How did I do?' chart (page 183) to assess the strategies they use to decipher new words.

175

Writing

1 **Imagine you are one of the people in the picture. Write an entry for your journal about clearing up your yard.**

1 Brainstorm words and phrases you can use in your journal entry. Use an organiser like the one on page 185.

2 Plan your journal entry. Include:
   • the date of your journal entry.
   • some information about how your yard became so untidy.
   • what you and the other people in the picture did to clean it up.
   • how you felt about clearing the yard.

3 Write your journal entry.
   • Write a first draft, then revise it to make it more interesting.
   • Write or type a neat copy and proofread it for mistakes.

2 **Write a letter to your local newspaper in support of ONE on the statements below.**
   • All drivers should have the air-conditioning units in their vehicles checked.
   • People who burn garbage in their backyards should have to pay a fine.

1 Plan your letter.
   Note down reasons and evidence which support the statement you selected.

2 Write the first draft of your letter. Remember to
   • use the format for a formal letter shown on page 96.
   • state your reason for writing your letter.
   • write two or three paragraphs in support of this reason.
   • write politely, using formal language.

3 Revise your letter. Write or type a neat copy.

> Create a poster to show the elements of the different types of writing you practised in this book.

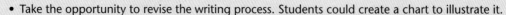

• Take the opportunity to revise the writing process. Students could create a chart to illustrate it.
• **Journal entry:** Students can work individually or in pairs in the brainstorming session to generate ideas for their journal.
• **Letter:** Reasons and evidence supporting these statements can be found in the reading texts about air pollution. You may wish to run through them with students before they write.

Practice Test

Which response correctly completes each sentence in items 1-10?

1 The students told _____ parents about the Parents' Evening.

  A his   C their

  B her   D them

2 We _____ football every Tuesday after school.

  A is playing   C plays

  B are playing   D play

3 The boys _____ on a school trip yesterday.

  A been   C gone

  B went   D going

4 I saw a _____ of ants climbing up the tree trunk.

  A flock   C swarm

  B school   D group

5 Nobody _____ what will happen in the future.

  A knows   C know

  B knew   D known

6 That was the _____ film I have ever seen.

  A most funny   C funnier

  B more funnier   D funniest

7 Next year we _____ our holidays in St. Lucia.

  A were spending   C will spend

  B have spent   D spending

8 We waited _____ it was dark for the concert to start.

  A before   C since

  B until   D for

9 The boy's parents were vexed _____ him when he did not tell the truth.

  A against   B for   C with   D to

10 Neither Crystal ____ Ashley can play in the match tomorrow.

  A and   B nor   C but   D none

From the sentences given in items 11-14, identify which is grammatically correct.

11 A Each student have his or her own desk.

  B Each student has his or her own desk.

  C Each student having his or her own desk.

  D Each student is have his or her own desk.

12 A Kyle has gone on holiday to the USA.

  B Kyle have gone on holiday to the USA.

  C Kyle has went on holiday to the USA.

  D Kyle did go on holiday to the USA.

13 A Jordan is very pleased of her results.

  B Jordan is very pleased to her results.

  C Jordan is very pleased with her results.

  D Jordan is very pleased for her results.

14 A I could not see nobody outside.

  B I could not see anyone outside.

  C I could not see someone outside.

  D I never seen anyone outside.

What part of speech is the underlined word in each sentence given in items 15-17?

15 The sea is very <u>rough</u> today.

  A adverb   C adjective

  B noun   D verb

16 The children cannot swim <u>because</u> the waves are too high.

  A preposition   C pronoun

  B conjunction   D verb

17 Our teacher told <u>us</u> to finish our work quickly.

   A noun   **C** pronoun
   B preposition   **D** verb

Which sentence in items 18-21 is correctly punctuated?

18 **A** "Please come in and sit down" she said.
   B "Please come in and sit down, she said.
   C "Please come in and sit down." she said.
   D "Please come in and sit down," she said.

19 **A** Mrs. White my mother's friend is staying with us for a few days.
   B Mrs. White my mother's friend, is staying with us for a few days.
   C Mrs. White, my mother's friend, is staying with us for a few days.
   D Mrs. White, my mothers friend, is staying with us for a few days.

20 **A** Many fruits grow in Jamaica; bananas, pineapple, oranges and many more.
   B Many fruits grow in Jamaica: bananas, pineapple, oranges and many more.
   C Many fruits grow in Jamaica: bananas, pineapple, oranges, and many more
   D Many fruits grow in Jamaica, bananas, pineapple, oranges and many more.

21 **A** She ran too fast; she tripped on a stone.
   B She ran, too fast, she tripped; on a stone.
   C She ran too fast, she tripped on a stone.
   D She ran too fast she tripped on a stone.

For items 22-23, in which sentences are capital letters correctly used?

22 **A** Joelle's american cousins came to stay.
   B Joelle's American Cousins came to stay.
   C joelle's american cousins came to stay.
   D Joelle's American cousins came to stay.

23 **A** My favourite book is 'Treasure Island' by R.L. stevenson.
   B My favourite book is 'Treasure Island' by R.L. Stevenson.
   C My favourite book is 'Treasure island' by r.l. Stevenson.
   D My favourite book is 'treasure island' by R.L. Stevenson.

Which mark should be placed at the * in the sentence given in items 24-26?

24 Paul breathed a sigh of relief * He knew he was safe now.

   A "   **B** .   **C** :   **D** -

25 The shop sells several different ice cream flavours * coconut, mango, banana and vanilla.

   A ,   **B** ;   **C** !   **D** :

26 "Hurry up * We're going to be late," my sister shouted."

   A :   **B** ?   **C** !   **D** "

In items 27 and 28, which sentence is the apostrophe correctly used?

27 **A** The childrens' grandparents live in Portland.
   B The childrens grandparents' live in Portland.
   C The children's grandparents live in Portland.
   D The childrens grandparent's live in Portland.

28 **A** They didnt buy any vegetable's in the market.
   B They didnt buy any vegetables' in the market.
   C They didnt' buy any vegetables in the market
   D They didn't buy any vegetables in the market.

Which words can be used to replace the underlined words in items 29-32?

29 The boy wrote so quickly his writing was underline{illegible}.

   A untidy   **C** unreadable

   B difficult   **D** clear

30 The runner underline{attempted} to break the world record.

   A failed   **C** wanted

   B succeeded   **D** tried

31 My grandfather has underline{retained} a lot of the books he enjoyed as a child.

   A kept   **C** lost

   B sold   **D** destroyed

Which words in items 33-35 best complete the sentences?

32 The _____ Principal of the school has now retired.

   A future   **C** efficient

   B former   **D** ancient

33 The _____ student refused to obey the order.

   A obedient   **C** orderly

   B foolish   **D** defiant

34 Zackary is very _____; he always does what he promises.

   A reliable   **C** irresponsible

   B careful   **D** cautious

35 Ashley _____ that she would make more effort in future.

   A advised   **C** promised

   B warned   **D** refused

Which word is OPPOSITE to the underlined words in items 36-37?

36 Howard knew that he was underline{guilty} of causing the problem.

   A responsible   **C** forgiven

   B accused   **D** innocent

37 It is underline{forbidden} to bring valuable items to school.

   A banned   **C** arranged

   B permitted   **D** agreed

What prefix can be added to the words in items 39-40 to change their meanings?

38 advantage

   A un-   **B** im-   **C** pre-   **D** dis-

39 understand

   A dis-   **B** mis-   **C** re-   **D** pre-

In items 40-41 what is the correct spelling of the words which complete the sentences?

40 It is not _____ to bring any money.

   A necessary   **C** necessarry

   B nessesary   **D** necessry

41 Everyone will have the _____ to take part.

   A oppertunity   **C** opportunity

   B oportunity   **D** opportunitty

Use this sample dictionary entry to answer items 42-45.

valuable / ˈvæljʊəbəl *adj.*
1 worth a lot of money: *The necklace is very* **valuable.** 2 very useful and important: *a* **valuable** *lesson.*

value / ˈvælju: *noun*
1 the amount that something is worth: *The* **value** *of the painting was not known.* 2 amount something is worth compared to what it costs: *The meat is excellent* **value** *at $450 JD a kilo.*

value / ˈvælju: *verb*
1 believe that someone or something is important: *a* **valued** *friend* 2 state how much something is worth: *I had the necklace* **valued.**

179

42 What part of speech is the word 'valuable'?

A noun   C adjective

B verb   D adverb

43 Which word correctly completes the sentence below?

Candice was keen to know the _____ of her ring.

A valued   C value

B values   D valuable

44 Which of the following statements is true?

The word *value* _____

A is a verb.

B is an adjective.

C has only one meaning.

D can be either a verb or an adjective.

45 Which of the following words is a synonym for the word *valuable*?

A expensive   C useful

B precious   D worthless

Study this part of a Table of Contents and answer items 46–49.

Section	Unit 1	Page
1	Reading Maps	12
	Points of the Compass	15
	Lattitude and Longitude	16
2	Temperature	20
	Rainfall	22
	Drought	24
3	Highland areas	27
	Lowland areas	30
	Coastal areas	33
	Rivers and lakes	37

46 In what type of book would you expect to find this Table of Contents?

A a Science book

B an English book

C a Social Studies book

D a dictionary

47 What is the information in Section 2 about?

A landforms   C how to read maps

B crops   D the weather

48 On which pages would you to find information about mountains?

A 22-23   B 27-29   C 12-14   D 30-32

49 On which page can you find information about the cardinal points: north, south, east and west?

A 12   B 15   C 16   D 27

Read the advertisement, then answer items 50-53.

CHIN'S SUPPLIES

The cheapest prices in town

Open 8.00 – 8.00 Monday to Saturday

- Call in your grocery order.
- We'll deliver it to your door.
- Cash or credit acceptable.

Your convenience is our business!

Call 862-4976 to place your order.

Lines open 7.00 am – 10.00 pm

7 days a week.

50 The advertisement claims that prices at Chin's Supplies are:

A higher than supermarket prices.

B cheaper than in village shops.

C lower than in any other shop.

D about the same as elsewhere.

51 Which of these services is NOT provided by Chin's Supplies?

A home delivery service

B phone ordering service

C payment by cash or credit

D ordering goods by internet

52 What is the latest time you can place an order?
  A eight o'clock in the morning
  B eight o'clock in the evening
  C ten o'clock at night
  D before the shop closes on Saturdays

53 Which of these statements is true?
  A You can only pay in cash.
  B You cannot order groceries on Sundays.
  C You must collect groceries at the store.
  D You do not have to pay for groceries immediately.

Use the information in the pie chart to answer items 55-57.

Favourite Hobbies of Grade 5 Students at Sunnybank School

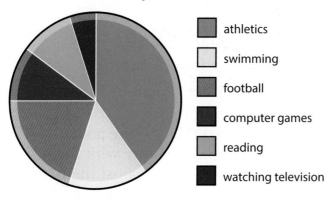

athletics

swimming

football

computer games

reading

watching television

54 The most popular hobby is:
  A swimming.   C athletics.
  B football.   D computer games.

55 Which hobby is liked by the smallest number of students?
  A computer games   C athletics
  B watching television   D reading

56 Which hobbies are preferred by equal numbers of students?
  A swimming and football
  B football and computer games
  C reading and swimming
  D reading and computer games

Read the passage, then answer items 57-61.

The West Indian Manatee is one of the most endangered species in the world. According to current estimates, there are only around four thousand of these huge sea cows still in existence. They are vegetarians and consume large quantities of sea grass and other aquatic plants. They live underwater, but as they are mammals, they need to come up to the surface every few minutes for air. A manatee can weigh as much as 2,000 pounds and lives for 50 to 60 years.

When Columbus and his sailors first sighted manatees, they thought they were looking at mermaids. Settlers in the Caribbean poached them for their meat and used their skin as leather. Today hunting manatees is illegal; their biggest threat is from boat traffic and from cold sea temperatures.

It is many years since manatees have been disappeared from the shores of Jamaica. In the 1980s Jamaican fishermen captured four manatees, which they took to a specially designed captive area at the Alligator Hole River in Clarendon. Three of the manatees are still alive, but as they have consumed all the vegetation in the river, supplies of sea grass have to be brought to them regularly.

57 What is the approximate size of the manatee population today?
  A 2,000   C 4,000
  B 50-60   D 3

58 How long do manatees stay underwater?
  A computer games   C watching television
  B athletics   D reading

59 What part of speech is the word endangered as it is used in line 2 of this extract?
  A noun   C adverb
  B verb   D adjective

60 Why were manatees hunted in the past?
  A People thought they were mermaids.
  B They were a useful source of food.

181

C They got in the way of boats.

D People were afraid of them.

61 Which of the following statements is false?

   A There are no manatees living in the wild in Jamaica today.

   B There is not enough food in the Alligator Hole River for the manatees to eat.

   C Most of the manatees caught by Jamaican fishermen have now died.

   D A special area was prepared to protect the manatees caught off the coast of Jamaica.

Read the following passage then answer items 62-67.

At one time Father was the village's big shot. Then he possessed most of the best lands and the finest cows and mules, and he alone was capable of loading four trucks of bananas on banana day and he had yams which he could sell five tons at a time and sugar cane as well.

There were mangoes and coconuts on his farm and people came and helped themselves to them. They hid of course. They'd go in the early morning and fill their baskets of mangoes or pick up the coconuts which had fallen ripe to the ground and sell them and make a few shillings.

They did this and when he caught them Father would say, 'Look here, don't you know not to do that? To ask me first?'

And they said, 'Mr Johnson, sir, I won't do it again. I beg you, sir.' And he let them go.

This was the only time, to my knowledge, that I heard them affix 'mister' to his name. And Father never minded, for laughingly, he would say: 'There's no mister to my birth certificate.' But what I'm getting at is that they called him mister only when they wanted him to be more lenient to them than he already was.

   Adapted from My Father, Sun-Sun Johnson,

   by C. Everard Palmer

62 At one time the writer's father:

   A owned a lot of land.

   B only had a small farm.

   C had no cattle.

   D was a poor man.

63 The expression *the village's big shot* (line 1) suggests that the writer's father:

   A could shoot very well.

   B was an important person in the village.

   C looked down on the other villagers.

   D was disliked in the village.

64 Which phrase tells us that the villagers did not have permission to take mangoes and coconuts?

   A 'fill their baskets'

   B 'sell them'

   C 'helped themselves'

   D 'make a few shillings'

65 When Father caught the villagers taking produce he:

   A reported them to the police.

   B became very angry with them.

   C took no action against them.

   D told them to take whatever they wanted.

66 The villagers only called the writer's father Mr. Johnson when:

   A they were trying to be polite to him.

   B they were trying to get away with something.

   C he was angry with them.

   D they were laughing at him.

67 Which of these adjectives best describes the writer's father?

   A mean   **C** good-tempered

   B proud   **D** careless

Learning Journal: Reading response chart

Title and text type	
Text features	e.g. *headings, bullet points, rhymes, dialogue*
Topic / theme	
Main ideas	
Text-to-self connection	e.g *This reminds me of when…*
Text-to-text connection	e.g. *This reminds me of something I read…*
Text-to-world connection	e.g *This makes me think about…*
What I learnt	
New words	
My opinion of the text	

Learning Journal: How did I do?

Date	
Task	e.g. *giving a presentation, comprehension, research*
What helped me to do the task?	e.g. *using context clues, creating research questions, story plan*
What did I do well?	
What was difficult?	
What did I learn?	
What do I need to get better at?	
What could I do differently next time?	

- Students copy these charts into their Learning Journals to help them to reflect on their learning.
- **Reading response**: This can be used with any type of text, but you do not need to use all the headings every time. You may wish to add a section on key words. For stories, you could substitute `story elements' for `text features'.
- **How did I do?**: This can be used after completing any task. To begin with, go through it with the class, thinking aloud and demonstrating how to make best use of it.

Comprehension: Think Aloud checklist

In a **Think Aloud** you voice your thoughts as you approach a reading text. This strategy helps to direct your reading and improves your comprehension. It encourages you to reflect on what you read as you go along.

Use the **Think Aloud** strategy with a partner or in groups. Ask and answer questions about texts using the signal words in the table below.

	Questions	Signal Words
Predicting	What do I know about this topic? What do I think I will learn about it?	I predict… In the next part I think…
Questioning	What did… Where was… How did… Why did… What did I learn from…	This told me that… I realised that…
Clarifying	Did I understand what I just read? How can I understand it more clearly?	I was surprised… I didn't expect…
Summarising	What is this paragraph / section about?	This is mainly about… The most important idea is…
Reflecting	What did I learn from this paragraph / section?	I realised that… I wonder if…
Text-to-self connections	How does this fit in with what I know already?	This is like… It reminds me of… If it were me…
Personal Response	How do I feel about this text?	My favourite part… I liked / disliked…

Context

You can conduct a Think Aloud to work out the meaning of unfamiliar words using the context. Ask yourself questions like these:

- What do I think this word means?
- Does it have a prefix or a suffix which will help me understand it?
- What clues can I find in the context which to help me? Read the previous sentences that follow your word.

Conduct a **Think Aloud** as a class exercise so that students become familiar with the strategy. They can then use the strategy independently to help them approach new texts. This strategy can be used for other purposes, e.g. using context to find the meaning of words, editing and revising compositions.

Brainstorming

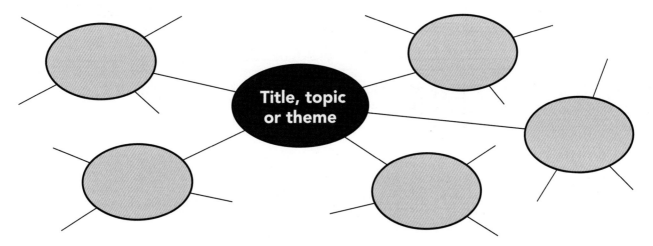

Write headings for your topic in the circles.
Draw as many circles and lines as you need for your topic.

Suggested topic headings:

- Stories: *characters, setting, events, problem, resolution*
- Characters: *personal details, appearance, actions, feelings*
- Animals: *size, appearance, habitat, diet*

Compare and contrast (Venn diagram)

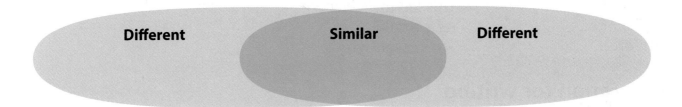

Signal words

the same as   different from
similar to   although
alike   however
compared to   on the other hand

- The brainstorming web can be used to help students generate ideas and structure their thoughts before writing. They can draw as many circles as they need to cover their topic.
- Students can compare two things in a Venn diagram, e.g. places, stories, characters. They write the names of the things being compared in the outer circles. They then write similarities in the middle and differences in the outer circles

185

Text structure: Problem and solution

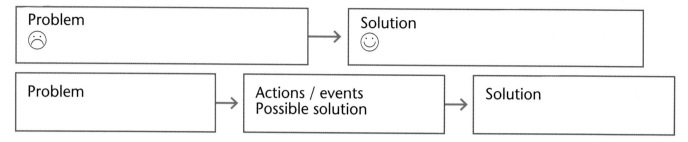

Signal words

If…then…
The question is…
One answer is…

As a result…
One reason for the problem is…
Because of…

Text structure: Cause and effect

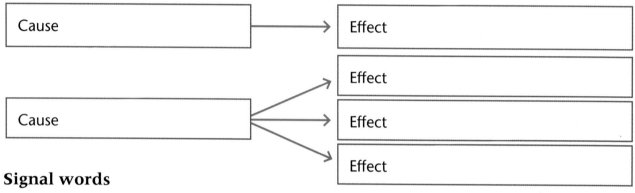

Signal words

So…
Because of…
Therefore…

This led to…
As a result…
The reason why…

Preparation for writing

RAFTs

Complete a RAFTs chart before making a detailed plan for your writing tasks to ensure that you understand the purpose and audience for the task.

Role	Audience
Who are you as the writer?	For whom are you writing?
Format	**Topic + strong verb**
What form will your writing take? (*a letter? a report? a story?*)	What are you writing about? Which verb best describes your purpose? (*to inform? to persuade? to entertain?*)

- Use the problem and solution and the cause and effect organisers to show the link between events and the effects they produce.
- The RAFTs strategy encourages students to consider audience and purpose when they prepare to write, and select the correct format for their task

Story maps

When you are writing a story:

- note down your ideas in a brainstorming web like the one on page 185.
- use a story map or a herringbone to help you plan.

Story Title	
Characters	
Setting	
Problem	
Event	
Event 2	
Event 3	
Resolution	

Herringbone

Title of story: _____

Who? **When?** **Where?**

What? **Why?** **How?**

Drafting

Use a DRAFT strategy poster to help you revise the first draft of your compositions.

D	**Delete** unnecessary words and sentences.	Have I repeated any words? Can I delete any phrases or sentences that don't add anything?
R	**Rearrange** words, phrases, sentences, ideas.	Have I formed my sentences correctly? Have I expressed my ideas in a logical sequence?
A	**Add** signal words to link ideas, new words to add interest.	Could I use signal words to link my ideas? Could I use different words to give my writing more impact?
F	**Form** correct sentences and correctly spelled words.	Have I used correct grammar, e.g. correctly formed verbs, plural nouns. Have I checked tricky spellings in the dictionary?
T	**Talk** about your work with other students.	Have I read out my work to see how it sounds? Have I asked another student to comment on what I have written?

- Encourage students to use either a story map or a herringbone to plan their stories.
- Practise using the DRAFT strategy poster with the whole class. When students are familiar with it, they can use it independently.

Ideas	Ideas are the heart of your message. Ask yourself: • Have I got enough information? • Are my main ideas clear and interesting? • Have I included evidence and supporting details?
Organisation	This is the *structure* of the piece. Ask yourself: • Have I got a clear *plan*? (E.g. introduction, development and conclusion, or a story map.) • Have I got a strong beginning? Does the ending tie it all together? • Are the details in an order that makes sense?
Voice	Voice is the way you express yourself on the page. Ask yourself: • Is my voice right for the *audience* and *purpose*? • Have I shown that I care about the topic?
Word Choice	This is the vocabulary you choose to interest your readers and create an effect. Good writers search for the right word or phrase. Ask yourself, Have I: • Used sensory words? • Used synonyms for words like *big, small, say, like*? • Included figurative language such as *similes* and *alliteration*? • Created a vivid picture of what I am describing? • Chosen the best words to explain it clearly?
Sentence Fluency	This is how you make well-constructed sentences that are easy to follow, and which flow into one another. Ask yourself, Have I: • used transitional words to link sentences? • used long and short sentences to provide variety? • used different types of sentences?
Conventions	Conventions help your readers to understand what you write. Ask yourself: • Are my *spelling, grammar and punctuation* correct? • Have I indented *paragraphs* and started speech on a new line?
+1 Presentation	Presentation is the overall look and layout of your writing. Try to make your work attractive and easy to read. Ask yourself: • How shall I set out my writing on the page? • Should I use underlining or larger letters to indicate headings? • Will illustrations or diagrams help to make my meaning clear? • Is my handwriting neat and easy to read?

• Focus on one trait at a time with students. You could have a lesson focusing on each trait. Link it to the writing process outlined on the next page.

The Writing Process

Choosing a topic, getting ideas, organising ideas, planning	**Pre-writing**	**Students can get ideas from:** • drawing a picture • talking to a partner • class discussion • creating a word web. **They can organise their ideas:** • in the order in which things happen • by sorting their ideas into groups.
Putting ideas into sentences	**Writing a first draft**	**Students can:** • write captions for a drawing • work with a partner of different ability • write independently. **Praise students for their efforts.** Don't expect 'correct' writing from early writers.

Making it more interesting	**Revising**	**Ask students to:**
		• reread their writing
		• read their writing to a partner
		• ask themselves:
		  o are the ideas clear?
		  o can I make it more interesting with adjectives or different verbs?

Checking punctuation and spelling	**Proofreading**	**Ask students to:** • reread looking just for one thing, e.g. full stops or capital letters • read again looking for something else, e.g. the spelling of tricky words.
Making a neat copy for others to read	**Publishing**	**Rewriting is hard work for students of all abilities.** • Select occasional pieces of writing for display or to put in a class book. • Explain why you would like them to make a neat copy *(purpose)* and who is going to read it *(audience)*.

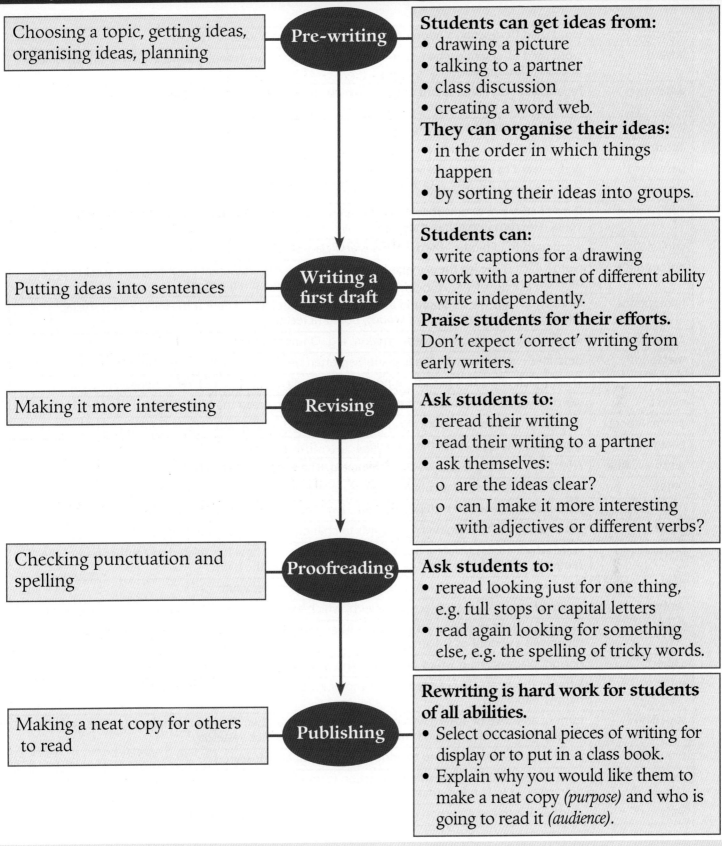

• It is important to demonstrate to young writers *how* people write.
• 'Think aloud' as you model the stages on the board. Involve students in drafting, revising and proofreading.
• Concentrate on one of these per session.

x

x

Glossary of Grammar Terms

adjective	word used to describe a noun or a pronoun, e.g. a big house, it was big.
adverb	word used to describe when, where, how or how often an action is done, e.g. The girl ran quickly. She came last night.
alliteration	repetition of the same sound in words which are close together, often used in poetry, e.g. the silver sands.
antonym	word that means the opposite of another word, e.g. beautiful - ugly
apostrophe	punctuation mark used to show ownership, e.g. Daniel's dog
base word	part of word to which a prefix or suffix can be added, e.g. honest (base word) – honesty/ dishonest
clause	group of words which includes a verb and a subject, e.g. The bus was late. While we waited for the bus
comparative	form of adjective or adverb which compares two things or people, e.g. My house is bigger than yours. Kim runs faster than me.
conjunction	word used to join other words, phrases and clauses, e.g. and, but, although
homograph	word which is spelled the same as another word but has a different meaning, and sometimes a different pronunciation, e.g. wind (type of weather), wind (an action)
homophone	word which has the same sound as another word but has a different meaning and is spelled differently, e.g. board (piece of wood), bored (a feeling)
interjection	word or phrase used to express emotion, e.g. Oh dear! Wow!
metaphor	describes one thing by saying it is another, often used in poetry e.g. The night was a black cloak.
noun	word which refers to a person, thing, place or quality, e.g. Paul, girl, river, honesty
object	word or words which receive the action of a verb, e.g. I read the book. We saw our friends.
onomatopoeia	A word which sound like the thing it describes, e.g. bang, splash
paragraph	group of sentences about the same idea
personification	referring to a thing as if it were a person, e.g. The wind whispered to me.
phrase	group of words which does not make sense on its own, e.g. the weather on Sunday, going to the beach
predicate	part of sentence which includes the verb, e.g. The cunning spider loved to play tricks.
prefix	letters added to the beginning of words to change their meaning, e.g. impossible, unhappy.
preposition	word which comes before a noun or a pronoun to show how it is related to another part of the sentence, e.g. The bag is on the table. The books are in the bag.
pronoun	short words used to replace nouns, e.g. they, them, mine, yours
sentence	group of words with a subject and a verb, which express a complete idea, e.g. It began to rain.
simile	phrase which compares one thing to another using like or as, e.g. The stars were like jewels. The moon was as bright as a diamond.
subject	person, place or thing which does what the verb describes, e.g. The boy kicked the ball.
suffix	letter or group of letters added to the end of a word to make a different word, e.g. friend/ friendly, happy/ happiness
superlative	form of adjective or adverb which compares more than two things or people, e.g. I live in the biggest house in the village. Paul ran the fastest in the race yesterday.
synonym	word with a similar meaning to another word, e.g. afraid/ scared
tense	form of verb which shows when the action takes place, e.g. I live in Kingston. (present tense) The boy travelled to London. (past tense)
verb	word which shows an action or state, e.g. The girl throws the ball. The ball is red.

Skills Index

Key syllabus skills	Page
ICT targets	
Use ICT tools to research and communicate information.	1, 2, 4, 5, 6, 13, 15, 18
Use ICT tools to source new words	4, 9
Conduct collaborative research	2
Locate information	1, 2, 5, 6, 10, 13, 15, 18
Record and playback information	1, 8
Digital citizenship: acknowledge sources	3, 7, 12
Speaking and listening	
Assume roles	41, 51, 119, 129, 132-3
Communication protocol	11, 17, 78, 98, 145
Create commercials/ adverts	81, 166
Debate	57, 130-2, 145
Discussion, description	11, 57, 64, 78, 136, 152 (included in most units)
Introduce speaker, give vote of thanks	61, 111, 152
Present / rebut arguments	130-2, 136, 145
Present information	17, 32, 44, 60-1, 98, 126, 159
Present talks and oral reports	44, 98, 126
Questions: formulate and ask	16, 32, 47, 53, 98, 108
Record audio or video	11, 51, 63, 78, 98, 159, 166
Recount details	17, 31, 159
Selectively use JC or SJE depending on audience and context	62, 91, 132
Share opinions	61, 126, 132-3
Speak fluently and confidently	17, 23, 44, 51, 84, 145, 159
Speak to inform or explain	32, 75, 78, 98, 118-19, 152
Take notes	14, 17, 23, 40, 48, 50, 57, 64, 70, 74, 81, 95, 98, 109, 115, 125-6, 136, 142, 145, 156
Tell/ retell stories	159
Use visual aids	17, 98
Word recognition and vocabulary development	
Affixes	107, 128
Antonyms	144, 147, 175
Blends and digraphs	127
Compound words	13, 40, 93
Context clues	125
Dictionary, use of	35
False homophones	156
Graphemes	127

Homographs	87, 107
Homophones	155, 175
Mnemonics	114
Morphemes	128
Phonics: blends and clusters	20, 127-8
Phrased / cued reading	158
Sight words	13
Spelling	20, 113-14, 135, 141, 162-3
Structural analysis	101, 128
Syllables	20, 170
Synonyms	67, 121, 144, 175
Thesaurus	67, 121
Word banks	13, 76, 80, 87, 101, 121, 144, 151, 162
Word structure: prefixes, inflectional endings	33-34, 40, 101, 107, 128, 147
Reading for meaning and enjoyment	
Audience	55, 97
Author's purpose	8, 14, 23, 55, 96-7, 132, 143
Cause and effect	44, 104, 144
Compare and contrast	56, 125, 137-8, 149, 165
Deducing	9, 43, 50, 57, 104
DRTA strategy	157-8
For and against	130-2, 136, 139
Inferences / inferring	9, 30, 50, 57, 63, 104, 123
Labels and advertisements	75, 77, 81
Main idea and supporting details	17, 21, 40, 111, 145, 166
Make inferences from labels	75
Predicting	8, 10, 15, 29, 62, 103, 150, 157
Problem and solution	31, 152
Question answer relationship (QAR)	9, 30, 43, 138, 172
Reader response logs, book reports/ journal entries on reading	9, 23, 28, 30, 37, 41, 44, 54, 66-8, 74, 83
SQ3R strategy	147
Story elements	31
Story map	31, 41, 74, 129, 159
Summaries	111, 145
Text to text/ text to self connection	8, 49, 124, 171
Text structure	44, 159
Reading for information	
Arguments: develop and organise	130-2, 136, 139, 145, 149
Classification	22, 28, 80, 88, 117-18, 108, 116

Formulate questions / collect data	16, 32, 47, 53, 98
Graphs, charts, diagrams	31, 60-1, 94, 125, 128, 162, 165
ICT: use to communicate information	10, 12, 14, 17, 24, 28, 32, 24, 44, 48, 67, 74, 76, 81, 87-8, 93-4, 102, 110, 115, 118, 126, 154, 156, 169, 172
KWL chart	109-10
Parts of books: table of contents, index	47-8-19
Research information	17, 21, 48, 50, 74, 81, 110, 152, 156, 159
Retrieve and synthesise information	152
Scan texts for specific information	75, 42, 48, 55, 62, 69, 76, 82, 137, 143
Skim for main idea	49, 56, 89, 96, 116, 130
SQ3R method to expository text	150
Summarise	111, 145
Support stance, rebut ideas	57, 61, 136, 176
Text features: identify, comment on function	15-16, 22-4, 55, 69, 76, 97, 151, 165

Grammar and conventions

Abbreviations	79-80, 107
Adjectives	465-6, 119
Adverbs: time, manner, place, comparative, superlative	46, 65-6
Apostrophes: possession, contractions	120, 140, 159-60
Clauses	59
Colons, semi colons	78, 106, 134, 154, 169
Comma splice	154
Commas with intervening phrases	100, 106, 127
Conjunctions	59, 112, 154
Connectives: because, but, so, also, therefore, similarly, however, in addition, furthermore, nevertheless, besides	44, 112, 134, 144, 169
Continuous present and past	84-5, 98, 105
Direct speech	58-9, 106
Exclamation marks	18, 58
Figurative language: similes, personification, metaphors	63, 66-8, 165
Fused sentences	154
Future tense	92, 98, 105
Interjections	27
Interrogative and negative sentences	18, 25-6, 38, 52, 147
Nouns: types, singular and plural, possessive	11-13, 26, 38, 40, 120, 140
Passive voice	153-4, 173-4
Pronouns: personal, indefinite, relative	27, 32-3, 39, 92, 126-7, 169
Possessive adjectives and pronouns	119-20
Predicate: simple and complete	19, 38

Prepositions	99, 161-2, 174
Present perfect tense	146-7, 173
Quotation marks	58, 73, 89, 106
Reported speech	92-3, 106
Sentence subject: simple and complete	19
Sentence types	18
Sentences: simple and compound	59
Signal words	15-16, 21, 44, 51, 94, 108, 130, 134, 136, 144, 169, 172
Subject–verb agreement	24-6, 168-9
Subject verb object	32
Tenses: identify past, present, future	24-5, 51-2, 71-2, 84-5, 92-3, 105, 146-7, 173-4

Writing

6 + 1 traits of writing	188
Advertisements: create	81, 166
Alliteration: identify and use	83, 165, 170
Arguments for and against	130-1, 136, 138, 143, 145
Book report / reading response chart	9, 23, 30, 83, 117, 122, 159
Cause and effect: reflect in writing	44, 169
Collaborative writing projects	28, 48, 156
Convert dramatic script to narrative	129
Debate: develop moots	145
Descriptive pieces	17, 68, 88, 149
Dialogues: compose	91
Editing check list	54, 68, 95, 115, 129, 136
Expository pieces: compose	48, 74, 142, 156
Generate / sort / classify ideas for writing	18, 35, 54, 61,73, 91, 102, 112, 133, 139, 140, 142, 176
Letters: compose	61, 95, 102, 108, 115, 142, 149, 176
Narratives: compose	35, 54, 129
Onomatopoeia: identify and use	23, 28, 37, 40, 165
Paragraphs: main ideas, supporting details	17, 21, 40, 74, 115, 136, 145
Peer editing	21, 54, 68, 81, 98, 102, 149, 170
Persuasive writing: use simple persuasive techniques	14, 130-2, 136, 139, 142
Poems	22-3, 28, 37, 62-3, 64, 66, 68, 82, 88, 164-5, 170
RAFTs strategy	186
Revise writing to meet identified criteria	54, 68, 74, 88, 95, 102, 108, 115, 129, 136, 142
Text features: use to lay out information	15, 22, 48, 55, 69, 76, 97, 150-1, 165-6
Writing process: follow flow chart, apply	21, 61, 74, 142, 176